# FREE AT LAST?

## THE GOSPEL IN THE AFRICAN-AMERICAN EXPERIENCE

## Carl F. Ellis Jr.

InterVarsity Press
Downers Grove, Illinois

*2nd edition:* ©*1996 by Carl F. Ellis Jr.*

*1st edition:* ©*1983 by Inter-Varsity Christian Fellowship of the United States of America, published under the title* Beyond Liberation.

*InterVarsity Press*® *is the book-publishing division of InterVarsity Christian Fellowship*®*, a student movement active on campus at hundreds of universities, colleges and schools of nursing in the United States of America, and a member movement of the International Fellowship of Evangelical Students. For information about local and regional activities, write Public Relations Dept., InterVarsity Christian Fellowship, 6400 Schroeder Rd., P.O. Box 7895, Madison, WI 53707-7895.*

*All Scripture quotations, unless otherwise indicated, are taken from the HOLY BIBLE, NEW INTERNATIONAL VERSION*®*. NIV*®*. Copyright* ©*1973, 1978, 1984 by International Bible Society. Used by permission of Zondervan Publishing House. All rights reserved.*

*Text of "Great Pax Whitie" from* MY HOUSE *by Nikki Giovanni. Copyright* © *1972 by Nikki Giovanni. By permission of William Morrow and Company, Inc.*

*Cover illustration: Roberta Polfus*

*ISBN 0-8308-1687-9*

*Printed in the United States of America* ♾

**Library of Congress Cataloging-in-Publication Data**

*Ellis, Carl F., 1946-*
    *Free at last?: the Gospel in the African-American experience/*
*Carl F. Ellis, Jr.*
      *p.   cm*
    *Includes bibliographical references.*
    *ISBN 0-8308-1687-9 (pbk.: alk. paper)*
    *1. Afro-Americans—Religion.    2. Afro-Americans.    I. Title.*
    *BR563.N4E45    1996*
    *277.3'0089'09673—dc20*
                                      95-48953
                                          CIP

| 20 | 19 | 18 | 17 | 16 | 15 | 14 | 13 | 12 | 11 | 10 | 9 | 8 | 7 | 6 | 5 |
|----|----|----|----|----|----|----|----|----|----|----|---|---|---|---|---|
| 13 | 12 | 11 | 10 | 09 | 08 | 07 | 06 | | | | | | | | |

*To my children*
*Carl III and Nicole*
*who have given me the joy of fatherhood*
*and to my mother*
*Mildred Ellis Protho*
*whose help and support I will always treasure*

## Acknowledgments

This book would never have been conceived or written without the influence of people who have been significant in my life. To them I will always be grateful.

From the day I was born to Carl F. Ellis Sr. and his lovely wife, Mildred, I was raised to feel loved and wanted in more ways than I can count. They took great care to supervise my development, exposing me to a rich variety of learning experiences and challenging me to think things through. I will never be able to fully express my loving gratitude to them.

Also I want to thank others whose positive influence is still felt and appreciated:

☐ Catherine Owens (my maternal grandmother), whose example of godliness inspired me to seek God with all my heart

☐ "Uncle James" (James McLain), whose affectionate love for God and for me has been a great source of strength

☐ His wife, Blanch (my paternal grandmother), who instilled in me the assurance that being Black should never block me from doing what I set my mind to

☐ Dr. Martin Luther King Jr., who opened my eyes to God's concern for justice and equality among people

☐ Malcolm X, who sensitized me to the beauty of my humanity

☐ The Reverend Robert Lowery, who showed me through his example that the pastoral ministry can be "peopley" and practical

☐ Robert Sykes and Gerald Garnett, who took time to share their faith with me, answering my intellectual questions and leading me to Christ

☐ Mr. Robert Crowe, my high-school math and science teacher, who relentlessly challenged my new faith, driving me to develop sound reasons for the hope that was in me

☐ Eric Fife, whom God used to call me into the ministry

☐ Dr. Clark Pinnock, who first helped me appreciate how the truths of Scripture can successfully confront human philosophies

☐ Dr. Francis Schaeffer, whose insights and writings equipped me to think in terms of a biblical world-and-life-view

☐ Tom Skinner, whose ministry has done a great deal to build a platform for the emergence of a national Black Christian movement

☐ Dr. William Pannell, my supervisor while I worked with Tom Skinner Associates (TSA), whose brilliant insights and feedback contributed much to clarify my theology

☐ my other TSA coworkers, including Roland Tisdale, Richard Parker, Henry Greenidge, Eric Payne and Curtis Goffe, whose fellowship and friendship have meant so much to me

☐ The Reverend Richard Woodward, whose teaching ministry was a great encouragement in a time of discouragement

☐ Dr. Columbus Salley, who provided the tools I needed to integrate my African-American awareness with my Christian commitment

☐ the Reverend Orlando Protho (my stepfather), who ordained me and whose enlightenment enabled me to appreciate the African-American church and its preaching in a new way (he went home to be with the Lord on August 20, 1992—I really miss him)

☐ Thom Hopler, whose impact on me was limited only by the brief time we had to share

☐ All my professors at Westminster Theological Seminary (WTS), who helped to further clarify my thinking—especially Dr. John Frame,

Dr. Harvie Conn, Dr. Robert Knudson and Bill Krispin (director of the Center for Urban Theological Studies)

☐ The Reverend Bill Link (dean at WTS), whose personal concern and financial sacrifice enabled me to enroll at WTS

☐ The brothers and sisters in the West Philly (Philadelphia) group, whose fellowship and warmth carried me through the difficult days of my senior year at seminary

☐ Prison Fellowship, which gave me, as a seminar instructor, a means of digesting the heavy things I learned at WTS

☐ New City Fellowship, which provided me, as pastor, an opportunity to implement some of the things I have written about

☐ InterVarsity Christian Fellowship, which brought me into contact with many of the influential people in my life

I also must acknowledge my children, Carl Francis Ellis III, born June 8, 1983, and Nicole René Elliott Ellis, born April 10, 1986. Only God knows how deep is my love and affection for them. They keep me young and on my toes as I watch them grow and develop. They have also inspired my faith and confidence in God's grace by reminding me of how God loves and delights in me.

Next I want to thank all those who did the typing, retyping, editing, reediting, critiquing and so on. For the first edition they include Isidra Smith, Carla Waiters, Michelle Black, Lesley Hamilton, Pat Ralston, Catherine Nordloff Tippens, Lunard and Sharon Lewis, David and Arlene Cadwell, Daniel Bockert, Mrs. Mildred Protho (my mother), E. Regina Elliott Smith, Edwina Morrison, Mrs. Estelle Elliott (whose helpful suggestions led to the development of the glossary), Joan Guest, Jane Wells and the rest of the editorial staff of InterVarsity Press (who were instrumental in the book's development), Mark Branson, Bob Hunter, Dr. Bennie Goodwin and others who reviewed the manuscript and gave many helpful suggestions.

This revised edition could not have been completed without the help of those who entered the book into the computer, including Clyde Price, who keyed in most of it at "warp speed," and Ray Beardsley, my computer consultant, who scanned key portions. Others helped with proofreading: Camille Hallstrom, Anna Trimiew, the Reverend and Mrs. Orlando Protho and Esther Dozier. I also want to thank those who helped with research, including Cynthia Hammiel, Michelle Williams and Trudy Roper.

Most of all I want to give special thanks to my Heavenly Father, whose infinite love and amazing grace made all this possible.

# 1
# Toward a Promised Land

*F*or four hundred years they had been oppressed. Their sense of history and destiny was all but wiped out. Their consciousness was blurred and distorted, their culture polluted with false values. Their knowledge of the one true God had become tangled up with a proliferation of man-made gods. Their sense of dignity had been overwhelmed by feelings of inferiority, feelings that came from the dehumanization inflicted by a racist society. The people felt forsaken by God.

Yet God remained faithful. He did not forsake them. In fact, he was already implementing his eternal plan of liberation. In ten demonstrations of judgment, God broke the back of a king who had used his technology to maintain a brutal system of slavery. God thus brought his people out of Egypt so that they might become his light to the nations.

This goal, however, could not be reached overnight. The people had to be prepared through gradual de-Egyptianization as they journeyed in the wilderness. God began to restore their culture, raising it to new heights through Moses and the law.

## Parallels in History

A survey of African-American history reveals that like the children of Israel, we have had a four-hundred-year collective trauma from which we have yet to fully recover. And like the children of Israel we have sojourned in a philosophical wilderness as our thinking has developed. The big question we face is, Has God been guiding us toward a promised land?

Martin Luther King Jr., in his *Memphis speech\** the night before he died, prophetically answered that question:

We've got some difficult days ahead. But it really doesn't matter with me now. Because I've been to the mountain top. I won't mind.

Like anybody, I would like to live a long life. Longevity has its place. But I'm not concerned about that now. I just want to do God's will.

And He's allowed me to go up to the mountain. And I've looked over, and *I've seen the promised land.*

I may not get there with you, but I want you to know tonight that we as a people will get to the promised land.

So I'm happy tonight. I'm not worried about anything. I'm not fearing any man. Mine eyes have seen the glory of the coming of the Lord.[1]

But questions still remain. What is this "promised land" like? Who is going to lead us there? How can we get there from here?

During the 1960s African-Americans had a real sense of direction. But by the time the eighties arrived our sense of direction had all but evaporated. More recently we've seen the emergence of a new militancy. Yet it seems we are still confused, like the children of Israel after they refused to possess the land God had given them (Numbers 13—14).

God had sent ten plagues to break the back of Pharaoh and discredit his pagan gods. He had dealt the mighty Egyptian army, with its superior technology, a major military setback at the Red Sea. He had fed the people from the sky. He had provided fresh water from a pool of poison. The Israelites reached the Promised Land one year after leaving Egypt. Yet they failed to believe that the same God who had done all this could defeat some fifth-rate Canaanite tribes.

What was so bizarre was that having decided not to take God and his word seriously, they wanted to return to Egypt—to slavery and oppression! They wanted to readopt the false values that had obliterated their culture and sense of worth.

### Where Have All the Leaders Gone?

Today the African-American community is in a similar situation. We are aware of the moral and legal victories of the sixties. But racism is still with us. In fact, it has even become "politically correct." Now we are in a state of theological and cultural disarray. We have a crisis of leadership, of identity. We are in a morass of me-ism. Where did this crisis begin?

Much of the generation of leadership that carried us through the sixties has died naturally, been assassinated or gone off into relative obscurity. Dr. King is gone. So is Malcolm X. *Huey P. Newton\** was blown away. Others have been co-opted by the establishment. Still others have lost touch with our people. We will not come into our own until a new generation inherits the mantle of leadership. But where will this new leadership come from? How will it build on the previous contributions?

### Where This Book's Discussion Will Take Us

These are among the questions we will examine in this book. In part I we will look briefly at a variety of concepts and issues that will be discussed more fully in the rest of the book. I want to lay some groundwork for a fresh analysis of some of the great issues in the African-American experience. Part II will touch on the major phases of African-American cultural history and point out some lessons we have learned.

In part III we will look at the root of *culture** as the human response to God's revelation. We will also look at the crippling effects of humanity's negative response to God, on consciousness in general and on the African-American consciousness in particular. In addition, I will discuss the nature of theology, along with some new ways it can empower our people to reach our cultural potential. Finally, part IV ties together what we have learned, suggesting how we can apply this knowledge toward developing a new agenda.

Though written from an African-American perspective, this work is not intended only for an African-American audience. Using the African-American cultural experience as the point of contact, I have attempted to forge a fresh understanding of how God by his *grace** is active in culture.

At the back of this revised edition is a glossary of people, events and terms. This is an alphabetical listing of (1) terms that either are used in a specialized sense or cannot be found in a standard dictionary, (2) historical information on events and organizations alluded to and (3) significant leaders (listed by last name), with biographical information. Names, events and terms included in the glossary are italicized and marked with an asterisk (*) the first time they appear in the text.

May you be encouraged to know God in new and deeper ways as you gain a fresh understanding of African-American *history** and culture. Whatever your background may be, I pray that this study will give you new insights to analyze the culture in which you live. Finally, it is my prayer that the principles contained in this book will play a role in building bridges of understanding and facilitating reconciliation where there has been alienation.

# Part I

# A Primer

# 2

# Picking Up
# the Pieces

*I*t used to be said that Western historians had sold us a bill of goods,
that what was portrayed as "objective" history was in reality
*White*\* history. *Black*\* history was almost completely glossed
over as if we did not exist. The same could have been said about the
other people-oriented disciplines, such as sociology, psychology and
anthropology. This White bias was unseen by White society until the
militant brothers of the sixties pointed it out.

These Black thinkers showed us that when people grow up in a
particular cultural context, they fail to see the cultural biases they have
inherited. They think of their own value system as neutral, the standard
for all people. But the Black leaders of the sixties showed us the folly
in this. They pointed out that the White American system of values
proclaimed that Black was not beautiful, that the system perpetuated
the daily degradation of African-Americans. The system was not
neutral when it came to us.

**The Great Rejection**

The Black militants rejected American culture and its bias toward everything White. Along with White American culture they rejected *Christianity.** To them, Christianity was the "White man's religion" and the biblical worldview was a White worldview. The militants of the 1960s looked at the past and found a well-documented case against *"Christianity"** in its poor treatment of our people. Even historic Black theology as expressed through the oral tradition of the African-American church did not escape being tagged as an expression of the White man's religion.

*Frederick Douglass,** the abolitionist, had also rejected "Christianity," but with one important difference:

Between the Christianity of this land, and the Christianity of Christ, *I recognize the widest possible difference*—so wide, that to receive the one as good, pure, and holy, is of necessity to reject the other as bad, corrupt, and wicked. To be the friend of the one, is of necessity to be the enemy of the other. I love the pure, peaceable, and impartial Christianity of Christ: I therefore hate the corrupt, slaveholding, women-whipping, cradle-plundering, partial and hypocritical Christianity of this land. Indeed, I can see no reason, but the most deceitful one, for calling the religion of this land Christianity. I look upon it as the climax of all misnomers, the boldest of all frauds, and the grossest of all libels.[1]

Unfortunately, the Black militants did not do the homework that one of their patron saints had done. They were thus unable to distinguish between the "Christianity of Christ" and the "Christianity of this land." The latter I call *White Christianity-ism.**

When Christianity was rejected, secularism and humanism filled the void. *Secularism* is the belief that human life is independent of God and his revelation and that the sociological struggles of a people transcend all forms of religion. *Humanism* is the belief that humans are the final judge of all truth.[2] Ironically, both of these are worldviews, with their own belief system and demands for faith. Since this is the essence of *religion,** secularism and humanism do not transcend religion. They are religions themselves.

Not realizing this, the secular militants ended up merely switching from a God-centered faith to a human-centered religion. They were justified in rejecting White Christianity-ism and asserting that we should replace White definitions of us with definitions of our own. But the militants did not stop there: for them, Black people replaced God himself as the ultimate judges of truth.

## A Limited Perspective

Leaving God out had significant results. Not least was that the Black thinkers of the sixties lacked an accurate picture of the world because they denied the reality of God.

In 1884 Edwin Abbott published the fable of "Flatland." Flatland is an imaginary country where everyone lives in only two dimensions. The people are circles, triangles and squares, and they live in pentagons. A line to them is like a wall to us. They do not know up or down, only north, south, east and west.

One day a sphere came to visit Flatland. At first the Flatlanders could not see him, because the sphere remained outside their plane. They were confused by a voice that was not associated with a line, and they did not understand when he told them that he was "above" them (figure 1). So the sphere entered Flatland. Of course to the Flatlanders he appeared to be a circle. But he talked to them about a three-dimensional world that was beyond their experience (figure 2).

One Flatlander reported that he had been transported temporarily out of Flatland and had experienced three dimensions. Let's call him Squarey. But the people mocked him because they couldn't understand what he was talking about. So Squarey stopped talking. To the Flatlanders, whatever is inconceivable in their two-dimensional world must be impossible.[3]

If the Flatlanders had acknowledged that their limited reality was an analogous part of a fuller reality, they could have had a meaningful discussion with the sphere and with Squarey about the third dimension. However, because they insisted that Flatland was the ultimate

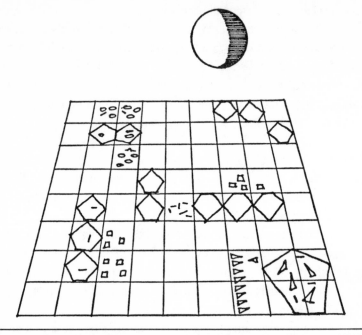

**Figure 1.** Flatland. Taken from *The Andromedans & Other Parables of Science and Faith* by Denis Osborne, © 1977 by Denis Osborne. Used by permission of InterVarsity Press, Downers Grove, Illinois.

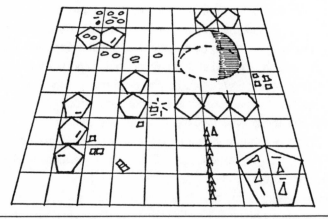

**Figure 2.** Flatland invaded. Taken from *The Andromedans & Other Parables of Science and Faith* by Denis Osborne, © 1977 by Denis Osborne. Used by permission of InterVarsity Press, Downers Grove, Illinois.

reality, they ended up with a distorted view of reality.

A secular worldview is like the Flatlanders' view. White historians had sold us a bill of goods by leaving Black folks out; Black secularists sold us a bill of goods by leaving God out. Some Black militants insisted that their reality was the ultimate reality. They did not see their reality as analogous to God's reality. God was not even a part of the world as they pictured it. They *should* have rejected Christianity-ism, but they had no reason for rejecting the one true God. Their perspective was limited, yet they presented this limited perspective as the whole truth. By so doing they distorted truth.

To a certain extent this limited viewpoint was propagated in the interest of religious neutrality. The secular humanists thought that people could talk about history, math, science, civil rights and so on while ignoring the reality of God. Decisions about morality were left up to the individual.

This is what tripped up Eve in the Garden of Eden (Genesis 3:1-6). She and Adam both knew what good and evil were on the basis of God's word (Genesis 2:16-17). But Satan tempted Eve to take a "neutral" stance toward God's word. Satan appealed to Eve as if she were independent of God: "Yo, God says one thing; I say another. Eve, you make the final determination of what is right and wrong."

Eve was not being neutral. She rejected God's word as her basis of judgment. She attempted to replace God as the ultimate judge. Eve became, in essence, the first secular humanist.

### History, Destiny and Consciousness

One of the major reasons God turned Israel back from the Promised Land and told them that they would have to wander in the wilderness for forty years was their lack of faith in God. They had balked at the border through lack of faith. According to their distorted perspective, the Canaanites were so big they made the Israelites look like grass-hoppers.

The Israelites needed a reconstruction of their culture. They needed to see things from God's point of view. But only Joshua and Caleb seem to have shown insight (Numbers 14:6-9), and they became the new generation of leadership. During the forty years of wilderness wandering, God restructured Israelite culture on the basis of the law and the covenant. He gave them a true way of looking at their history, their present situation and their *destiny.* *

We can learn something from what God taught the Israelites. First, through Moses God restored to Israel a correct view of their history (Genesis 12—50; Exodus 1—18). Many of God's dealings with the family of Abraham had likely been forgotten or distorted in the four-hundred-year ordeal of Egyptian slavery.

African-Americans, too, need to get back in touch with their history. But how? What is the meaning of African-American history?

History is never an account of all the events of the past. It is instead an account of events that have been sifted and evaluated to determine their significance. History might be called a collection of significant events. But what makes an event significant? To some extent an event is significant if it changed the course of history!

How can we understand what is and what is not significant in our past? It will certainly help if we have a God-centered view of the world. If we leave out God, we will have a distorted view, like the folks in Flatland. We need to "reflect back"[4] on the Word of God if we want to have an adequate understanding of our own past.

Second, God through Moses restored to Israel a correct view of destiny. After four hundred years in slavery and a few months wandering in the wilderness, the people had forgotten where they were going. God had to remind his people of his specially chosen direction for their lives.

What is the destiny of African-American people? Where are we going? I believe we will never know until we return to our roots, to the authentic aspects of African-American culture, which include the church. Our destiny will be found there as we "reflect back" on the Word of God. God is the Lord of destiny. If we leave God out, we lose our sense of direction.

History and destiny for us are like the third dimension for the

Flatlanders. God is not limited by the flow of history, just as the sphere was not limited by the Flatlanders' plane of existence. If Flatland were warped or curved, the Flatlanders would be unconscious of it. They are limited by being *within* their world. The only way to know the contours of Flatland is from the sphere's perspective (figure 3).

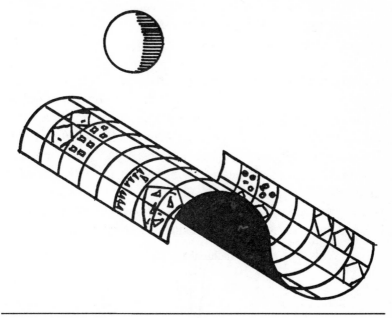

**Figure 3.** Warped reality

Because of our limitations we have no way of knowing the contours of history. We are incapable of knowing what our destiny points to. Since God has the ultimate perspective and knows all things, he alone is able to guide us through the flow of history toward our true destiny. The Word of God must be our guide to history and destiny. The Word corrects our understanding of reality and completes our picture of the world.

Finally, God, through Moses, restored to Israel what they needed for a renewed *collective consciousness.** What is a collective consciousness? It consists of the standards adopted by a people. An essential aspect in the life of a people, it determines what people do and how they do it in every area of life. The collective consciousness is the grid a people uses to understand the world. It gives rise to their sociology, psychology, anthropology and so on. It is also the key to a people's sense of history and destiny.

How can African-American consciousness be defined? What should we as a people recognize as our standards, our values? Only by seeing ourselves as God sees us will we be able to avoid false, self-destructive values. Our values must come from the Word of the one true God.

Culture embodies the cumulative effect of history, destiny and consciousness in the life of a people. Although some have defined culture as "the patterned way in which people do things,"[5] these visible actions are more the manifestation of culture than culture itself (figure 4). Culture itself is made up of commitments, values and beliefs about the world and people. If our underlying basic commitment is that we are not involved in God's world, then our entire culture will end up with a distorted view of reality. Godlessness will affect every area of life, and this godlessness will be a kind of cultural death.

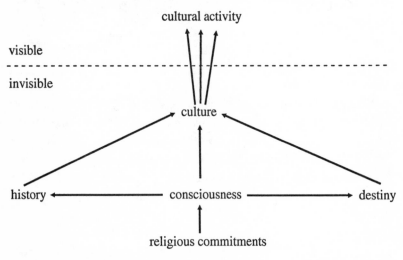

**Figure 4.**   The relation between cultural activity and a people's values

## By Grace

It is unfortunate that the militant Black thinkers attempted to reconstruct our culture on a commitment to a so-called religiously neutral, secular worldview. Because of this, the militant movement that developed in the sixties fell apart. Much Black consciousness degenerated into do-your-own-thing-ism. Much of our history was forgotten. By the dawn of the eighties many of our young people knew little of what Martin Luther King and Malcolm X had stood for.

Today we must ask ourselves, What is the new militancy based on? Will it too fall apart because of an inadequate foundation?

Earlier Black militants rejected the scriptural worldview without really examining it. They failed to see that Scripture did not come to us from a European or White American context. Today's militants seem to be repeating this same mistake.

Though the leaders of the sixties left God out, by God's grace they were able to make some valuable contributions to us. However, because of the onslaught of do-your-own-thing-ism, we lost the cultural framework to tie these contributions together.

In order to pick up the pieces and reconstruct African-American culture, we will have to "reflect back" on what God has revealed about himself and about us. This must be the task of a new generation of leadership. Such a noble task will require the wisdom and understanding available only from God. "The fear [reverence] of the Lord—that is wisdom, and to shun evil is understanding" (Job 28:28).

# 3
# "Oh, Freedom!"

When people lack a basic commitment to God, unrighteousness follows. Scripture describes at least two types of unrighteousness: *ungodliness* and *oppression*. Ungodliness happens when people rebel against God and his revelation. Disregarding their responsibility toward God and others, they themselves suffer the consequences of their wrongdoing. Oppression occurs when people impose their ungodliness on others, causing them to suffer the consequences. For example, if a person has a racist attitude, he or she is guilty of ungodliness. If, however, that person imposes his racism on others, forcing them to live in substandard conditions, then he is guilty of oppression.

Unrighteousness is seldom exclusively one or the other; it is usually a combination of both. Oppressors are people whose unrighteousness is primarily, but not exclusively, oppression. The unrighteousness of oppressed people is primarily, but not exclusively, ungodliness.

## Grace as a Base

Unrighteousness is toxic. It destroys humanity. It is only by the grace of God that our humanity has not been totally destroyed—that we can still resist unrighteousness at all. If we had lost that ability, the oppressed would be unable to resist oppression.

How does resistance relate to *righteousness,* * oppression and our need for God's salvation and grace? Let's look at this next.

1. *Resistance and the righteousness of God.* Theologian James Cone has affirmed that God is on the side of the oppressed.[1] What does this mean? It means that the oppressed, when they resist oppression, are resisting unrighteousness. It does not mean that the oppressed are more righteous than the oppressors. It does mean, however, that they have the opportunity to *demonstrate* more righteousness. Why? Because resisting oppression is more righteous than giving in to it or inflicting it on others, especially if the oppressed resist righteously. (This will be discussed in chapter fourteen.) God is the God of righteousness, and in resisting oppression the oppressed align themselves with God. They advance God's justice.

2. *Resistance and the ungodliness of the oppressed.* If ungodliness is imposed on people whose own ungodliness has already diminished their humanity, then the imposed ungodliness is in harmony with their own ungodliness. Consider the prostitute. If she "turns a trick" she cannot charge her "john" with rape. Though her sexuality has been abused, it was her willful intention to execute the transaction. Her intentions complemented the intentions of her john. Nevertheless, the fact that her intentions matched those of her oppressor does not mean that she has simply gotten "what she asked for" or that the oppressor ought not to be judged for his oppression. She became a prostitute in the first place partly because her sense of humanity had been brutalized by oppression and mistreatment.

There is never perfect harmony between oppression and the ungodliness of the oppressed. God set a limit to this unrighteous harmony after the Fall, when he put hostility between Satan, the ultimate oppressor, and humans (Genesis 3:15). By so doing God ensured that for every oppression there will be a corresponding resistance.

3. *Resistance and the oppressed's need for salvation.* If the oppressed focus on their humanity (which oppression is trying to destroy) and try to defend that humanity, they will be acting righteously. Their own ungodliness will be driven beneath the surface. When liberation comes, however, their ungodliness will resurface with all its negative effects. The oppressed *must* fight to break the back of oppression so they can seek God's solution to their *own* unrighteousness.

Israel learned this lesson under the judges. They disobeyed God in the first place by not driving out the Canaanites (Deuteronomy 7:1-6; Judges 1:27—2:2). The Canaanites regrouped, regained their strength and came back to oppress the Israelites. Israel resisted. They cried out to God for help, sought God's ways and were delivered from oppression. But each time they were liberated, their ungodliness resurfaced, and they betrayed their call to be a light to the nations. They had to face their own need for salvation.

4. *Resistance and the grace of God.* It is God who has preserved our humanity from total destruction by unrighteousness. He has not let ungodliness and oppression whittle down to nothing his image in people. God cares about justice and has compassionate love for suffering people (Isaiah 58:3-12; Amos 5:10-15, 21-24). God's compassion is rooted in his grace. It is because of God's grace that oppression will ultimately cave in to the resistance of the oppressed.

Thus it is God's grace alone that provides the *basis* for resisting oppression. It is his grace that provides the *power* to resist oppression. It is God's grace that provides the *will* to resist oppression. If we leave God out, we leave out the very possibility of freedom.

### An African-American Quest

A central theme in the flow of African-American history has been the quest for freedom and dignity. There is only one basis for human dignity: the scriptural teaching that man and woman were created in the image of God (Genesis 1:26-27). God's personal dignity is the original personal dignity. Our dignity is derived from the dignity of God. In other words, if God is somebody, which he is, then I am somebody because I in some ways resemble God.

But what is the nature of freedom? Some would say that freedom equals independence. Independence from the oppression of other people is a valid goal, but to attempt independence from God is utterly futile. Think of how an airplane flies. Does a wing produce lift because it becomes independent of gravity? Of course not. The wing produces lift precisely *because of* gravity. A wing's lift is an expression of the law of gravity.[2] Trying to be independent of gravity would be as foolish as stepping off the top of a building and trying to walk on air. For a few fleeting seconds you might think you had succeeded, but your illusion would end abruptly when you reached the pavement below.

God's rule over us is like gravity: our attempts to resist it are utterly foolish. God laughs at the nations' plots to rid themselves of his sovereignty, because God knows that they simply cannot escape his lordship (Psalm 2). "In him we live and move and have our being" (Acts 17:28).

Perhaps we can best learn what his lordship means by determining what it does *not* mean. We are not robots. God's sovereignty does not mean manipulation. Manipulation is our human way of controlling things. For example, as I type this on my computer, I control what it does with the keyboard and the mouse. I can make the computer do exactly what I want—that is, I can manipulate the computer. Because we tend to see God as having our limitations, we may imagine that God's sovereignty means that he manipulates us the same way I manipulate my computer. But this is not the case.

There are aspects of the creation which God controls through manipulation. I'm thinking here of the physical and biological laws that determine the behavior of the inanimate world, plants and lower animals. But that is not the way God chooses to control us. He exercises lordship over us through *freedom*. Human freedom is derived from God's lordship and not independent of it, for by definition nothing can be outside God's sovereignty. As Jesus says, "If the Son sets you free, you will be free indeed" (John 8:36).

Our difficulty in understanding freedom as a function of God's sovereignty is like the difficulty the Flatlanders had in understanding the third dimension. That it is hard for us to understand "freedom control" does not mean that it is not true. To rebel against God's lordship is to rebel against our own human freedom. If we leave the *freedom function* of God's lordship, we find ourselves under the *manipulation function.* To be under manipulation is to be under the slavery of sin (Romans 6:16; Galatians 5:1). These are our only two options.

When Adam sinned, for example, he was not exercising free choice; he was rebelling against freedom of choice. "You are free to eat from any tree in the garden" (Genesis 2:16): this was the range of freedom. "But you must not eat from the tree of the knowledge [determination] of good and evil, for when you eat of it you will surely die" (Genesis 2:17): Adam and Eve were not free to choose to eat the fruit of the forbidden tree so long as they lived under the freedom function of God's sovereignty. Death in this context was not the result of a free choice. On the contrary, it required a willful rejection of freedom in order to partake of this fruit and die.

If our cultural quest for freedom has been a quest for God's lordship, then Martin Luther King's parting words to us will be fulfilled. We will cross the River Jordan into God's rest—a rest with worldwide implications. But if our cultural quest for freedom has been a quest for independence from God, we will end up on the junk heap of the nations—a junk heap of slavery far worse than what we have ever experienced.

### A'nt Jane
> Oh, Freedom,
> Oh, Freedom,
> Oh, Freedom over me!
> And before I'll be a slave
> I'll be buried in my grave
> And go home to my Lord and be free.

This old freedom song is a clear indication that historically our struggle has not been a quest for independence from God. On the contrary, it shows that our quest has been rooted in a desire for God's lordship. Here freedom is not seen as something to be "over," as in recent humanistic thinking, but as something to be "over me." Freedom is being under the right authority; it is being home with my Lord and under the freedom function of God's lordship.

The strength and resilience of the African-American church are another indication that our historic struggle has been a quest for God's freedom. Let's not be hasty to jettison the biblical perspectives of our heritage, as the secular militants did. Maybe we should have listened to *A'nt Jane\** a little more closely.

It is time for a new generation of Joshuas to learn from what has gone before us and, while "reflecting back" on the Word of God, to build the basis of a renewed African-American culture—a renewed culture that will give us a new vision. For "where there is no vision, the people perish" (Proverbs 29:18 KJV).

# Part II

# "Reflecting Back"

# 4
# Soul Dynamic

W hen the people of Judah were captured and taken from Canaan to Babylon, they were confused, to say the least. They had in their possession the Scriptures stating God's promise that the land of Canaan would be theirs forever. Yet here they were, having lost Canaan, captive minorities in the land of a foreign superpower.

Big questions preyed on the minds of the captive people: If God promised the land to us forever, how did we end up in this Babylonian predicament? What happened to God's covenant promises? How could God let us down?

Someone was inspired by God to deal with these questions. He plunged into this awesome task by getting hold of three books: *The Annals of Solomon, The Annals of the Kings of Israel* and *The Annals of the Kings of Judah.* He proceeded to select material out of these scrolls, analyze it and arrange it into a theological framework. As he did this he "reflected back" on God, who is absolutely faithful and trustworthy to keep all his promises. In his work he demonstrated that it was not God who failed the covenant, but the people. His work became the books of 1 and 2 Kings.[1]

African-Americans have essentially the same question: What are we doing here? It cannot be demonstrated that our arrival in chains was a direct result of our failure. On the contrary, it was the slave traders who were more unfaithful to God. However, the example of how 1 and 2 Kings were written can give a clue to help us reconstruct African-American history.

As we study our history, we need to select material out of the body of knowledge, analyze it and arrange it into a theological framework. At the same time we must "reflect back" on the God who has revealed himself in the Scriptures as the true and living God, absolutely faithful, just and trustworthy. We need to evaluate the contributions made by outstanding people in our history and see what we can learn from the history of our quest for freedom and dignity.

We need to do this work by building on the insights of individuals like Martin Luther King Jr., who told us that in God's economy undeserved suffering can be redemptive (in a narrow sense). With this kind of insight we may discover some new things about freedom and dignity, some new dimensions of truth in Scripture. A dynamic theology will emerge with the understanding of the meaning of African-American history as we both study it and "reflect back" on the Scriptures. With this theology we will be able to weep with righteous anger as we see how our people have suffered, knowing all the time that the suffering has not been in vain.

It is a disgrace that we have not learned to preach "the full counsel of God" through our history, the way Stephen and later Paul were able to preach through Jewish history (Acts 7:2-53; 13:16-41). We talk today about getting back to our roots. But have we shown our roots to be in God? It is a disgrace that we have not taken African-American history seriously. It is also a disgrace that we have not learned to disciple the African-American community through other cultural phenomena besides history.

We must begin somewhere to accomplish this neglected task. Why not here? To begin, let's take a look at a few aspects of church history from an African perspective.

## The Gospel in Africa

Africa was no stranger to the *gospel\** in the early days of the church. Nor was the African a stranger to the biblical writers.

Africans were not unknown . . . to the writers of the Bible. Their peculiarities of complexion and hair were as well known to the ancient Greeks and Hebrews as they are to the American people today. And when they spoke of the Ethiopians, they meant the ancestors of the black-skinned and wooly-haired people who . . . have been known as laborers on the plantations of the South. It is to these people, and to their country, that the Psalmist refers, when he says, "Ethiopia shall soon stretch out her hands unto God."[2]

As Jesus was carrying his cross through the streets of Jerusalem, he stumbled under its weight. Simon, a Black man from Cyrene, Africa, was enlisted to carry the cross the rest of the way (Luke 23:26). On the day of Pentecost, people from every nation (including African nations) heard the gospel and were converted (Acts 2:5-12). An Ethiopian government official was converted on his way home (Acts 8:26-39). The church at Antioch had several African members, among them two prophets or teachers: Simeon, called the Black man, and Lucius the Cyrenian (Acts 13:1). What were those two Africans doing in Antioch? We find in Acts 11:19-21 that they had gone there when they learned that non-Jews were not hearing the good news from the Jewish missionaries; the young African church may have been sending missionaries like Simeon and Lucius to plant churches. It was out of that Antioch church that Paul and Barnabas were sent to evangelize Turkey, Greece and Italy. So the European church partly has the African church to thank for its missionary faithfulness.

Great early scholars like Augustine, Tertullian and Origen were Black men from Africa.[3] Augustine was a major influence on John Calvin. So the Reformation theologians have the African church to thank for a great deal of their theology. At one time there were over five hundred bishops in the African church. In the third century the Coptic church was formed; however, by the sixth century it had become spiritually dead. The Muslim conquest finally wiped out much of the church in North Africa.

In those days the Sahara Desert was not as extensive as it is today. Given the well-traveled trade routes that crisscrossed Africa from east to west, the gospel could have penetrated deep into the interior of Africa. Even now an unbroken line of communication links the West Coast of Africa, through the Sudan and the so-called Great Desert, to Asia.

Africa is no vast island, separated by an immense ocean from other portions of the globe and cut off through the ages from the men who have made and influenced the destinies of mankind. Africa has been closely connected, both as source and nourisher, with some of the most potent influences which have affected for good the history of the world. The people of Asia and the people of Africa have been in constant intercourse. No violent social or political disruption has ever broken through this communication. No chasm caused by war has suspended intercourse.[4]

The foundational truths of the gospel could well have been part of the basis for the great Mali civilization that arose in West Africa in the thirteenth century. A Muslim historian described the people of Mali as

seldom unjust, and [having] a much greater horror of injustice than any other people. Their sultan shows no mercy to anyone who is guilty of the least act of it. There is complete security in their country. Neither traveller nor inhabitant in it has anything to fear from robbers or men of violence. It is a real state whose organization and civilization could be compared with those of the Musselman kingdoms, or indeed the Christian kingdoms of the same period.[5]

We have a rich African heritage of which we can be proud. We should learn about the great eastern civilizations such as Ethiopia, Makuria and Alwa, and about the great western civilizations such as Ghana, Mali and Songhay.[6]

Many of us who have studied our African roots with pride have unfortunately looked at our American experience with shame. Though slavery itself is nothing to rejoice about, the remarkable survival of our people through all the phases of our American experience should be a great encouragement. Our survival reflects God's active grace. American slavery was the beginning of racism in our experience. But by grace we resisted these oppressions as we sought for freedom and dignity.

### Progress of Consciousness

The historic African-American resistance to oppression in the quest for freedom and dignity can be divided into five major phases. Though they were initiated in historical sequence, each still exists today. These phases represent various ways of understanding ourselves and our situation. They are as follows: (1) *Colored,* (2) *Neo-Colored,* (3) *Negro,* (4) *Neo-Negro* and (5) *Black.* The Black phase included five subphases: (a) *Black awareness,* (b) *Black power,* (c) *Black revolutionism,* (d) *Neo-Black revolutionism* and (e) *Neo-Pan-Africanism.** By the 1980s the quest stalled as we slipped into a post-Black lull. Today, however, the rise of the new militancy may indicate the dawning of a sixth phase—the *African-American* phase, with *Afrocentrism* as its initial subphase. The fulfillment of each or all of these quests will be what I call the *Joshua phase.*

I have chosen these names for convenience and simplicity, although other names could have served just as well. I do not intend my survey to be exhaustive but to point out some things that God taught us through our history.

Each of the pre-Joshua phases has brought us closer to the "River Jordan," yet none has been able to take us across. Only those whose African-American consciousness is reconstructed around the Word of God will be able to implement the Joshua phase. They are the ones who can disciple our community through a similar reconstruction of

African-American culture. At the end of any of the previous phases, the Joshua phase could have been implemented. But it didn't happen. And if the discipler of the African-American culture does not address the legitimate concerns of today's new militants with a Joshua-phase reconstruction, the present quest too will fall short. We will wander in philosophical circles.

Before we examine the actual phases of our history, let's review the context out of which grew the early forms of African-American consciousness.

**Slave Resistance**

Columbus Salley and Ronald Behm write about the experience of slavery:

> The series of traumatic shocks involved had such an effect upon the Africans that their personality development was altered to suit the image and likeness of a system that assumed their inferiority.
>
> First, there was the shock of being captured. "The second shock—the long march to the sea—drew out the nightmare for many weeks. . . . Hardship, thirst, brutalities, and near starvation penetrated the experience of each exhausted man and woman who reached the coast." It was also shocking to be sold to foreign traders and then branded and herded into a strange ship. Then came the protracted and stupefying Middle Passage from Africa to the Americas. This dread transportation involved severe overcrowding, frequent rape, fatal disease and cruel beatings, all of which served to establish a master's absolute domination. The final shock came with a seasoning period in the West Indies during which slaves were taught obedience and cringing submission to their masters. . . .
>
> As an African came to America he was easily "fitted" for his work because he was divorced from his native culture and language. His number was inexhaustible, and his physical characteristics made identification unmistakable. As rationale and justification for the system, he was reputed (falsely) to come from an uncivilized

world, thus making slavery the means to the graces of white, Western . . . civilization.[7]

The whole basis of this dehumanizing practice was an illegitimate view of humanity—a view in which skin color determined not only a person's status but indeed the presence or lack of the image of God. It became a time-honored belief among many adherents of White Christianity-ism that the uprooted African had no soul. Black people were therefore classified as nonhuman—in later history as three-fifths human. So raping a female slave was not a crime, nor was it considered fornication or adultery.

Yet something positive began to develop in the consciousness of the enslaved Africans, something so significant that it would have a profound effect on African-American culture from the days of slavery up to the present. The slaves learned new things about God.

The early masters, with few exceptions, had never intended that their slaves should become Christian. However, this did not prevent the slaves from experiencing the power of the Word of God. As I pointed out in chapter three, resistance to oppression is itself an expression of God's grace. When a people are subjected to such oppression, they are driven inward, to the depths of the very humanity the oppression is trying to negate. Any cultural expressions that emerge from such a suffering people will come from those human depths. Other human beings who encounter these expressions will be affected at comparable depths. This, I believe, is what LeRoi Jones meant when he described us as the "Blues People."[8] This cultural depth and the skills to express such depth are what is today popularly known as "soul."

Humanity is made in the image of God, and through it God reveals his personhood and power. The deeper we go into our humanity, the more we experience God's power. This is part of the reason soul culture is so penetrating. It is also one reason the existence of God was never a matter of argument in our historic thinking. African-American culture always presupposed God. Soul culture thus became fertile ground for the gospel.

From various sources, many slaves began to pick up bits and pieces of biblical truth. By God's grace they were able to put these gospel fragments together and derive some interesting ideas. These early Black theologians began to set their fellow slaves on fire as they shared their insights. They began to get the notion that they were created in the image of God. This confirmed their sense of human worth and reaffirmed their awareness that being a slave was a contradiction to their dignity as human beings.

Black *spirituals** like "Swing Low, Sweet Chariot" and "Free at Last" became examples of historic Black theology. The writings and sayings of Frederick Douglass expressed the practical outworking of Black theology. Douglass, *Sojourner Truth,** *Harriet Tubman** and many other Black exponents of freedom were committed to Christ. The *Underground Railroad** itself became an application of the "good news."

As the fires of revival began to spread among the slaves, freedom from slavery came to symbolize human dignity, the outworking of salvation in this life. This, of course, presented a problem:

Christianity was a major barrier to be hurdled on the way to chattel racial slavery. There was an unwritten law that a Christian could not be held as a slave. Therefore, if Blacks were allowed to be converted, they could no longer be slaves, and baptism would be tantamount to emancipation. . . . To settle any doubt, the leading colony of Virginia in "a series of laws between 1667 and 1671 laid down the rule that conversion alone did not lead to a release from servitude." Finally, the Church of England accepted the position stated by Morgan Godwyn in 1680 that "Christianity" and slavery were *fully compatible*.[9]

This fully compatible "Christianity" was in reality slavemaster Christianity-ism. This is what the Black militants of the 1960s and the new militants of today have identified as the White man's religion. Since the slavemasters' attempt to stamp out or suppress the slave revival had proved to be futile, they tried instead to preempt it. They attempted to force on the slaves their own "more appropriate" Christianity-ism.

With the problem of the status of Christian slaves settled, efforts were made to spread ["Christianity"] among Blacks. In 1701 the Society for the Propagation of the Gospel in Foreign Parts (S.P.G.) was organized as a missionary arm of the Anglican Church. Its missionaries who worked among the slaves were opposed by slavemasters who were reluctant to allow time to their slaves for religious instruction. . . .

Those who were influenced were taught doctrine designed to support slavery, almost to the exclusion of the historic dogmas of the Christian faith. So, very early in colonial life an intimate and inseparable union between "Christianity" and the institution of slavery was effected.[10]

The Scriptures themselves warn us that "the time will come when men will not put up with sound doctrine" (2 Timothy 4:3). Slavery had opened the door for the emergence of unchristian Christianity-ism. But 2 Timothy goes on to say, "Instead, to suit their own desires, . . . they will turn their ears away from the truth and turn aside to myths" (vv. 3-4). Such myths became the basic ingredients of slavemaster Christianity-ism. Let's look at some of these myths.

### A Mark, a Curse and a Spook

First, a myth was created about the "mark of Cain." According to Genesis 4:1-15, Cain, a farmer, rebelled against God and killed his brother Abel, a shepherd. In response God punished Cain by putting the ground under a curse. Nothing would grow for him. Cain was condemned to be a homeless wanderer for the rest of his life.

Cain appealed to God on the grounds that (1) the punishment was too hard for him to bear and (2) he was afraid he'd be killed by anyone who found him. As an act of grace, God put a mark on Cain as a warning to everyone not to kill him. God told Cain that if anyone killed him, God would take seven lives in revenge.

The slavemasters' myth declared that the mark on Cain was dark skin. But the Bible neither says nor implies that this mark had anything to do with skin color. The Scripture just says that the mark was a warning not to kill Cain. (If the mark of Cain was dark skin, as some have dogmatically believed, then woe to those who have hurt or killed dark-skinned people, for they will be avenged by God sevenfold!) Of course, we will never know what the mark of Cain really was. Besides, all of Cain's descendants were killed in the flood.

A second myth revolved around a *curse on Ham** and his descendants. This myth is rooted in a twisted interpretation of Genesis 9:18-28. According to this passage, Noah had three sons: Shem, Ham and Japheth. (Ham was the father of Canaan.) Noah planted a vineyard, made some wine, got drunk, took off his clothes and lay naked in his tent. Ham discovered his father in his drunken, naked state; he told his brothers to take care of their father, and they did.

This was no sin on Ham's part. However, according to the myth, Ham laughed at Noah and mocked him. But Scripture neither records nor implies such irreverence on Ham's part.

When Noah sobered up and learned "what his youngest son had done to him," he cursed Canaan and his descendants. Advocates of the Ham myth deliberately ignore the fact that the Hebrew language had no word for grandson. Noah's "youngest son" was really his youngest male descendant. This was Canaan, Ham's youngest son and Noah's youngest grandson. It was Canaan and not Ham who irreverently took advantage of Noah's drunken condition and did something horrible to Noah. It was Canaan who left Noah naked in his tent.

Thus the curse fell on Canaan and the Canaanites, who followed his perverted example (Genesis 19:1-9). All the Canaanite kingdoms were eventually destroyed, fulfilling the curse on Canaan (2 Samuel 8:1; 1 Chronicles 18:1-14; Psalm 135:1-12).

One thing is clear. Ham and his other descendants had nothing to do with this curse. Ham was also the father of Cush, Egypt and Put (or Libya; Genesis 10:6-14), who are the fathers of the peoples of Africa. This curse has absolutely nothing to do with Africans or African-Americans.

A third myth pictured a totally otherworldly Jesus. If the slave system was to be preserved, then the slavemasters could not afford for the slaves to have a biblical Jesus who was fully human and fully divine. Such a Jesus might have something to do with salvation in this life. The slaves might get some dangerous ideas from Jesus' statements like "The Spirit of the Lord is on me, because he has anointed me . . . to proclaim freedom for the prisoners and . . . to release the oppressed" (Luke 4:18).

The humanity of Christ in particular presented a problem. If Jesus was really a man of southwest Asian or northeast African descent, he might have looked more like the slaves than like the slavemasters. Thus an exclusively White Jesus was substituted, a "man" who was totally otherworldly. This Jesus offered a salvation restricted to the hereafter. Jesus' humanity was diminished almost to nothing, and his divinity was rendered abstract. This fake Jesus was nothing more than a spineless spook and bore little resemblance to the biblical Christ. According to Scripture, Jesus came by way of incarnation (John 1:14); the slavemasters' mythological Jesus, however, was an invention of the spirit of antichrist, according to 1 John 4:1-3.

### Soul Force

Slavemaster Christianity-ism was rejected by most Christian slaves, but under its cover they began to develop an indigenous theological outlook and practice. Because slaves were not allowed to meet together without the presence of Whites, they began using "double-meaning" language. When the master was present in Black worship, he would think the slaves were singing and shouting about one thing (spiritual freedom, perhaps) when in reality they were thinking of another (freedom this side of heaven). This double-meaning language was passed down in our oral tradition.

Because the African-American church has not produced written confessions and creeds, some have said that it has not produced a theology. It is true that for many reasons, including the fact that our people were long denied access to reading and writing, we have been an oral and not a literary people. But to say that we have no theology because we have not produced it in literature is like saying that the

Jews of the exodus had no revelation before Sinai. The Jews were always singing about something, and some of these songs came to be recorded in the five books of Moses. It is within our oral tradition that we find historic Black theology. The rich oral tradition of the Black church—its music and its preaching—is the locus of theology in African-American culture.

The power of soul force was greatly multiplied by the power of God's Word, because the only indigenous channel of expression we had was the church. We learned to transform the Bible from its written form into an oral form, using soul culture. We produced a *theological dynamic** that captured nuggets of biblical truth in forceful phrases and images from life experience; we created a *cultural dynamic** of deeply moving expressions of Black consciousness reflecting the image of God in us. These two merged to become the *soul dynamic** that simmered, grew and mellowed through the days of slavery.

For our people, the written Word of God was like powdered milk, having all the nutrients of whole milk yet undrinkable because it was in the wrong form. Transforming the written Word of God into an oral Word of God was like adding water.[11] Though this transformed Word of God does not have the same authoritative weight as Scripture, it made the Word of God "drinkable" and had a powerful effect. Viewed comparatively, this theological dynamic was to classical Christian theology as art is to science, as intuitive knowledge is to cognitive knowledge, as the concrete is to the abstract, as the multidimensional is to the linear, as a mental image is to a concept.[12]

Since the African-American struggle has been against ethical wrongdoing, the theology of the African-American church has been essentially ethical. Since the major theme that runs throughout our history is the quest for true freedom and human dignity, the early days of this quest were a struggle to be consistent to God's image despite the forces of dehumanization. Thus from the days of slavery up to the present moment, the African-American experience has been a struggle against personal, institutional and legal wrongs that attempt to negate our humanity, our culture and our constitutional rights. Though the topic will be discussed more fully in chapter twelve, it will be helpful at this time to take a brief look at this theological dynamic from three perspectives: its content, its context and its experience.

*Content.* In Black theology, redemptive history is not treated as information merely to be analyzed and imparted. The events are dramatized by the preacher so that the whole congregation can join him in celebrating God's present grace and faithfulness while "reflecting back" on God's grace and faithfulness as revealed in the scriptural accounts. This is the genius of Black preaching. James Cone describes it in *God of the Oppressed:*

> The form of Black religious thought is expressed in the style of story and its content is liberation. . . . [Black people during slavery] intuitively perceived that the problem of the auction block and slave drivers would not be solved through philosophical debate. The problem had to be handled on the level of concrete history as that history was defined by the presence of the slavemasters. Slaves therefore had to devise a language commensurate with their social situation. That was why they told stories. Through the medium of stories, Black slaves created concrete and vivid pictures of their past and present existence, using the historical images of God's dealings with his people and thus breaking open the future for the oppressed not known to ordinary historical observation.[13]

*Context.* Black theology emphasizes the event of worship empowered by "the move of the Spirit" and our participation in the event. This is why expressions are chosen not for their rational value but for their emotive value, not for accuracy but for beauty.

Historic Black theology is not a spectator sport. The response of the listener is as much a part of preaching as the proclamation itself: "Can I get a witness?" asks the preacher. Celebration is the very cornerstone of Black worship; it is commonly called "having chu'ch."

*Experience.* Black theology is experiential and collective. When you listen to Black preaching, you hear "I" a great deal. It would be easy but wrong to conclude that this is individualistic. Rather, in good traditional Black preaching there is an intercourse between the preacher's proclamation and the congregation's response, which reaches its climax when the preacher becomes one with the congregation. At this point the preacher becomes prophet for the people. When he says "I," it becomes a collective "I" for the congregation. It is an experience that illustrates the mystical union of Christ and his church.

## A Unifying Force

This dynamic became the heart of the collective expression of Black resistance to White oppression. It was also the driving force behind the emergence of African-American culture. We were a people of different languages and cultures in Africa. Yet when the attempt was made to strip us of all humanity through oppression, the soul dynamic of resistance by God's grace emerged, not only giving us what we needed to survive the horrors of slavery but also galvanizing us into a cultural nation.

We have not always been good stewards of our soul dynamic. Witness our neglect of its ethical implications or the hostility that has existed among various groups based on complexion or status. Witness too our failure on occasion to apply the cultural power of the soul dynamic to resisting oppression. At various times in our history we have misapplied it to accommodating oppression instead of overcoming it.

Yet the soul dynamic was there, drawing us together as a people. We must remember that no nation has ever been a good steward of the gracious gifts of God. We are all unrighteous. However, in spite of human attempts to cut us off from God and make us nobodies, God made us somebody by bringing forth the African-American cultural nation so that by his grace we would "seek him and perhaps reach out for him and find him, though he is not far from each one of us. 'For in him we live and move and have our being' " (Acts 17:27-28).

# 5

# A Formative Phase

*O*ur quest for freedom and dignity has been shaped by the theological dynamic. Thus when we've been true to it, our quest for freedom has been a quest for the freedom of God's lordship. And our quest for dignity has been a quest for the being of God, because we have our being, our dignity, in him.

When we look at the phases of African-American history from this perspective, we will see that though ultimate freedom and dignity eluded us, we learned some valuable lessons about what it means to possess them in this life. Let's now take a closer but brief look at our formative phase and its aftermath.

## Colored

The Colored phase of our history was born in slavery. In it the myth of White supremacy was imposed on us, along with White standards. *Colored* (*darky* and *nigger* are equivalent terms), a label chosen for us by the slavemasters, allowed for division among our people.

"House slaves" were usually the products of the masters' sexual exploitation of the slaves. They were lighter in complexion and enjoyed a better quality of life than other slaves. Consequently they tended to be more devoted to the master than were the other Black brothers and sisters. "Field slaves," the workers and overseers, were usually darker in complexion and shared a contempt for the master.

The sexual exploitation of the slave woman caused a tangled net of trouble for everyone. (1) The Black man suspected the White man of having designs on his woman; (2) the Black man suspected the Black woman because he was never sure that she could be all his, even if she wanted to be; (3) the White woman suspected the Black woman of being the object of her husband's exploitation; and (4) the White man suspected the Black man, fearing that his male slave might do to his White woman what he was doing to the slave woman. The male slavemaster who sexually neglected his wife to exploit Black women was also afraid that his wife might seek satisfaction from a male slave. The portrayal of the Black male as a "stud" only aggravated his fear. Ironically, this White-generated fear was blamed on the Black male. By the time of the Reconstruction it had evolved into a mass paranoia that became the main rationale for the formation of the *Ku Klux Klan*\* and contributed to the roots of postslavery racism.

Suspicion between the house slaves and field slaves, as well as between Black women and Black men, established a pattern of intra-Black mistrust that lasted through many years. This negative self-image tended to keep anger and frustration internalized and served to free the masters from much of their worry of a slave revolt. Though the hearts of most slaves longed for freedom, the brute force of the institution of slavery prevented all but a very few from actualizing it. So the hope of freedom in the Colored phase became tied mostly to the hereafter.

In the early foundations of Southern Black theology, the *second exodus*\* became a major theme. The River Jordan represented death. On this side of the Jordan we lived in the Egypt of slavery, where we were the least among the American cultures. On the other side of the

Jordan we would be free to be with our Lord in the Promised Land, and we'd be first among the American cultures (figure 5).

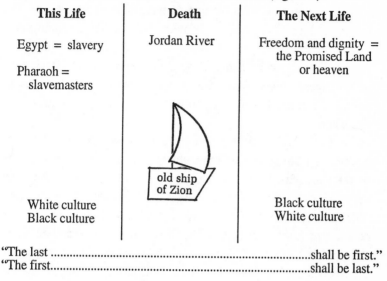

| This Life | Death | The Next Life |
|---|---|---|
| Egypt = slavery<br><br>Pharaoh =<br>slavemasters | Jordan River | Freedom and dignity =<br>the Promised Land<br>or heaven |
| White culture<br>Black culture | old ship<br>of Zion | Black culture<br>White culture |

"The last ..................................................................shall be first."
"The first..................................................................shall be last."

**Figure 5.** Structure of early Black theology

Though we did not achieve true freedom and human dignity at this time, we did learn several things during the Colored phase. Through the pain of exploitation we realized that slavery as practiced could never allow Black people the personal dignity the Bible declares open to all. We saw the parallel between our oppressed condition and that of the ancient Hebrews. Though faith in Christ promised us freedom on the other side of death, we were awakened in *faith* * also to pursue freedom on this side of the Jordan. We learned that life cannot be lived on an otherworldly basis, with hope only for the hereafter. In short, we learned that the God of the Bible was truly God, while the god offered us in Christianity-ism was no god at all.

### Nonslavery to Neoslavery

After the Civil War (1861-1865) and *Emancipation,* * the end of slavery was no longer a dream but reality. The remarkable political and social progress made by Blacks during Reconstruction gave our people hope that the scars of slavery would soon be eliminated from our collective psyche. This progress was largely inspired by the positive theological outlook that emerged in the 1820s among free Blacks in the North.[1]

An ex-slave, Blanche Kelso Bruce, was representing Mississippi in the United States Senate. Pinckney Benton Stewart Pinchback, young, charming, daring, was sitting in the governor's mansion in Louisiana.

In Mississippi, in South Carolina, in Louisiana, Negro lieutenant governors were sitting on the right hand of power. A Negro was secretary of state in Florida; a Negro was on the state supreme court in South Carolina. Negroes were superintendents of education, state treasurers, adjutant generals, solicitors, judges and major generals of militia. Robert H. Wood was mayor of Natchez, Mississippi, and Norris Wright Cuney was running for mayor of Galveston, Texas. Seven Negroes were sitting in the House of Representatives.[2]

However, the "freedom" wrought by the Emancipation Proclamation turned out to fall short of true freedom. It was diminished as the Reconstruction lost momentum. It was demolished with the final *death blow to the Reconstruction** in 1877, at the inauguration of President Rutherford B. Hayes. Hayes, for political reasons, withdrew the federal troops that had been enforcing the provisions of the *Thirteenth, Fourteenth and Fifteenth Amendments** to the Constitution in the South. The former slaves were thereby abandoned to the devices of those who wanted to reestablish White supremacy. As a result, a neoslavery emerged—a system of oppression rooted in political disenfranchisement, racial segregation and exploitative economic relationships that subjugated Blacks to Whites. This became known as the *Jim Crow backlash,**[3] and the laws that undergirded it were known as the "black codes."

Roughly contemporary with the Jim Crow backlash in the South was the Industrial Revolution of the North. The Industrial Revolution had a far-reaching impact on the American population. During the last quarter of the nineteenth century a wave of immigrants from Europe had washed over the United States. America was becoming a multi-ethnic, multicultural and multilingual society, especially in the North-eastern cities. In the minds of many, American society had to find a way to stay culturally American. Thus the concept of the *melting pot*\* was born. The public school system became the ideal vehicle for inculcating the melting-pot value system.

What the Jim Crow backlash achieved in the South, the melting-pot concept achieved in the North: the exclusion of Black people from mainstream American life. Not everyone could melt into the pot, only the European immigrants. And their ability to melt was directly related to their closeness to Anglo-Saxon culture.[4] This bleak situation was further aggravated because the Jim Crow movement spilled over into the North and the melting-pot movement spilled over into the South.

**The White Church in Transition**

Many White Christians had been faithful to the cultural mandate of Jesus Christ during Reconstruction. They brought education and other forms of help to the former slaves. When the pressure of Jim Crowism arose in the late 1870s, however, they were forced to abandon the African-American community, leaving us to face the horrors of the Southern racist backlash alone.

Another concern was drawing White Christians' attention. Just after the turn of the twentieth century, the "battle for the Bible" was heating up. On one side were those following in the footsteps of others who a century earlier had given in to the basic assumptions of secular humanism. As a result, their Christianity had eroded into an empty Christianity-ism, with a god whose substance depended on human definition and human opinion. For them Jesus was a mere man—a prophet at best—and the Bible was merely a human book containing some passages that might be considered "inspired" in some vague way. These people became known as "liberals" or "modernists."

The liberals had lost their theological direction and had nothing to do but play connotation word games. This all changed in 1907, when Walter Rauschenbusch published *Christianity and the Social Crisis.*[5] Advocating social action and neglecting personal salvation, his "social gospel" breathed new life into the liberal movement.

On the other side of the battle were those who, reacting against the liberals, advocated personal salvation and orthodox doctrine over social action. They became known as *fundamentalists** or "conservatives." Those who stood for the *conceptual* authority of Scripture took the fundamentalist side, while those who stood for the *ethical* authority of Scripture took the liberal side. To make a sharp distinction between themselves and the liberals, many fundamentalists abandoned all social involvement and concentrated on merely getting people "saved." They wrongly identified social action with *liberalism** rather than Christian action. Furthermore, the fiascoes of *Prohibition** and the *Scopes trial** made fundamentalists feel the heat of cultural defeat. This effectively closed the books on fundamentalist cultural involvement and opened the door for secular humanism.

The Bible itself never sets up such a dichotomy between personal salvation and social action, between conceptual and ethical authority. So in essence both sides lost the battle of the Bible. Between 1877 and 1930 the White Bible-believing churches developed a double isolation from the Black community: They capitulated to White racism, and they adopted a socially impotent gospel. The rift was deep, because social ethics and the quest for freedom and dignity lay at the heart of historic Black theology. The social retreat of White Bible-believing Christianity made it resemble White Christianity-ism.

### Advance and Retreat
In spite of the abandonment of the White Christians, the Black church had the theological dynamic that had been brewing throughout the days of slavery. By the time of the Emancipation we had seen one of the most powerful examples of the spread of the gospel since the days of Paul. America witnessed a "most astonishing success of Protestantism" in the overwhelming conversion of the African-American com-

munity.[6] This explosive growth of the African-American church be-tween 1860 and 1910 (the harvest of seed planted a century or more earlier) has remained, thus far, unparalleled in American history.

The Black church was utterly bewildered by the abortion of Recon-struction and the onslaught of the Jim Crow backlash. By the 1880s and 1890s it had yet to apply Black theology to the realities of disenfranchisement. Because the practice of the old, practical Black theology had been lost, Jim Crow Christianity-ism was imposed on large segments of the Black church in the South. So the Black church degenerated into an "accommodative church."[7] "The preachers in these churches oriented their members to White domination in society. As Black ministers had played the role of mediator and spokesperson before the Civil War, so they continued during this period. In terms of race relations, the Black churches' main function was to accommodate their members to their subordinate status in White society."[8]

The attempt to apply the theological dynamic to accommodation temporarily crippled the Southern church. But that did not stop the quest for freedom and dignity. It continued, but no longer within the bounds of church culture. The church would later partially recover from this paralysis and again become a major force in the quest, but the next two phases developed without leadership from the church. In the next chapter we will look at these phases, as well as the branches into which the quest divided.

# 6
# Two Streams

With the emergence of post-Reconstruction oppression, Black resistance moved toward two goals: to overcome the effects of Jim Crow in the South and to enter into the melting pot in the North. The quest would now flow in two streams, northern and southern. Both streams have attempted to achieve freedom and dignity by two strategies, integration (or desegregation) and consolidation around Black cultural resources. The southern stream first tried a consolidation strategy in the Neo-Colored phase of our history.

### The Neo-Colored Phase

*Booker T. Washington** was the main exponent of the Neo-Colored strategy. He told us that we needed to consolidate around the skills and resources we had gained from slavery and earn freedom and dignity. In his 1895 address to a White audience at the Atlanta Exposition, Booker T. said,

A ship lost at sea for many days suddenly sighted a friendly vessel. From the mast of the unfortunate vessel was seen a signal, "Water, water; we die of thirst!" The answer from the friendly vessel at once came back, "Cast down your bucket where you are." A second time the signal, "Water, water; send us water!" ran up from the distressed vessel, and was answered, "Cast down your bucket where you are." And a third and fourth signal for water was answered, "Cast down your bucket where you are." The captain of the distressed vessel, at last heeding the injunction, cast down his bucket, and it came up full of fresh, sparkling water from the mouth of the Amazon river. To those of my race, . . . I would say: "Cast down your bucket where you are"—cast it down in making friends in every manly way of the people of all races by whom we are surrounded.

Cast it down in agriculture, mechanics, in commerce, in domestic service, and in the professions. . . . No race can prosper till it learns that there is as much dignity in tilling a field as in writing a poem. It is at the bottom of life we must begin, and not at the top. . . .

To those of the white race . . . I say . . . you can be sure in the future, as in the past, that you and your families will be surrounded by the most patient, faithful, law-abiding, and unresentful people that the world has seen. As we have proved our loyalty to you in the past, in nursing your children, watching by the sickbed of your mothers and fathers, and often following them with tear-dimmed eyes to their graves, so in the future, in our humble way, we shall stand by you with a devotion that no foreigner can approach, ready to lay down our lives, if need be, in defense of yours, interlacing our industrial, commercial, civil, and religious life with yours in a way that shall make the interests of both races one. In all things that are purely social we can be as separate as the fingers, yet one as the hand in all things essential to mutual progress.[1]

In other words, if we proved ourselves worthy and industrious enough in our humble manual and skilled labor, the White folks would eventually welcome us. This optimism about the goodwill of White people was the major premise of *White humanism*\* among Blacks. It did not bear fruit. White folks refused to accept our hard work. And after the European immigrants learned our skills, which we freely shared with them, we were systematically eliminated from the skilled labor force. By the early 1920s this system of elimination was well established through White-only trade unions. Hence a major portion of the southern-based Neo-Colored strategy was nullified by racism, and the rest of this phase slowly faded.

Though it did not work for us, the Neo-Colored movement did set a workable pattern for other ethnic groups. And we learned several things for ourselves during this phase. First, mere nonslavery provided neither true freedom nor human dignity. Second, we needed to consolidate around our existing resources as a people. Third, it was essential that we develop the resources we already had if we were going to achieve our goal. White humanism had proved to be a farce as far as we were concerned; White standards gave us no ground for or means of dignity. If we wanted to melt in, we'd have to find another way than the good graces of Whites and the honest labor of our hands.

Around 1900, Northern men like *W. E. B. Du Bois\** and *W. Monroe Trotter\** began to fire blistering criticisms at Booker T. Washington. They saw the need to pull together as a cultural nation, demand our rights and deal with our situation from a position of militant educational strength. However, the window of opportunity had passed for these militant ideas to catch on. The trauma that accompanied the end of Reconstruction caused African-Americans to once again become preoccupied with issues of survival.

On the other hand, the concept of an educational base for consolidation proved to be too far ahead of its time. This idea did not have broad enough acceptance among the Northern Black population of that time to fuel a major movement. The North had been a haven for Southern Blacks during slavery. It was harder for them to see the deep problems of life in the North, since they had seen much worse in the South.

Following World War I, large numbers of Black people migrated from the South to the Northern cities in search of jobs and a better way of life. This migration swelled the population, especially in the North-eastern cities, and the time came when Black people would no longer be satisfied with the slight measure of dignity allotted them there.

## The Negro Phase

As selected European cultures began to melt into the melting pot, the African-American cultural nation, lacking European roots, began to burn, crushed by the weight of the melting pot against the hot coals of oppression. Freedom and dignity were taken from our grasp—they appeared to be locked inside the melting pot. Entering the pot became the new hope of achieving freedom and dignity.

For some Northern Blacks getting into the melting pot by any means necessary was all that mattered. As a result, in the early 1920s a consensus began to develop among those who were seriously trying to enter. This consensus I call the Negro phase.

Those involved in the strategy learned some lessons from the failure of the Neo-Colored phase. But they never saw the need to consolidate our people, nor did they jettison the baggage of White humanism. They thought the problem was not White humanism but rather the strategy we had employed to make it come alive. They agreed that to achieve melting-pot status, one had to become just like the melting-pot folks. So the key strategy of the Negro phase became imitation.

A certain young man observed this when he lived in Boston during the late 1930s:

I saw those Roxbury Negroes acting and living differently from any black people I'd ever dreamed of in my life. . . . What I thought I was seeing . . . were high-class, educated, important Negroes, living well, working in big jobs and positions. . . . These Negroes walked along the sidewalks looking haughty and dignified, on their way to work, to shop, to visit, to church. . . . They prided themselves on being incomparably more "cultured," "cultivated," "dignified," and better off than their black brethren down in the ghetto, which was no further away than you could throw a rock. Under the pitiful misapprehension that it would make them "better," these Hill Negroes were breaking their backs trying to imitate white people.

Any black family that had been around Boston long enough to own the home they lived in was considered among the Hill elite. It didn't make any difference that they had to rent out rooms to make ends meet. Then the native-born New Englanders among them looked down upon recently migrated Southern home-owners who lived next door . . . .

In those days on the Hill, any who could claim "professional" status—teachers, preachers, practical nurses—also considered themselves superior. . . .

I'd guess that eight out of ten of the Hill Negroes of Roxbury, despite the impressive-sounding job titles they affected, actually worked as menials and servants. "He's in banking," or "He's in securities." It sounded as though they were discussing a Rockefeller or a Mellon—and not some greyheaded, dignity-posturing bank janitor, or bond-house messenger. "I'm with an old family" was the euphemism used to dignify the professions of white folks' cooks and maids who talked so affectedly among their own kind in Roxbury that you couldn't even understand them. I don't know how many forty and fifty year old errand boys went down the Hill dressed like ambassadors in black suits and white collars, to down-town jobs "in government," "in finance," or "in law." It has never ceased to amaze me how so many Negroes, then and now, could stand the indignity of that kind of self-delusion.[2]

Hence some of us began to "talk proper," desire a pale complexion, avoid getting suntans and straighten our hair.

The same young observer described what he went through in his pre-Black days to get a hairstyle (a "conk") that looked like straight White hair.

The congolene [a mixture of eggs, potatoes and lye] just felt warm when Shorty [his best friend] started combing it in. But then my head caught fire.

I gritted my teeth and tried to pull the sides of the kitchen table together. The comb felt as if it was raking my skin off.

My eyes watered, my nose was running. I couldn't stand it any longer; I bolted to the washbasin. I was cursing Shorty with every name I could think of when he got the spray going and started soap-lathering my head.

He lathered and spray-rinsed, lathered and spray-rinsed, maybe ten or twelve times, each time gradually closing the hot-water faucet, until the rinse was cold, and that helped some.

"You feel any stinging spots?"

"No," I managed to say. My knees were trembling.

"Sit back down, then. I think we got it all out okay."

The flame came back as Shorty, with a thick towel, started drying my head, rubbing hard. *"Easy, man, easy!"* I kept shouting.

"The first time's always worst. You get used to it better before long. You took it real good, homeboy. You got a good conk."

When Shorty let me stand up and see in the mirror, my hair hung down in limp, damp strings. My scalp still flamed, but not as badly; I would bear it. He draped the towel around my shoulders . . . and began again vaselining my hair.

I could feel him combing, straight back, first the big comb, then the fine-toothed one. . . .

My first view in the mirror blotted out the hurting. I'd seen some pretty conks, but when it's the first time, on your *own* head, the transformation, after the lifetime of kinks, is staggering. . . .

On top of my head was this thick, smooth sheen of shining red hair—real red—as straight as any white man's. . . .

How ridiculous I was! Stupid enough to stand there simply lost in admiration of my hair now looking "white."

This was my first really big step toward self-degradation: when I endured all of that pain, literally burning my flesh to have it look like a white man's hair. I had joined that multitude of Negro men and women in America who are brainwashed into believing that the black people are "inferior"—and white people "superior"—that they will even violate and mutilate their God-created bodies to try to look "pretty" by white standards.[3]

Because *Negro* was a label chosen for us by Whites, it allowed for gradation in color. We even learned to discriminate against ourselves on the basis of color. If a Negro happened to have a very pale complexion, naturally straight hair and a mastery of "proper talk," he was able to "pass for White" and melt into the pot. Some estimate that we lost at least fifty thousand Negroes a year this way.

The Negro strategy of the urban North had bought a pseudosophisticated lifestyle. And the religious expression of this movement I call "Polly Parrot Christianity-ism." It was an imitation of the old "White Man's religion" minus the supernatural. In it God was unimportant. An ultracold style of worship replaced the practices of historic Black theology. Heaven and hell were considered myths, and jumping, shouting, rhythm and other expressions of emotion were considered uncivilized. Those who practiced Polly Parrot Christiany-ism were ashamed of the soul dynamic and tried to distance themselves from it.

But how can people be free if they are not free to be themselves? How can people find dignity if they are ashamed of their cultural and ethnic heritage? Pretending to be White is bondage to a lie and demeaning to a person's character. After all, what would the Negro who was "passing" do if his White associates found out that he was not White?

In spite of the obvious failures of the Negro strategy, many who practiced it continued to do so for several decades. From the late fifties through the early sixties there was a great defection with the rise of the next southern phase. In the late sixties and early seventies the Negro strategy received its death blow as the next northern phase erupted.

Though we did not achieve freedom and dignity, we learned several things through the Negro phase. We learned that the strategy of imitation is unworkable for most of our people because it is based on factors of genetics and environment over which we have no control. And we learned that imitating the melting-pot lifestyle, racism and standards leads to intra-Negro complexion consciousness, self-hatred, feelings of inferiority and economic stress. Though it did not work for us, the Negro movement set a pattern for other ethnic groups that did prove successful for them.

Along with urbanization came ghettoization, which victimized those who did not have the imitational skills, physical characteristics, money or willingness to practice the "Negro" lifestyle. Housing discrimination killed any chance for Black people to escape the ghetto the way some other ethnic groups were doing.

Obviously these folks did not practice Polly Parrot Christianityism, and from them emerged a new type of African-American church that was in some ways the forerunner of the Neo-Negro church (see chapter seven). "The Black church, which had given Black people a survival style in a hostile White world, responded to urbanization and White withdrawal by developing a new mental outlook concerning its role in American society. The increasing economic diversity of the Black community in the city transformed the accommodative Black church into a secular church."[4]

As this new urban church began to recover from the crippling effects of being squeezed into the role of accommodation, it began to take a more active role in the life of the African-American community.

As large middle-class and mixed-class congregations grew up in the urban center, the preacher was expected to devote more time to community affairs and the advancement of the race. These activities, as always, were within the accepted limitations of the White power structure. They therefore consisted largely of improvements in housing, education and the like rather than in "social equality and integration with whites."

Even within this change of perspective by Black churches, traditional loyalty to the Baptist and Methodist churches prevailed. But the predominantly otherworldly outlook and concern for the purely "spiritual" was diminished. A number of the northern Black ministers became influential in politics and in protest.[5]

Ghettoization had produced an urban Black population that was increasingly frustrated and angry over being crowded into substandard housing and trapped in the cycle of poor schooling, underemployment and poverty. From the next phase in the northern stream would emerge a philosophy focusing this anger and causing a sweeping cultural change—a change that would fan the flames of this smoldering resentment into an urban eruption.

Meanwhile, in the South, cultural forces were already converging to usher in the next southern phase. Chapter seven will focus on this strategic phase and its heroic spokesperson.

# 7

# "De Lawd"

*B*uilt on the ruins of the Neo-Colored phase and based on historic Southern Black theology, another strategy emerged. In its early days the Neo-Negro strategy was an attempt to bring to the South the same level of freedom that African-Americans in the North seemed to enjoy. Desegregation was the goal. This phase came to the fore shortly after the Supreme Court ruled *segregation unconstitutional** in 1954. It quickly became obvious, however, that desegregation was not going to come about through the goodness of people's hearts. We had learned through the Neo-Colored and the Negro phases that as far as we were concerned, White humanism was on its deathbed. The only way for us to enter the American mainstream was through law.

### The Spirit of the Time

We had no idea how to mobilize the kind of cultural power needed to overcome hard-core Jim Crowism and legally break the patterns of segregation. The Neo-Negro consensus, however, was that once we achieved desegregation, racial tension would subside. The ignorance that had been the basis for racial prejudice would be wiped out through understanding. "Men often hate each other because they fear each other; they fear each other because they do not know each other; they do not know each other because they cannot communicate; they cannot communicate because they are separated."[1] The stage was set for a new movement to meet the challenge. It was the right time.

On December 1, 1955, an attractive Negro seamstress, Mrs. Rosa Parks, boarded the Cleveland Avenue bus in downtown Montgomery [Alabama]. She was returning home after her regular day's work in a leading department store. Tired from long hours on her feet, Mrs. Parks sat down in the first seat behind the section reserved for whites. Not long after she took her seat, the bus operator ordered her, along with three other Negro passengers, to move back in order to accommodate boarding white passengers.

By this time every seat in the bus was taken. This meant that if Mrs. Parks followed the driver's command she would have to stand while a white male passenger, who had just boarded the bus, would sit. The other three Negro passengers immediately complied with the driver's request. But Mrs. Parks quietly refused. The result was her arrest. . . .

She was anchored to that seat by the accumulated indignities of days gone by and the boundless aspirations of generations yet unborn. She was a victim of both the forces of history and the forces of destiny. She had been tracked down by the *Zeitgeist*—the spirit of the time.[2]

This was the first of a sequence of events that would consolidate and bring to national attention the Neo-Negro phase of our history. The arrest of *Rosa Parks*\* sent waves of outrage throughout the African-American community of Montgomery. For the first time in anybody's memory, the Black community was of one mind on what to do about the situation. This oneness was recognized at the meeting of Montgomery's Black ministers: "Something unusual was about to happen."[3]

Though the meeting lacked coherence, no one present questioned the validity of the proposed response: a bus boycott. Almost all the influential Black ministers were present at that meeting, and they agreed to speak to their congregations on Sunday morning about the proposed boycott. A citywide meeting was planned for Monday night, December 5, to determine how long they would refuse to ride the buses.

The first day of the boycott was a total success. As one eyewitness described it,

All day long it continued. . . . During the rush hours the sidewalks were crowded with laborers and domestic workers, many of them well past middle age, trudging patiently to their jobs and home again, sometimes as much as twelve miles. They knew why they walked, and the knowledge was evident in the way they carried themselves. And as I watched them I knew that there is nothing more majestic than the determined courage of individuals willing to suffer and sacrifice for their freedom and dignity.[4]

### The Right Man

Present at the ministers' meeting that night of Mrs. Parks's arrest was a young preacher who had just finished his doctoral thesis. He had devoted a great deal of time to its writing and was looking forward to giving more attention to his church work. Because of this he had turned down an opportunity to run for president of the local chapter of the *National Association for the Advancement of Colored People (NAACP)*.* But now he was caught by the current of history; leadership for the protest had to be chosen.

As soon as [Roy] Bennett had opened the nominations for president, Rufus Lewis spoke from the far corner of the room: "Mr. Chairman, I would like to nominate Reverend M. L. King for president." The motion was seconded and carried, and in a matter of minutes I was unanimously elected.

The action had caught me unawares. It had happened so quickly that I did not even have time to think it through. It is probable that if I had, I would have declined the nomination.[5]

Events had moved too fast. It was unanimously agreed that the protest should continue until certain demands were met. These demands were drawn up in the form of a resolution to be presented at the December 5 meeting for approval. Dr. King was to make the main address.

"I was now almost overcome, obsessed by a feeling of inadequacy," confessed King. He had nowhere to turn but to God, "whose matchless strength stands over against the frailties and inadequacies of human nature."[6] He prayed for guidance.

I faced a new and sobering dilemma: How could I make a speech that would be militant enough to keep my people aroused to positive action and yet moderate enough to keep this fervor within controllable and Christian bounds? . . . Could the militant and the moderate be combined in a single speech?

I decided that I had to face the challenge head on, and attempt to combine two apparent irreconcilables. I would seek to arouse the group to action by insisting that their self-respect was at stake and that if they accepted such injustices without protesting, they would betray their own sense of dignity and the eternal edicts of God Himself. But I would balance this with a strong affirmation of the Christian doctrine of love.[7]

In accepting the responsibility of spokesperson, King found his mind being "driven back to the Sermon on the Mount and the Gandhian method of nonviolent resistance. This principle became the guiding light of our movement. Christ furnished the spirit and motivation and [Mahatma] Gandhi furnished the method."[8]

When Monday night came, the cars and people were lined up as far as the eye could see. They were all headed to the meeting. With TV cameras running, Dr. Martin Luther King Jr. began to deliver a speech that would change the course of history.

Without referring to notes, he told the story of what happened to Mrs. Parks. Then he reviewed the long history of abuses that Black citizens had experienced on the city buses. He continued:

But there comes a time that people get tired. We are here this evening to say to those who have mistreated us so long that we are tired—tired of being segregated and humiliated; tired of being kicked about by the brutal feet of oppression. We had no alternative but to protest. For many years, we have shown amazing patience. We have sometimes given our white brothers the feeling that we liked the way we were being treated. But we come here tonight to be saved from that patience that makes us patient with anything less than freedom and justice. . . .

Our method will be that of persuasion, not coercion. . . . Our actions must be guided by the deepest principles of our Christian faith. Love must be our regulating ideal. Once again we must hear the words of Jesus echoing across the centuries: "Love your enemies, bless them that curse you, and pray for them that despitefully use you." If we fail to do this our protest will end up as a meaningless drama on the stage of history, and its memory will be shrouded with the ugly garments of shame. In spite of the mistreatment that we have confronted we must not become bitter and end up by hating our white brothers. As Booker T. Washington said, "Let no man pull you so low as to make you hate him."

If you will protest courageously, and yet with dignity and Christian love, when the history books are written in future generations, the historians will have to pause and say, "There lived a great people—a black people—who injected new meaning and dignity in the veins of civilization." This is our challenge and our overwhelming responsibility.[9]

As Dr. King sat listening to the long applause, he realized that his speech had evoked more response than any speech or sermon he had ever delivered, and yet it had been virtually unprepared. He came to realize for the first time what the older preachers meant when they said, "Open your mouth and God will speak for you."[10]

To parallel Mordecai's statement to Queen Esther (Esther 4:14): If Martin had kept quiet at that time, help would have come from another quarter. But Dr. King was ready at the right time, and he gave the people a message they could act on.

## The Right Message

Nonviolent protest was the tool Dr. King introduced in Montgomery. Through the years he became more and more convinced of the power of nonviolence to bring about justice. Montgomery became a testing ground, a crucible. *Truth force* and *love force* consolidated in African-American culture as "soul force." In Montgomery were thousands of Black folks whose "feets was tired" but whose "souls was at rest"— and many empty buses. White folks frequently harassed them, while the KKK stirred up violence.

The result, after 384 days, was the birth of a powerful movement that overflowed from the Montgomery crucible throughout Alabama, the South, the United States—and ultimately to the ends of the earth.

What was it that gave the Civil Rights Movement and its main prophet the uncanny power to transform a downtrodden people into a mighty army, to bring the most powerful government on earth to its knees in repentance?

To many Whites in the South who thought their "Coloreds" were happy with the status quo and well cared for, the Civil Rights Movement was incomprehensible. It caught them completely off-guard. Many Whites expressed complete bewilderment at the transformation of Black folks as they became caught up in the new Southern winds that were beginning to blow down the mighty citadels of segregation: "I dawn't unda-stay'en what's goin' awn. T's like some'mm dun jumped inta awva nigras ova'night."

Many have tried to explain the Civil Rights Movement merely as a people movement, but it doesn't work! As Brother Martin himself explained, this movement, which suddenly catapulted him into world-wide recognition, cannot be explained without God. In 1958 he wrote:

Every rational explanation breaks down at some point. There is something about the protest that is suprarational; it cannot be explained without a divine dimension. . . . God still works through history His wonders to perform. It seems as though God had decided to use Montgomery as the proving ground for the struggle and triumph of freedom and justice in America. And what better place for it than the leading symbol of the Old South? It is one of the splendid ironies of our day that Montgomery, the Cradle of the Confederacy, is being transformed into Montgomery, the cradle of freedom and justice. . . .

In the first days of the protest none of these expressions was mentioned; the phrase most often heard was "Christian love." It was the Sermon on the Mount, rather than a doctrine of passive resistance, that initially inspired the Negroes of Montgomery to dignified social action. It was Jesus of Nazareth that stirred the Negroes to protest with the creative weapon of love.[11]

## A Tale of One City

As early as the post-World War II years, several African-American leaders had begun to contemplate the significance of 1963, the one-hundred-year anniversary of the Emancipation Proclamation (January 1, 1863). It was painfully obvious to them that after all the years of legal freedom, we were still under the yoke of racism. Many leaders began to call for the full implementation of the Fourteenth and Fifteenth Amendments. Montgomery had awakened the nation, and now "Free by '63" became the rallying cry, echoing through the Black nation during the 1950s and into the early 1960s. Thus our focus was on 1963. King wrote:

Yet not all of these forces conjoined could have brought about the massive and largely bloodless Revolution of 1963 if there had not been at hand a philosophy and a method worthy of its goals. Nonviolent direct action did not originate in America, but it found its natural home in this land, where refusal to cooperate with injustice was an ancient and honorable tradition and where Christian forgiveness was written into the minds and hearts of good men. Tested in Montgomery during the winter of 1955-56, and toughened throughout the South in the eight ensuing years, nonviolent resistance had become, by 1963, the logical force in the greatest mass-action crusade for freedom that has ever occurred in American history.[12]

Nowhere was this crusade for freedom in 1963 seen more clearly than Birmingham, Alabama. Birmingham's brutal system of segregation was well known throughout the South. It had thoroughly intimidated all who lived under its yoke. It was in the Birmingham of Theopholis Eugene "Bull" Connor, the public safety commissioner, that the power of soul force was most visibly demonstrated.

In Connor's Birmingham, the silent password was fear. It was a fear not only on the part of the black oppressed, but also in the hearts of the white oppressors. Guilt was a part of their fear. There was also the dread of change, that all too prevalent fear which hounds those whose attitudes have been hardened by the long winter of reaction.

Many were apprehensive of social ostracism. Certainly Birmingham had its white moderates who disapproved of Bull Connor's tactics. Certainly Birmingham had its decent white citizens who privately deplored the maltreatment of Negroes. But they remained publicly silent. It was a silence born of fear—fear of social, political and economic reprisals. The ultimate tragedy of Birmingham was not the brutality of bad people, but the silence of the good people.[13]

### Lessons from Birmingham

The movement in Birmingham can teach us a number of things. It teaches us about *ethics*. * Dr. King, along with hundreds of others, had been arrested for demonstrating against segregation. In his "Letter from the Birmingham Jail" King not only answered his critics but also provided a definitive ethical basis for the whole civil rights movement, an apologetic I will discuss later.[14] Birmingham demonstrated that to go to jail in the cause of freedom was both an honor and a spiritual experience. Behind the Birmingham bars, the older participants led Bible studies that spoke to the events transpiring about them. They led the demonstrators in prayer and thanksgiving, for they could see the hand of God at work in their midst. Thus the theological dynamic was part of the very fabric of the Birmingham event.

An important part of the mass meetings was the freedom songs. In a sense the freedom songs are the soul of the movement. They are more than just incantations of clever phrases designed to invigorate a campaign; they are as old as the history of the Negro in America. They are adaptations of the songs the slaves sang—the sorrow songs, the shouts for joy, the battle hymns and the anthems of our movement. I have heard people talk of their beat and rhythm, but we in the movement are as inspired by their words. "Woke Up This Morning with My Mind Stayed on Freedom" is a sentence that needs no music to make its point. We sing the freedom songs today for the same reason the slaves sang them, because we too are in bondage and the songs add hope to our determination that "We shall overcome, Black and White together, We shall overcome someday."

I have stood in a meeting with hundreds of youngsters and joined in while they sang "Ain't Gonna Let Nobody Turn Me 'Round." It is not a song; it is a resolve. A few minutes later, I have seen those same youngsters refuse to turn around from the onrush of a police dog, refuse to turn around before a pugnacious Bull Connor in command of men armed with power hoses. These songs bind us together, give us courage together, help us to march together.[15]

**The Red Sea**
As the Birmingham drama unfolded, tensions increased. Adult demonstrators by the hundreds were rounded up by the police. As these protestors were jailed, teenagers and children quickly stepped in to replace them. The Birmingham jails overflowed. In repeated skirmishes with the police, the marchers were brutalized with clubs and fire hoses.

It was inevitable that all this would climax in a violent and deadly confrontation with Bull Connor and his men. People throughout the city began to pray earnestly for God's special intervention to prevent the anticipated bloodshed.

The dreaded climax came, but God manifested his grace. For even those under the direct authority of Bull Connor were moved by the

Spirit to obey God rather than man. Connor became so frustrated that
he was driven into a frenzy of fury as the whole world looked on.

*It was a Sunday afternoon, when several hundred Birmingham
Negroes had determined to hold a prayer meeting near the city jail.
They gathered at the New Pilgrim Baptist Church and began an
orderly march. Bull Connor ordered out the police dogs and fire
hoses. When the marchers approached the border between the
white and Negro areas, Connor ordered them to turn back. The
Reverend Charles Billups, who was leading the march, politely
refused.*

We asked everybody to get down on their knees. And they got
down on their knees in their Easter Sunday go to meet'n [clothes].
Somebody just started praying in these old traditional chants of the
Black community [the theological dynamic]. People were moan-
ing, crying and praying. . . . Bull Connor was totally difficult and
said he was going to throw us all in jail.

All of a sudden some old lady got up and said "God is with this
movement, we goin' on to the jail." She got up and everybody
started [getting up].

*Enraged, Bull Connor whirled on his men and shouted:*
"Dammit. Turn on the hoses."[16]

What happened in the next thirty seconds was one of the most fantastic
events of the Birmingham story.

*Bull Connor's men, their deadly hoses poised for action, stood
facing the marchers.*

If they had turned [the hoses] on, the pressure from that close
distance would have broken people's ribs. Bull Connor was [yell-
ing], "Stop 'em, Stop 'em!!!"

*The marchers, many of them [still] on their knees, stared back,
unafraid and unmoving. Slowly the Negroes stood up and began to
advance.*

These firemen, . . . who really didn't know any better, had been
so moved by this experience, that . . . they never turned the hoses
on.

*Connor's men, as though hypnotized, fell back, their hoses sagging uselessly in their hands while several hundred Negroes marched past them.*

The dogs that had been straining at the leash, jumping at us, all of a sudden just stopped, and we walked right on through. And somebody hollered out, "Great God Almighty done parted the Red Sea one more time!!"[17]

This broke the back of segregation in Birmingham. It brought the White leaders to the conference table, and in the end, even the opposition could not withstand the power of soul force.

Birmingham taught us not only about ethics and the dynamic of the situation, but also about people. The movement had a profound effect on Blacks who had previously been intimidated. There was a new spirit in the air. King wrote of the oppressed at this time:

When, for decades, you have been able to make a man compromise his manhood by threatening him with a cruel and unjust punishment, and when suddenly he turns upon you and says: "Punish me. I do not deserve it. But because I do not deserve it, I will accept it so that the world will know that I am right and you are wrong," you hardly know what to do. You feel defeated and secretly ashamed. You know that this man is as good a man as you are; that from some mysterious source he has found the courage and the conviction to meet physical force with soul force.[18]

Of the effect on the oppressor, Dr. King wrote:

Nonviolent resistance paralyzed and confused the power structures against which it was directed. The brutality with which officials would have quelled the black individual became impotent when it could not be pursued with stealth and remain unobserved.

It was caught—as a fugitive from a penitentiary is often caught—in gigantic circling spotlights. It was imprisoned in a luminous glare revealing the naked truth to the whole world.[19]

What happened in Birmingham was a classic confrontation between actions derived from righteousness and those derived from oppression. It was an ethical debate carried out in the streets. "Discernment can come about in unexpected ways. It may, of course, come about in expected ways: perhaps in a verse of Scripture coming to mind, perhaps a fact of experience not noticed before. . . . But since one may know all the verses, and all the facts, without knowing the *patterns,* often the insight will come in odd ways."[20]

The nonviolent demonstrations dramatized the teachings of Jesus. Those who participated in the drama were walking in the shoes of Jesus and proclaiming his Word through their actions. Those who opposed the demonstrations found themselves trying to hold back the same Word of God that brought forth the universe and upholds it.

Ethical discourse is never merely a matter of setting forth facts and verses. In an ethical debate, one or both parties may be very knowledgeable about Scripture and experience, but unable to make the connections because of immaturity.

Thus, it is useful, not only to reason, but also to tell stories, to pray, to sing, to share analogies, to do odd things for "shock value" (Ezekiel), to teach by example.[21]

Teaching by example was the essence of the Birmingham experience for the demonstrators. Shock value came when the opposition saw their own bigotry and violence exposed in plain sight to the world.

White America was forced to face the ugly facts of life as the Negro thrust himself into the consciousness of the country, and dramatized his grievances on a thousand brightly lighted stages. No period in American history, save the Civil War and the Reconstruction, records such breadth and depth to the Negro's drive to alter his life. No period records so many thaws in the frozen patterns of segregation.[22]

Dr. King had become the leader, motivator, spokesperson and focus of this dramatic movement. Who was this voice from the South?

### "We Didn't Know Who You Was"

Martin Luther King Jr. was ideal for the role assigned to him by the Lord of history. His character was strong, his dedication and brilliance deep-rooted. These traits made him highly respected in the African-American community.

Andrew Young, former United Nations ambassador and former mayor of Atlanta, Georgia, recalls,

I think he made no distinctions between people. He was not interested in their education. He saw straight through to the heart of a human being, and that was where he tried to relate to people. . . . He was so basically humble and unassuming and yet he was so obviously talented. The man would become transformed once he got behind a pulpit and [people] could see the brilliance of his leadership.[23]

This is why those close to Dr. King affectionately called him "De Lawd."

### A Time of Training

Brother Martin did not go to an evangelical seminary. Had he applied to one, he might well have been rejected on racial grounds. But since our Lord is sovereign over history, Dr. King received the preparation needed to become the leader, theologian and prophet of the Civil Rights Movement.

Having been raised in a strict fundamentalist tradition, in his senior year at Crozer Seminary (where he earned an M.Div.) Dr. King began to journey through new doctrinal lands. But the theological dynamic was alive in this third-generation preacher, providing "theological antibodies" against the infections of all that he would study—liberalism, *neo-orthodoxy*\* and, later, existentialism. His Black church background had equipped him to "eat the fish and spit out the bones."

Although Dr. King did not accept everything liberalism encompassed, he was impressed with its intellectual vigor, something he had never found in fundamentalism. But he questioned the liberal doctrine that humanity is basically good. The more he "observed the tragedies of history and man's shameful inclination to take the low road," the more he came to see the depths of sin. Liberalism for Dr. King was "all too sentimental concerning human nature and it leaned toward false idealism." Liberalism had optimistically overlooked "the glaring reality of collective evil" and "the fact that reason was darkened by sin."

Brother Martin found neo-orthodoxy to be "a helpful corrective for a sentimental liberalism," but "it did not provide an answer to basic questions." Where liberalism "was too optimistic concerning human nature, neo-orthodoxy was too pessimistic." For him, neo-orthodoxy went too far in "stressing a God who was hidden, unknown, and 'wholly other.' "

Existentialism was the next step in his intellectual journey, but Dr. King acknowledged that "the ultimate Christian answer could not be found in existential assertions."

Social ethics increasingly commanded his interest. In his early teens Brother Martin had been very concerned about the problem of racial injustice. During his doctoral studies at Boston University Divinity School, the "social gospel" expressed by Walter Rauschenbusch left an indelible imprint on King's thinking. But Brother Martin never bought Rauschenbusch's "unwarranted optimism concerning human nature." Rauschenbusch also came "perilously close to identifying the Kingdom of God with a particular social and economic system." This Brother Martin vigorously opposed. He believed that "the gospel at its best deals with the whole man, not only his soul but also his body, not only his spiritual well-being but also his material well-being." In other words, "a religion that professes a concern for the souls of men and is not equally concerned about the slums that damn them, the economic conditions that strangle them, and the social conditions that cripple them, is a spiritually moribund religion."

After studying several social and ethical theories, Brother Martin almost despaired of the power of love to solve social problems. "The turn-the-other-cheek and the love-your-enemies philosophies are valid," he felt, "only when individuals are in conflict with other individuals; when racial groups and nations are in conflict, a more realistic approach is necessary."[24]

It all came together for him in the next stage of his journey. He explains:

> I was introduced to the life and teachings of Mahatma Gandhi. As I read his works I became deeply fascinated by his campaigns of

nonviolent resistance. The whole Gandhian concept of *satyagraha* [*satya* is truth that equals love, and *graha* is force; *satyagraha* thus means truth force or love force] was profoundly significant to me. As I delved deeper into the philosophy of Gandhi, my skepticism concerning the power of love gradually diminished, and I came to see for the first time that the Christian doctrine of love, operating through the Gandhian method of nonviolence, is one of the most potent weapons available to an oppressed people in their struggle for freedom.[25]

## A Dysfunctional Church

Dr. King was misunderstood by many in both the Black community and the White. The most acute misunderstandings came from the predominantly White, so-called Bible-believing community. Dr. King's theological dynamic gave him a biblical message and method that conformed neither to the White conservative agenda nor to the White liberal agenda.

Sadly, many White *evangelical,* * *fundamentalist** and *Reformed** churches were caught sleeping with no oil in their lamps at the outbreak of this move of God in the land. They had evidently been rendered dysfunctional by a defective view of theology and culture. They failed to distinguish between White standards and scriptural standards. Their theology had led them to a preoccupation with private salvation.

The importance of personal salvation should never be diminished. But the whole counsel of God revealed in the Scriptures goes far beyond the scope of the private realm. According to God's Word, even salvation itself finds its significance in terms of a much larger picture—namely, the praise of God's glory (Ephesians 1—2). But many leading evangelicals never came to grips with the big picture of God's purposes. They never saw the broad cultural implications of the Great Commission. This is why their Christianity never had application beyond the private aspects of life. Many believed that America's racial injustices would fade away automatically as more individuals had conversion experiences. This naive view completely ignored the patterns of racism that had been woven into the American system.

The fundamentalist reaction was much harsher. Fundamentalists and right-wing politicians branded Dr. King and the Civil Rights Movement as "communistic." Though there was no evidence for such allegations, the label effectively scared off some potential supporters. The Civil Rights Movement and the words of King were beginning to strike at the very root of the White Christianity-ism that supported the political, economic and social system in which they had a vested interest.

Many fundamentalists and evangelicals saw the message of Brother Martin as an experience in futility in light of the total dichotomy between "the sweet by-and-by" and "the nasty now-and-now."[26] They saw Dr. King as absurdly "bothering to polish the brass and rearrange the furniture on the *Titanic.*" According to them, "he should have been getting people 'saved' in these 'last days' and not been concerned with eating at lunch counters."

Those in the Reformed church community, who pride themselves on having a wholistic theology, were better equipped to understand the phenomenon of Brother Martin. Dr. King was trying to bring the reality of the biblical world-and-life-view to bear on the real problems in society, such as racism and segregation. He firmly believed that history was neither autonomous nor a chance occurrence of events, but that God was sovereign over all things. He believed in the power of the Spirit of God to quicken people to respond positively to the Word. Dr. King was firmly rooted in the life of the church and saw the kingdom of God as having a broad sphere of influence in its theology and ethics.

Yet the Reformed Christians who shared Brother Martin's outlook did not recognize him. They were caught in the "paralysis of analysis."[27]

When Dr. King listed the churches that endorsed the Civil Rights Movement, the so-called Bible-believing churches were conspicuously absent.[28] Was it too much to expect them to recognize the ethical and theological nature of the movement when it was at its peak?

Without input from the Black community, the White church was unable to see the structural sin in the American system. Reformed thinkers like J. Marcellus Kik who attempted to apply theology to social problems tended to be negative.[29] Other thinkers said things like "Immediate integration would be destructive to Blacks and Whites alike," or "The problems of racism will eventually disappear under the present system of preaching the Word." The same arguments were being offered by proponents of apartheid in South Africa.

Thus the mainline, Bible-believing community generally misunderstood the significance of Dr. King—the fundamentalists and evangelicals primarily because of their defective theological position and the Reformed Christians primarily because of their defective cultural position.

This dysfunctionality of the conservative churches was due in part to the nature of Western theology itself. It had developed under the challenge of unbelieving philosophy and science, and thus it was much more concerned with *epistemological* issues (what we should know about God) than with *ethical* issues (how we should obey God). The White church had generally been isolated from the African-American community for almost a hundred years, and Brother Martin was the product of the African-American church—a church with a distinctly different growth and flavor. Hence, just as the kingdom of God had caught the scribes and Pharisees unawares, the Civil Rights Movement caught the predominantly White, Bible-believing communities unawares. Ironically, the liberals, who had apparently departed from God's written Word, were able to recognize this move of God better than those who were supposed to be committed to God's Word.

### Ideal Methodology
Brother Martin had been tracked down by the spirit of the time. He had been tracked down by the Spirit of God operating in our lives and times by the grace of God—a grace rooted in Jesus Christ (John 1:16).

That same Spirit has been at work throughout history in general, and in African-American history in particular. That same Spirit of grace brought us through Montgomery in 1955-1956, the pinnacle of the Civil Rights Movement in the triumph in Birmingham, and the *March on Washington** in August 1963.

"It is an axiom of social change that no revolution can take place without a methodology suited to the circumstances of the period."[30] Nonviolent direct action was developed and honed by *James Farmer** in Chicago. Yet it proved to be the ideal methodology for the Southern Neo-Negro strategy, given the overwhelming power of the forces arrayed against our people. Many had offered violent strategies, but the power of the Word of God, dramatized in the streets of the South, proved far more powerful than all the forces of segregation put together.

**The Word Applied**

We cannot discuss the Civil Rights Movement without discussing theology. But what is theology, and why were so many theologians caught napping by this movement?

Theology has been traditionally defined as "the study of God." Since the study of God would be impossible without his Word, we can define theology as "the application of God's Word to all areas of life,"[31] including the study of God.

Another theological area of concern has been the defense of the faith, historically called apologetics. In line with our broader perspective on theology, apologetics would be best defined as "the application of God's Word to controversy."[32] I have already noted that historic Black theology has been more ethical than epistemological. "Ethics is not a branch of theology but *equivalent to theology* because all theology answers ethical questions."[33] The Civil Rights Movement applied the theological dynamic to the controversy of Southern injustice. Thus what we had in Dr. King's message was the best example to date of an *ethics apologetic*. It had individual, collective and social implications.

## Pointing to Jesus

The center of this ethics apologetic was the Sermon on the Mount. Sadly, some Bible-believing Christians had relegated the Sermon on the Mount to a bygone age, while others had simply never gotten around to its social implications. But Brother Martin did. Dr. King was an ethics apologist after the pattern of an Old Testament prophet. He called the United States to repentance and obedience to God.

Brother Martin's message separated the wheat from the tares. He gave us a vehicle for rediscovering the ethical dimensions of "kingdom life" (for example, Isaiah 58:1-14; Matthew 7:21-27; 25:34-46). He reminded us that the judgment of God had ethical aspects (Luke 6:20-38) that were to be worked out in society (Isaiah 2:1-5; Luke 4:18-19).

Brother Martin looked for God's answer to racial injustice. Fundamentalism did not have it; and though he learned some valuable things from fundamentalism, he did not remain a fundamentalist. Liberalism did not have it; and though he learned some valuable things from liberalism, he did not become a liberal. Neo-orthodoxy did not have it; and though he learned some valuable things from neo-orthodoxy, he did not become neo-orthodox. Evangelicalism did not have it; and because evangelicalism stayed within its comfortable non-Black cultural niche, he did not become an evangelical. Reformed theology could have had it, but its theologians stayed within the bounds of their traditional confessions.

Gandhi had discovered some of the answers and offered them to Brother Martin. But though Mahatma Gandhi, a Hindu, equipped Dr. King with a method, Dr. King never bought into the religion of Hinduism. Brother Martin was too thoroughly saturated with the theological dynamic, the integration point for all he learned.

We must remember that the primary test of orthodoxy in the historic Black church is different from what it is in predominantly White, conservative church circles. In White culture the test tends to be *conceptual*—that is, how one articulates one's theology in confessions, creeds or statements of faith. In the African-American church the test tends to be *existential*\*—that is, how well one personally knows God or uses the theological dynamic. According to Scripture there is a third test which is *situational*—that is, how sensitive and committed one is to actualizing the truth of God's Word, or how obedient one is to the ethical implications of Christ's teachings.

We must also remember that in Scripture orthodoxy is most often measured on ethical grounds. Most in the Bible-believing community were more consistent with Scripture individually and conceptually than they were socially and ethically. But Dr. King was perhaps more consistent with Scripture socially and ethically than he was individually and conceptually. From an individual and conceptual perspective Brother Martin appeared to be less than orthodox; from a social and ethical perspective, however, many Bible-believing Christians appear less than orthodox. The ideal for all of us should be total scriptural consistency in all aspects of faith.

Brother Martin was often criticized for trying to get Black non-Christians to be nonviolent and White non-Christians to obey Jesus' words by implementing the Golden Rule. However, this criticism is based on a faulty view of the Christian's duty in this fallen world. As Cornelius Van Til said, we are called both to restrain sin and to destroy its consequences in this world as much as may be possible.

It is our duty not only to seek to destroy evil in ourselves and in our fellow Christians, but it is our further duty to seek to destroy evil in all our fellow men. It may be, humanly speaking, hopeless in some instances that we should succeed in bringing them to Christ. This does not absolve us, however, from seeking to restrain their sins to some extent for this life. We must be active first of all in the field of special grace, but we also have a task to perform with respect to the destruction of evil in the field of common grace.

Still further we must note that our task with respect to the destruction of evil is not done if we have sought to fight sin itself everywhere we see it. We have the further obligation to destroy the consequences of sin in this world as far as we can. We must do good to all men, especially to those of the household of faith. To help relieve something of the sufferings of the creatures of God is our privilege and our task.[34]

Dr. King was also criticized for not preaching the gospel and not getting people saved. But we can't always preach the gospel at sixty-five miles an hour. When road and weather conditions are bad, we have to slow down to a safe or understandable speed. In the case of the Civil Rights Movement the goal was to eliminate segregation (to apply the gospel at five miles per hour). How did the Civil Rights Movement relate to the gospel? Segregation points to racism; racism points to human depravity; depravity points to human rebellion against God; rebellion brings God's judgment and wrath; judgment points to our need for salvation; and our need for salvation points to Jesus Christ, our only hope for it. Martin Luther King Jr. applied the Word of God to the evils manifested in society without letting us forget that Jesus was the ultimate fulfillment of the Civil Rights Movement.

The only real problem with the Southern *theological dynamic* * had been its limited application to the social problems faced by Black America. From the end of the nineteenth century until the time of Dr. King, its only social application had been a passive one—survival and accommodation to the atrocities of racism. Brother Martin gave us a fresh and aggressive application of the dynamic to the Southern cause of justice. No one could remain neutral to its ethical and social implications. Our people had the will to resist oppression, but they had not had the method. God raised up Brother Martin to give us that method, renewing our will to resist.

God's grace pervaded this important phase of our quest. If the meaning of the African-American nation's history is rooted in searching for God (Acts 17:26-28), then Dr. Martin Luther King's ethics apologetic was a great stride in that direction.

### Agenda for Justice

Once the back of legal segregation was broken, there was truly cause for celebration. The federal government responded to the call to repentance with the passage of the civil rights and voting rights bills, along with the establishment of the Commission on Civil Rights to ensure the implementation of these laws. African-American people were now more able to pursue freedom and dignity. We could now broaden our quest for true personhood—a status we had hoped to find in the melting pot.

For the first time, a few "visible" Black people actually entered the melting pot and began to report back what life was like inside. And the story was not very promising. It was not the freedom and dignity we were looking for; it was a rat race. In mainstream life, African-American culture was still unacceptable, so many who "integrated" found that they could not enter authentically. Integration for them meant that they had to "give up their identity and deny their heritage."[35] What we thought of as the Promised Land was in sight—but it was a desert.

For the ghettoized underclass, alienated from the institutions of America, mere access to the melting pot made little difference. Louis E. Lomax explained what had happened:

> By marching, singing, praying and suffering, Martin Luther King let America out of the prison of legal segregation. Only after the prison walls fell was it fully laid bare that the inmates of segregation had been maimed for life. Their tortured souls could be heard groaning in agony and despair from Mississippi to Cleveland's Hough, from Georgia to Watts, from Alabama to Harlem. King . . . had opened the door but the newly freed men were too crippled by experience to walk in.[36]

Though freedom and dignity were not to be found in the melting pot, we learned several things from the Neo-Negro phase. First, we discovered how essential the soul dynamic was for our cause, as evidenced by its profound effect not only on Black folks but on America at large. Second, we learned that segregation, though a form of oppression, was not the total picture of oppression, and that desegregation, though a fruit of liberation, was not the total picture of liberation; for racism in the hearts of people is not negated by laws. Third, the cultural price of entering the melting pot was too high; and, in fact, the melting-pot system could never produce freedom and dignity for our people.

Most of us felt a gnawing within our guts as we came to realize the truth that a fiery young man articulated superbly:

It's impossible for a chicken to produce a duck egg—even though they both belong to the same family of fowl. A chicken just doesn't have it within its system to produce a duck egg. It can't do it. It can only produce according to what that particular system was constructed to produce. The system in this country cannot produce freedom for an Afro-American. It is impossible for this system, this economic system, this political system, this social system, this system, period. It's impossible for this system, as it stands, to produce freedom right now for the black man in this country.

And if a chicken did produce a duck egg, I'm quite sure you would say it was certainly a revolutionary chicken![37]

## Post-Martin Crisis

Those who followed Brother Martin have tried to continue his work in two ways. Some looked to the institutions that originally responded to the Civil Rights Movement as vehicles to advance our people. Among these groups were the *Southern Christian Leadership Conference (SCLC),* * founded by Dr. King himself; Operation Breadbasket, the economic arm of SCLC; *People United to Save Humanity (PUSH)*; the *National Urban League*; and the NAACP. A second group looked to the nonviolent strategy and the memory of Brother Martin as the keys to continuing progress. The Martin Luther King Jr. Center for Social Change in Atlanta, Georgia, represents this perspective.

All of these groups have contributed to our people since the assassination of Brother Martin in 1968, but they lack the prophetic power that Dr. King possessed. Some lack his power because they have tied in too closely with the federal government. We can be thankful for the response of the federal government, but we should not have declared ourselves "free at last." Other American institutions—schools, clubs, churches and labor unions, to name a few—also have racist structures that need to be reformed.

And other levels of government still needed to be tackled by the Civil Rights Movement. Many state and local governments had proven themselves incapable of guarding the rights of African-Americans. While liberal politicians have worked to make the federal government a watchdog over the racial practices of lower levels of government, conservatives have been fighting to take such watchdog power away from Washington. Events since 1980 have borne out our need to be guaranteed freedom through state and local structures also, and not to depend on the federal government.

While Dr. King looked to nonviolence as a means of unleashing the power of God, his followers looked to the strategy of nonviolence itself as the answer. Hence they lacked Dr. King's prophetic power. We can be thankful for the method of nonviolence, but nonviolence was not the force. Nonviolence succeeded in changing structures not because it was nonviolent, but because it had a strength derived from God. American culture, like all cultures, has a way of accommodating itself to new expressions of truth the way the human body accommodates itself to dope. With the first hit comes an initial, blissful "rush"; but with succeeding hits, an increasing numbness sets in, and the body no longer responds. This was the case with nonviolence. Initially it was a powerful means of cultural discipleship, but as time passed and the American culture became acclimated to it, numbness crept in. The shock value was lost. We needed new methods of applying God's Word and power.

Brother Martin was concerned about God's righteousness and justice wherever they were needed. He showed us that God's Word could be applied to other social issues, like the Vietnam War and hunger. He saw that biblical ethics must be applied to *every* area of life. When Dr. King took aim at the war, many thought he had abandoned the cause of Black people. When he planned the Poor People's March on Washington, many did not understand why the issue was poverty, not just racism.

Time has vindicated Dr. King. Ultimately it is not Black versus White. It is justice versus injustice, haves versus have-nots. As long as Dr. King talked only about African-Americans he was relatively safe, but when he began to pull poor Whites and poor Blacks together he became a threat to the power and wealth elite. If he had been allowed to live, he might have even been able to articulate the frustrations of today's shrinking middle class. Thus Brother Martin could have been a prophet of a sizable slice of America. This would have been a formidable challenge, but it was never allowed to materialize.

We can thank God for Martin Luther King Jr. and for his ethics apologetic, which gave God's worldwide church a valuable tool for making disciples of all nations. Yes, we can be thankful for this prophet who had a love ethic like Jesus', a cultural brilliance like Paul's, a poetic speech like Jeremiah's, an agenda for justice like Amos's, a direct-action drama like Ezekiel's and a mode of leadership like Moses'. God had spoken to Brother Martin:

God has spoken to me, and I'm not going to run from the responsibility.

May mean going through the floods and through the waters, but I'm going if it means that!

May mean going through the storms and the winds, but I'm going, if it means that!

May mean going to jail, but I'm going if it means that!

It may even mean physical death, but if it means that, I will die standing up for the freedom of my people!

God has spoken to me![38]

# 8

# "A Shining Prince"

*O*nce we had uncovered the well-kept secret that freedom and dignity were not to be found in the melting pot, many began to rethink the whole direction of the quest. Rumblings of discontent increased among the more militant Northern thinkers during the later stages of the Civil Rights Movement. Among the first to become disenchanted with nonviolence, they condemned Martin Luther King Jr. for his action in 1964-1965 during an African-American voter registration drive in Selma, Alabama (see *Battle of Selma\**). *Eldridge Cleaver,\** minister of defense of the *Black Panther Party,\** considered this incident the beginning of the end of the Civil Rights Movement:

[Dr. King] denied history a great moment, never to be recaptured, when he turned tail on the Edmund Pettus Bridge and refused to all those whites behind him what they had traveled thousands of miles to receive. If the police had turned them back by force, all those nuns, priests, rabbis, preachers, and distinguished ladies and gentlemen old and young—as they had done the Negroes a week earlier—the violence and brutality of the system would have been ruthlessly exposed. Or if, seeing King determined to lead them on to Montgomery, the troopers had stepped aside to avoid precisely the confrontation that Washington would not have tolerated, it would have signaled the capitulation of the militant white South. As it turned out, the March on Montgomery was a show of somewhat dim luster, stage-managed by the Establishment.[1]

## Shock Waves

After the turnaround at the Edmund Pettus Bridge, some of the more militant participants in the Selma-to-Montgomery march (1965) began to deemphasize moral force as the means of achieving freedom. They asserted the need for power. Midway through the *Memphis-to-Jackson march** (1966) many began to chant "Black Power, Black Power!" *Stokely Carmichael,** the new leader of the *Student Non-violent Coordinating Committee (SNCC),** openly challenged Dr. King to take a stand for Black Power.[2]

Shock waves spread across America. A consciousness change was taking place among Black leaders, signaling the beginning of the Black phase. With it, White humanism was dead and buried, and *Black humanism** was born. Just as the death, in 1877, of the post-Civil War Reconstruction marked the beginning of the "melting-pot" era, so the Black Consciousness Movement marked its end. For the first time, White society was unable to avoid dealing with us on our terms or on mutually acceptable terms.

During this transitional stage, our complexion consciousness melted. We simply regarded each other as "Black." We also began to discover the richness of our heritage. These new discoveries made us acutely aware that the American system had "run a number on us." This new consciousness was

> the bold assertion of the fact that the humanity of Blacks is a non-negotiable, indisputable reality. The humanity of Black people IS!

[It was] initially the psychological realization that White oppressive, dehumanizing institutions are only capable of making Blacks insensitive to their humanity. No man or institution has the power to destroy the basic humanity of Black people. The reality of the humanity of Blacks is independent of racist attitudes and values. The humanity of Blacks is as certain as the forces used by God to regulate the universe, as real as the principles that dominate life and death.[3]

So began the search for historical roots that were authentically Black. This new quest carried some back to the writings and sayings of Frederick Douglass, the great abolitionist. For others the quest went beyond Douglass to *Nat Turner** and *Denmark Vesey,** who led slave revolts.

The militant Black thinkers failed to realize that their disenchantment with the Civil Rights Movement was due to their viewing Southern desegregation from a Northern perspective. They assumed that desegregation was another way of facilitating integration by means of imitating White folks. After all, this had been the best-known Northern strategy. The Southern leaders of the Civil Rights Movement, however, never thought of desegregation as a means of becoming culturally White or losing their identity. Imitation had no history in the South. Blacks of the South wanted to desegregate but remain culturally Black.

From Frederick Douglass, the Northern quest continued through W. E. B. Du Bois, whose aim was to consolidate the African-American community into a cultural nation—not through servitude and menial labor, as Booker T. Washington had suggested, but on the basis of education. Du Bois was a strong advocate of Pan-Africanism and saw that the Black nation could be led by what he called the "talented tenth." He founded the *Niagara Movement** in 1905 and was a key organizer of the NAACP in 1909. While Du Bois met with limited success, the idea of a Black cultural nation survived. But since education was still beyond the reach of the masses of African-Americans, a different basis for cultural nationalism was needed.

In the 1920s *Marcus Garvey,** as head of the United Negro Improvement Association (UNIA), attempted to consolidate the Black nation around what most of us had in common—namely, religion. Instead of seeking a nationalism in America, he resurrected the idea of founding a political nation in Africa.[4] Before his back-to-Africa movement was sabotaged and Garvey deported, he managed to attract thousands of followers. Most were in Northeastern cities, particularly in Harlem, New York City. With the *Harlem Renaissance** in the 1920s, Blacks began to affirm in art, literature and music what Douglass, Du Bois and later Garvey had taught—that our non-Whiteness is something to be proud of.

Patterned on the defunct Garvey movement were three Black religious sects—two were forms of Christianity-ism, and one was a form of *Islam-ism.** These were, respectively, the Peace Mission Movement, founded and headed by *Father Divine,** the United House of Prayer for All People, founded and headed by *Bishop Charles Emmanuel "Daddy" Grace,** and the Nation of Islam, founded by W. D. Fard and headed by Elijah Pool, who changed his name to *Elijah Muhammad.** All three were moderately successful.

## Mr. Little

In Omaha, Nebraska, on May 19, 1925, a boy was born to the Reverend and Mrs. Earl Little. They named this fourth child Malcolm. The Reverend Little, a Baptist preacher, was a dedicated organizer in the Garvey movement and often took his son with him to UNIA meetings. What little Mr. Little heard at those meetings made a profound impression on him. So did the violence that surrounded his family. When the KKK drove his family out of Omaha, they moved to Milwaukee, Wisconsin, and then to Lansing, Michigan—always followed by violence.

The Littles' boy grew up to be one of the most influential Black leaders, a spokesperson for the militant North, the inaugurator of the Black phase.

Malcolm Little's formative years were disastrous. He was emotionally damaged, and his understanding of himself and his people was grossly distorted because he gave in to the assumptions of White racism. Malcolm later wrote that his father, in spite of his pro-Black philosophy,

> was subconsciously so afflicted with the white man's brainwashing of Negroes that he inclined to favor the light ones, and I was his lightest child. Most negro parents in those days would almost instinctively treat any lighter children better than they did the darker ones. It came directly from the slavery tradition that the "mulatto," because he was visibly nearer to white, was therefore "better." . . .
>
> Out in the world later on, . . . I was among the millions of negroes who were insane enough to feel that it was some kind of status symbol to be light-complexioned—that one was actually fortunate to be born thus. But, still later, I learned to hate every drop of white rapist's [his grandfather's] blood that is in me.[5]

After the murder of their father, the family was forced to go on welfare, and Malcolm became involved in petty thefts around Lansing. As his mother was slowly driven insane by the pressure of her situation, the Little family fell apart.

When Mrs. Little was institutionalized, Malcolm was placed in a series of foster homes and detention homes. During the summer of 1940 he visited his half-sister Ella in Boston, Massachusetts. There his eyes were opened to the oppression he had been subjected to in Lansing.

Malcolm began to feel restless around White people, and his White friends noticed it. He was a brilliant student, but when he expressed a desire to be a lawyer, his eighth-grade teacher responded: "That's no realistic goal for a nigger." Instead carpentry was suggested as an appropriate career. Malcolm reflected:

> The more I thought afterwards about what he said, the more uneasy it made me. It just kept treading around in my mind. . . .
>
> It was a surprising thing that I had never thought of it that way before, but I realized that whatever I wasn't, I *was* smarter than nearly all of those white kids. But apparently I was still not

intelligent enough, in their eyes, to become whatever I wanted to be.

It was then that I began to change—inside.[6]

Malcolm began to draw away from White people. It became a strain even to sit in his eighth-grade classroom. "Where 'nigger' had slipped off my back before, wherever I heard it now, I stopped and looked at whoever said it. And they looked surprised when I did."[7]

Like a time bomb, experiences like this would later explode.

## Years of Deterioration

From that time Malcolm began a general downhill slide. Eventually he went to live with his sister Ella in Boston, where he worked several odd jobs. His downhill slide continued through a two-year stay in Harlem, where his activities included drug abuse, hustling and assorted crimes, and his return to Boston, where he continued his life of crime. He was eventually busted on several counts of grand theft and sentenced to ten years in prison. Malcolm described himself at his lowest point in prison:

I preferred the solitary. . . . I would pace for hours like a caged leopard, viciously cursing aloud to myself. And my favorite targets were the Bible and God. But there was a legal limit to how much time one could be kept in solitary. Eventually, the men in the cell-block had a name for me: "Satan." Because of my antireligious attitude.[8]

Malcolm Little's life changed direction in 1947, when he met fellow inmate Bimbi, who made a strong impression on him. Bimbi's opinions on any given subject were highly respected, even by the prison guards.

Out of the blue one day, Bimbi told me flatly, as was his way, that I had some brains, if I'd use them. I had wanted his friendship, not that kind of advice. I might have cursed another convict, but nobody cursed Bimbi. He told me I should take advantage of the prison correspondence courses and the library.[9]

Malcolm began to study English and penmanship through correspondence courses, and after about a year he could write a decent letter. "About then, too, influenced by having heard Bimbi often explain word derivations, I quietly started another correspondence course—in Latin."[10] Malcolm Little's life had turned decisively.

## Undoing the Damage
One day in 1948 Malcolm received a letter from his brother Philbert, who had been involved in a holiness church and had often told Malcolm that he and his church were praying for him. Only now the message was different. Philbert said "he had discovered the 'natural religion for the black man,' . . . something called 'the Nation of Islam.' "[11] A letter from his brother Reginald instructed him not to eat any more pork or smoke any more cigarettes. (Reginald also told Malcolm he'd show him how to get out of prison. This struck a responsive chord.) Reginald visited Malcolm and began to explain some of his new beliefs:

"Malcolm, if a man knew every imaginable thing that there is to know, who would he be?"

"Well, he would have to be some kind of a god—"

Reginald said, "There's a *man* who knows everything."

"Who is that?"

"God is a man," Reginald said. "His real name is Allah."

Reginald went on. He said that God had 360 degrees of knowledge, . . . "the sum total of knowledge. . . . The devil has only thirty-three degrees of knowledge—known as Masonry."

He told me that this God had come to America, and that he had made himself known to a man named Elijah—"a black man, just like us." This God had let Elijah know . . . that the devil's "time was up."

"The devil is also a man," Reginald said.

"What do you mean?"

"The white man is the devil."

I will never forget: my mind was involuntarily flashing across the entire spectrum of white people I had ever known. . . .

I said, "Without any exception?"

"Without any exception."[12]

Malcolm went on to think about all his encounters with White people, and without exception they had been negative. The time bomb was exploding! On a subsequent visit Reginald expounded on what "white devils" had kept hidden from African-Americans. Concurring, Malcolm was dramatically converted. He wrote:

The truth can be quickly received . . . only by the sinner who knows and admits that he is guilty of having sinned much. Stated another way: only guilt admitted accepts truth. The Bible again: the one people whom Jesus could not help were the Pharisees; they didn't feel they needed any help.

The very enormity of my previous life's guile prepared me to accept the truth.

Not for weeks yet would I deal with the direct, personal application to myself, as a black man, of the truth. It still was like a blinding light.[13]

In an attempt to document Elijah Muhammad's teachings, Malcolm began an intensive program of self-education. His vocabulary increased by leaps and bounds as he copied the entire dictionary by hand.

Why did Malcolm's brothers describe the Nation of Islam as the "natural religion for the black man"? Elijah Muhammad had begun with his perceptions of the Black situation and had developed a mythology to explain it. According to his mythology, the moon had been separated from the earth, and then Allah created the first humans, a Black people who founded the Holy City of Mecca.

Thirty percent of this Black race was dissatisfied. Mr. Yacub, whose head was unusually large, began preaching dissatisfaction in Mecca and gained a large following. Eventually he and his 59,999 followers were exiled to the island of Patmos. Yacub became bitter toward Allah and decided to create a devil race in revenge. He knew that the Black man contained two germs, black and brown, and that the brown germ was the morally weaker because it was lighter.

Mr. Yacub died before completing his task, but he left rules for his followers by which Brown people could marry only with other

Browns, and Blacks with Blacks. All Black babies were killed at birth so that the race would gradually grow lighter—first Brown, then Red, then Yellow, then White.

Because Whites were morally weakest, they were most susceptible to evil influence. They became a race of devils. When they eventually returned to the mainland, they began to turn the peaceful heaven on earth into a hell torn by quarreling and fighting.

Allah sent Moses to civilize the Whites, who would rule for six thousand years. Blacks would experience their devilishness firsthand through enslavement in America. But Allah did not forget his people: he sent Master W. D. Fard to tell Allah's message to Elijah Muhammad, who was to tell it to North America.[14]

This bizarre mythological explanation of the origin of the White race was in part a reaction to White Christianity-ism's own bizarre myths about the mark of Cain and the curse of Ham.

Upon his release from prison in the spring of 1952, Malcolm went to Detroit, Michigan, where he became Malcolm X, a minister of Temple No. 1. From then until 1964 Malcolm X was the main exponent of Elijah Muhammad's doctrine. He built the Nation of Islam from the least successful into the most formidable of the post-Garvey religious movements. Malcolm's power of persuasion, his extensive knowledge of history, his remarkable ability to express complicated issues in simple parables and his wit and energy in organizing new temples made the Nation of Islam one of the most powerful Black organizations in history.

### Rearrangement

For twelve years Malcolm X followed Elijah Muhammad and worked in the cause of the Nation of Islam, becoming minister of Harlem's prestigious Temple No. 7. Then a rift began to develop between Malcolm and the Nation.

Los Angeles, July 3 [1963] (UPI)—Elijah Muhammad, 67-year-old leader of the Black Muslim movement, today faced paternity suits from two former secretaries who charged he fathered their four

children. . . . Both women are in their twenties. . . . [They] charged
they had intimacies with Elijah Muhammad from 1957 until this
year. [One] alleged he fathered her two children and said she was
expecting a third child by him . . . [and] the other plaintiff said he
was the father of her daughter.[15]

Hints of such problems had occurred as far back as 1955, but Malcolm
had refused to believe them. At the same time Elijah Muhammad
began to cut down Malcolm's character and work behind his back. On
December 2, 1963, Elijah Muhammad suspended Malcolm from the
Nation for ninety days following a controversial statement made about
the assassination of President John F. Kennedy (see *chickens roost\**).
He began to get reports that his closest associates were calling for his
death. In his words, "My head felt like it was bleeding inside, I felt
like my brain was damaged."[16]

### Racism Jettisoned

On March 2, 1964, Malcolm's suspension from the Nation of Islam
was not lifted as scheduled. Finally, on March 8, when it appeared that
his suspension would be indefinite, Malcolm called a news conference
and announced his formal break with Elijah Muhammad and the
Nation. From that time Malcolm lived under the threat of assassination. He said, "Now, each day I live as if I am already dead."[17]

To gain a fresh perspective, Malcolm made a pilgrimage to Mecca,
looking for answers to his questions about the African-American
situation. His experience there was profoundly enlightening and led
him into a prophetic role. He wrote his wife, Betty:

Never have I witnessed such sincere hospitality and the overwhelming spirit of true brotherhood as is practiced by people of all
colors and races here in this Ancient Holy Land. . . . For the past week,
I have been utterly speechless and spellbound by the graciousness I
see displayed all around me by people *of all colors.* . . .

You may be shocked by these words from me. But on this
pilgrimage, what I have seen, and experienced, has forced me to
*re-arrange* much of my thought-patterns previously held, and to

*toss aside* some of my previous conclusions. This was not too difficult for me. Despite my firm convictions, I have always been a man who tries to face facts, and to accept the reality of life as new experience and new knowledge unfolds it. I have always kept an open mind, which is necessary to the flexibility that must go hand in hand with every form of intelligent search for truth. . . .

I could see from this, that perhaps if white Americans could accept the Oneness of God, then perhaps, too, they could accept *in reality* the Oneness of Man—and cease to measure, and hinder, and harm others in terms of their "differences" in color. . . .

Never have I been so highly honored. Never have I been made to feel more humble and unworthy. Who would believe the blessings that have been heaped upon an *American Negro?*[18]

Of course his notoriety in the press and his renown as an uncommon "American Muslim" had opened many key doors for him. Several officials and influential people in Jidda, Saudi Arabia, rolled out the red carpet for Malcolm because they saw him as the forerunner of an indigenous American Muslim community. His association with Muhammad Ali, the widely admired heavyweight boxing champion of the world, served to enhance his reception among his fellow pilgrims in Mecca.[19]

Yet this was a significant stage in the deprogramming of Malcolm X. Since he had swallowed the poisons of White racism, it may have taken the bitter medicine of Black racism to make him vomit the poison up. After a twelve-year dose, he was ready to see that humanity is not determined by race.

It wasn't the teachings of Islam that opened his eyes. It was seeing, outside America, relationships among people of all colors. Here were human relationships that had not been destroyed by the type of bigotry that had marked his life. Malcolm reported the following:

There was a color pattern in the huge crowds. Once I happened to notice this, I closely observed it thereafter. Being from America made me intensely sensitive to matters of color. I saw that people who looked alike drew together and most of the time stayed together. This was entirely voluntary; there being no other reason for it. But, Africans were with Africans, Pakistanis were with Pakistanis. And so forth. I tucked it into my mind that when I returned home I would tell Americans this observation; that where true brotherhood existed among all colors where no one felt segregated, where there was no "superiority" complex, no "inferiority" complex—then voluntarily, naturally, people of the same kind felt drawn together by that which they had in common.[20]

"Malcolm X was an acute and sensitive observer . . . though the beliefs which he had acquired and still cherished at that time prevented him from realizing the full implications of what he saw."[21] The phenomenon he experienced abroad has been observed within America. A casual survey of American history will reveal that the North and the South have had distinctively different manifestations of racism. Thus those who grew up in the segregated South tended to equate racism with Southern segregation. On a first visit to the North they might get the impression that racism was not a problem there. In time, however, they would come to recognize Northern institutional racism.

Likewise, if Malcolm had had the chance to familiarize himself with the history of the Islamic world, he would have discovered that the "color patterns" he observed were partly the result of racism and slavery (see *racism in the Muslim world\**). In fact, Muslims enslaved Black Africans long before America existed. And slavery is still widely practiced in the Arab Islamic world today[22] (see *slavery in the Muslim world\**).

Nevertheless, without the distractions of *American* racism Malcolm was able to see things more clearly. He gained a fuller understanding of how the attitudes and motives of White people in America had affected Black people. "In my thirty-nine years on this earth," he said, "the Holy City had been the first time I had ever stood before the Creator of All and felt like a complete human being."[23]

In one step he embraced the humanity of all people and jettisoned racism.

## Living Manhood

After his return, Malcolm X spoke in Chicago about his radical change of mind:

> In the past, I have permitted myself to be used to make sweeping indictments of all white people, and these generalizations have caused injuries to some white people who did not deserve them. Because of the spiritual rebirth which I was blessed to undergo as a result of my pilgrimage to the Holy City of Mecca, I no longer subscribe to sweeping indictments of one race. My pilgrimage . . . served to convince me that perhaps American whites can be cured of the rampant racism which is consuming them and about to destroy this country. In the future, I intend to be careful not to sentence anyone who has not been proven guilty. I am not a racist and do not subscribe to any of the tenets of racism. In all honesty and sincerity it can be stated that I wish nothing but freedom, justice and equality: life, liberty and the pursuit of happiness—for all people.[24]

With his nonracist stance he began to reevaluate other concepts and values. His understanding of power and leadership opened up new dimensions.

> Mankind's history has proved from one era to another that the true criterion of leadership is spiritual. Men are attracted by spirit. By power, men are *forced.* Love is engendered by spirit. By power, anxieties are created. . . .
>
> I am in agreement one hundred per cent with those . . . who say that no government laws ever can *force* brotherhood. The only true world solution today is governments guided by true religion—of the spirit.[25]

Clearly Malcolm's philosophy was changing—but to what? That we will never know. One thing is sure: the only way to account for Malcolm X's rise from the cesspool of society to become one of the most influential men in American history is the grace of God. Malcolm, having himself been humanized, gave us a new meaning to being Black: we were human. He liberated truths that had been locked up in the mythological doctrines of the Nation of Islam and delivered them to the smoldering victims of ghettoization.

Malcolm seems to have been a genuine seeker of truth, but the distortions of un-Christian Christianity-ism prevented him from seeing the Bible as the real source of the truth about humanity. He functioned as a cultural prophet, enlightening us and condemning Christianity-ism with its view of African-Americans. This enlightenment used "borrowed capital"[26] from Christian truth, but in the name of Islam.

The challenge of Malcolm X forced Black Christians to search the Scriptures for new insights about humanity. Without realizing it, Malcolm X reoriented the African-American collective consciousness toward a truer scriptural view of ourselves, opening our eyes to the image of God in us. He became the symbol and embodiment of that new consciousness. In a way, Malcolm was our humanity. Ossie Davis said, "Malcolm was our manhood, our living, black manhood! This was his meaning to his people. And, in honoring him, we honor the best in ourselves. . . . He was and is—a prince—our black shining prince!"[27]

Eldridge Cleaver wrote:

It was not the Black Muslim movement itself that was so irresistibly appealing to the true believers. It was the awakening into self-consciousness of twenty million Negroes which was so compelling. Malcolm X articulated their aspirations better than any other man of our time. When he spoke under the banner of Elijah Muhammad he was irresistible. When he spoke under his own banner he was still irresistible. If he had become a Quaker, a Catholic, or a Seventh-day Adventist, or a Sammy Davis-style Jew, and if he had continued to give voice to the mute ambitions in the black man's soul, his message would still have been triumphant: because what was great was not Malcolm X but the truth he uttered.[28]

## "Let's Cool It, Brothers"

As long as Malcolm X was speaking under the banner of the Nation of Islam, he was not considered a serious threat to the wealth and power elite. But when he founded the Organization of Afro-American Unity (OAAU) and began to speak under his own banner, the perceived threat increased. He began to affirm that people are people regardless of color, that the issue is not Black versus White but oppressed versus oppressor, exploited versus exploiter. The powerful feared he would eventually attract a broad-based, even international following. His intention to bring charges of human rights violations against the United States on the floor of the United Nations made him too much of a threat. He had to be removed from the scene.

Even the powerful in the Islamic world who warmly received Malcolm could not afford for him to continue to evolve and develop. If Islam turned out to be only a phase in Malcolm's ongoing quest for truth and freedom, their plans to Islamize America through an African-American Muslim community would suffer a major setback. Thus they stood to benefit if Islam appeared to be Malcolm's final destination. For this to happen, though, Malcolm's quest had to be frozen in its tracks.

Intensely consumed with the pursuit of a quest whose end seemed in view, Malcolm saw that the OAAU needed a new program. A series of three public meetings was planned to "arouse interest." The site chosen was the Audubon Ballroom, an upstairs dance hall on 166th Street, between Broadway and St. Nicholas Avenue, in Harlem (New York City). Malcolm was to speak at each meeting.

At the first meeting, scheduled for Sunday, January 24, 1965, Malcolm would trace the roots of Black history from the great African civilizations through slavery to the present. At the second meeting, scheduled for Sunday, January 31, Malcolm would discuss the current African-American situation and the devices used to keep our people oppressed. At the third meeting, scheduled for Sunday, February 7, Malcolm would reveal his long-awaited vision for the African-American community and present the new OAAU program.

The January 24 and 31 meetings were held as planned. Because of a conflict in Malcolm's schedule, however, the February 7 meeting had to be postponed to February 15. But early on the morning of February 14, Malcolm's home was fire-bombed while he, his wife and their four children were asleep. No one was hurt. Naturally, the February 15 meeting turned into a discussion of the bombing and who was behind it. Malcolm believed it was the Nation of Islam. The discussion of the new OAAU program and Malcolm's new vision was moved to the following Sunday, February 21. That day became the day to remember.[29]

"The people who entered the ballroom were not searched at the door. In recent weeks, Malcolm X had become irritable about this, saying, 'It makes people uncomfortable' and that it reminded him of Elijah Muhammad. 'If I can't be safe among my own kind, where can I be?' "[30] Malcolm arrived just before two o'clock. He told a small group of his assistants that

he was going to state that he had been hasty to accuse the Black Muslims of bombing his home. "Things have happened since that are bigger than what they can do. I know what they can do. Things have gone beyond that. . . . The way I feel, I ought not to go out there at all today," Malcolm X said. . . . "I'm going to ease some of this tension by telling the black man not to fight himself—that's all a part of the white man's big maneuver, to keep us fighting among ourselves, against each other. I'm not fighting anyone, that's not what we're here for."[31]

Malcolm could hear himself being introduced from the anteroom where he sat: "And now, without further remarks, I present to you one who is willing to put himself on the line for you, a man who would give his life for you—I want you to hear, listen, to understand—one who is a *trojan* for the black man!"

There was applause, and he walked out, smiling and nodding. The applause diminished. Then came

the familiar ringing greeting, "*Asalaam-alekum,* brothers and sisters!"

"Wa'aleikum-salaam!" some in the audience responded.

Then there was a disturbance about eight rows from the front. Amid

a sudden commotion, a man called out angrily: "Take your hand out
of my pocket!" The audience turned to look.

"Hold it! Hold it! Don't get excited," Malcolm X said crisply. "Let's
cool it, brothers . . ."[32]
A deafening hail of gunfire suddenly exploded in the midst of the
confusion. The horrified audience scrambled for cover while Malcolm
clutched his chest. His bullet-riddled "body fell back stiffly, knocking
over two chairs; his head struck the floor with a thud." The assassins
ran "backward toward the door . . . firing at the same time." They
rushed down the stairs and disappeared onto West 166th Street, though
one had been wounded by return fire from Malcolm's bodyguards. It
was over.

Many ran toward Malcolm, among them Sister Betty, who had been
shielding her hysterical young daughters. "My husband!" she cried.
"They're killing my husband!"[33]

But Malcolm was already gone. And so were our hopes of discov-
ering his new vision for us as a people.

What was Malcolm's vision? The answer to that question could be
the key to understanding why we are here—why God in his sovereignty brought us forth as a cultural nation out of the horrors of slavery.
It may have also revealed to us our future significance, both nationally
and globally.

But our "Black shining prince"—the one who exemplified such
promise and potential, who touched something deep within us—was
tragically snatched from us in his prime. He was thirty-nine.

What the KKK had been unable to do, what institutional racism had
failed to stifle, a number of "brothers" were able to accomplish in a
volley of gunfire reminiscent of the Wild West. These former Muslims
were eventually convicted for the crime, but the identity of the person
or persons who ultimately masterminded Malcolm's murder may
never be fully known.

Amidst our shock, outrage and grief one woman said, "It looked
like a firing squad."[34]

The audience had come to hear a man who preached a message of actualization that didn't involve putting down someone else. Many had come to appreciate the potential of true brotherhood and saw in Malcolm a foreshadowing of that future reality.

I imagine that some lamented, like the two on the road to Emmaus (Luke 24:21), "We thought Malcolm was the one to show us the way to liberation." Having tasted the firstfruits of freedom and dignity, they had no interest in returning to bankrupt ideology or inflammatory rhetoric.

The movement was built on Malcolm. But where could they go now?

### A Flash in the Pan

On that balmy yet bleak February afternoon of Malcolm's death, the task of seeking the foundation of Malcolm's vision fell to us—and this task still remains. Many have attempted to fulfill Malcolm's vision. Unfortunately, without knowing the true basis of his vision, their attempts, noble as they were, have fallen short.

Along with the OAAU, Malcolm founded Muslim Mosque, Incorporated. He intended these to function in the Black Consciousness Movement as a political (secular) arm and as a religious arm, respectively. Consequently, those who tried to carry on Malcolm's work after his assassination did so according to these two perspectives. In this section we will examine the secular approach; in the "Oil and Water" section, the religious approach.

### The Black Phase: A Secular Approach

Those who followed the secular approach well remembered when Malcolm said,

> No religion will ever make me forget the condition of our people in this country. No religion will ever make me forget the continued fighting with dogs against our people in this country. No religion will make me forget the police clubs that come up 'side our heads. No God, no religion, no thing will make me forget it until it stops, until it's finished, until it's eliminated.

Although I'm still a Muslim, . . . I'm not here to try and change your religion. I'm not here to argue or discuss anything that we differ about, because it's time for us to submerge our differences and realize that it is best for us to first see that we have the same problem, a common problem—a problem that will make you catch hell whether you're a Baptist or a Methodist, or a Muslim or a nationalist. . . . You're going to catch hell just like I am.[35]

If I discover that I am caught up in a religion that will not allow me to fight the battle for black men, then I say to hell with that religion![36]

Black people would need to forget about differences if they were to combat racism. Malcolm called this "the Gospel of Black Nationalism." It was to transcend all groups, churches and clubs in the Black community, just as the gospel of Christ that Billy Graham preached transcended denominations. He encouraged his followers to "join any organization that has a gospel that's for the uplifting of the Black man."[37]

Many remembered the scathing indictments Malcolm brought against "Christianity" (Christianity-ism) during his days in the Nation of Islam. They also remembered the hostility between him and the Nation after his break with Elijah Muhammad. After the bombing of his home, Malcolm went so far as to say, "I'm waking up America to the great Muslim menace."[38] So those who had been attracted to Malcolm but not to Islam carried on with an antireligious bias in general and an anti-Christian bias in particular.

What started out as an open-minded approach, however, quickly turned into secular humanism. The Black secularists, holding no truth as absolute, hoped to see all the variant elements of our culture merge into agreement and unity through a process of gradual synthesis. A religiously neutral Black culture would emerge, a unified whole, excluding the theological dynamic and the Black church.

**Black Awareness**

Nothing short of a cultural revolution resulted as these ideas trickled down to the folks on the street. For the first time we chose our own term by which to be known. That term was *Black,* and we tried to consolidate around it. As if following the principle alluded to in 1 Corinthians 1:27-28, we took the word *(Black) that was most despised in melting-pot culture and confounded America as we redefined it as a term of dignity.*

Whether we knew it or not, the choice of the term *Black* was a very clever one. As an ideal in African-American culture, Black was beautiful by definition. As a concept in the larger, White-oriented culture, Black was ugly, evil and dirty. This set up an immediate and continuous values confrontation in the minds of those who adopted the term *Black,* a confrontation between our newfound positive view of *Blackness\** and the traditional value system's negative view (figure 6). It had two effects, especially on the youth of Black America. First, it radicalized the urban masses. Thus we suddenly had a vast army of militant-minded people ready to be led by new Black leadership—a vast army also open to manipulation in the name of Blackness.

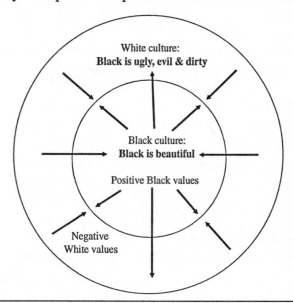

**Figure 6.** Confrontation between Black and White values

Among the alienated victims of ghettoization, however, the values confrontation had a second effect: it heaped frustration on frustration. Their expectations had been heightened by the social upheaval of the sixties. Yet they had experienced no real benefit from either the Civil Rights Movement or the Black Consciousness Movement.

To them the only alternative was to strike out and vent their pent-up anger. For the first time in our history, the hostility and suspicion we generally perpetuated among ourselves was now focused outside, at White society and at the White-owned businesses in our communities.

The *Watts riot*\* (Los Angeles, California), August 11-16, 1965, was followed by other *urban riots in 1965,*\* the *Cleveland riot*\* in 1966 and the *Detroit riot*\* in 1967. Amazingly, despite the passion and heat of these early riots, the businesses that had "Soul Brother" on their windows were untouched by the destruction.

The assassination of Martin Luther King Jr. on April 4, 1968, triggered another wave of riots in at least 150 American cities (see *post-Martin riots*\*). The hundreds of years of hatred poured into the Black community was suddenly regurgitated, and America for the first time felt its effect and was shocked.

Many of the newly radicalized militants believed that freedom and dignity were within our grasp. According to the new consensus, to assert one's Blackness was to demonstrate that one had achieved the goals of the historic Black quest. We soon discovered, however, that mere assertiveness could not bear the freight of our whole humanity.

Though we did not achieve the fullness of freedom and dignity, we learned several things from Black awareness. We learned, for instance, that we have human dignity, as we are, in our non-Whiteness. We also learned that the African-American community has characteristics as a nation, that our culture and consciousness are worth affirming and preserving. Finally, we learned that racism, like sin, has been institutionalized in American society at all levels and in every area of life.

**Black Power**
Among us were those who thought our people would find freedom

and dignity when we organized and consolidated our political, economic and social power into a unified force. The exercise of power by Black people was thought to be the key. This became known as Black Power. Though Malcolm X was the real father of this movement and Marcus Garvey coined the term "Black Power," it was *Stokely Carmichael\** and *Floyd McKissick\** who made it popular.

Those in the Black Power movement advocated five things:

☐ that we deal with the melting-pot system not on a moral base but on a power base, from a position of strength (because by this time White America was considered amoral)

☐ that we form coalitions with other groups only at points of agreement, and not as allies

☐ that we maintain control in our own communities—economically, politically and socially

☐ that we develop a Black melting pot

☐ that we form new institutions to express the new realities of a Black-conscious people (see figure 7)

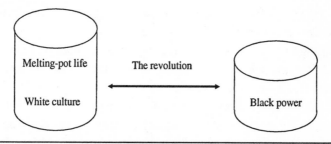

Melting-pot life

The revolution

White culture

Black power

**Figure 7.** Black Power

Stokely Carmichael and Charles Hamilton wrote:
Black people must redefine themselves, and only they can do that. Throughout this country, vast segments of the black communities are beginning to recognize the need to assert their own definitions, to reclaim their history, their culture; to create their own sense of community and togetherness. . . .

The next step is what we shall call the process of political modernization. . . .

We mean by it three major concepts: 1) questioning old values and institutions of the society; 2) searching for new and different forms of political structure to solve political and economic problems; and 3) broadening the base of political participation to include more people in the decision-making process. . . .

The concept of Black Power rests on a fundamental premise: *Before a group can enter the open society, it must first close ranks.*[39] By this time we were also beginning to see some negative effects of our own unrighteousness. If the militant thinkers had a functioning biblical worldview, they could have anticipated this.

Thus the closer we came to our goal of overthrowing White oppression, the more our own ungodliness surfaced to oppress us. Negro pimps became Black pimps, Negro dope pushers became Black dope pushers. In the words of the Last Poets, "Niggers change into doing 'Black' nigger things."[40]

Ethical content could have saved the Black Power movement. But the leaders had already swallowed secular humanism. Thus all moral decisions were left up to the individual. The movement was drowned out by *do-your-own-thing-ism*. We fell short of true freedom and human dignity as our own ungodliness began to hold us back. This shouldn't have surprised us, since this is the natural effect unrighteousness has on all people and all nations.

But the Black Power movement gave us some other valuable insights. It showed that it is necessary to demonstrate the beauty of being Black corporately (body life). We also learned that Black Power alone could not keep us from substituting the rule of "a hateful honky for a nasty nigger."[41] And finally, we saw that Black economic power at best would still be dependent on the American economic system.

## Black Revolutionism

Many of us saw that in spite of the reforms of Black power, the American system was still having a negative effect on African-American people. Many thought we were on the right track in looking for freedom and dignity within ourselves; the trick was to remove the overwhelming influence that was preventing us from being "us." The American system had to be replaced. All political and economic power had to be transferred to Black people. Enter the Black revolution.

The revolutionaries weren't concerned about what would happen after the revolution, because optimism was still strong; we would cross that bridge when we got there. After the revolution everything would be reversed. Black folks would be on top, and the melting-pot folks would feel the flames for a change while they followed Booker T. Washington's advice, *earning* a place in the new order.

The River Jordan was replaced by "the struggle." On this side of the struggle we were oppressed. On the other side we would be liberated, along with our oppressed brothers and sisters; we would be first among the cultural nations (figure 8).

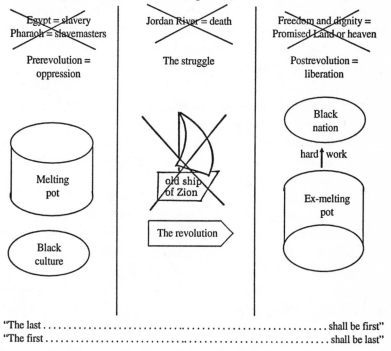

"The last . . . . . . . . . . . . . . . . . . . . . . . . . . . . . . . . . . . . . . . . . . . . . . . . . . . . . . . shall be first"
"The first . . . . . . . . . . . . . . . . . . . . . . . . . . . . . . . . . . . . . . . . . . . . . . . . . . . . . . . shall be last"

**Figure 8.** Black revolutionism compared to historic Black theology

Black revolutionism resembled early Black theology in structure. In Black revolutionism the main question was not "What are you going to do when the *judgment* comes?" but "What are you going to do when the *revolution* comes?" Instead of the Garden of Eden the revolutionaries harked back to an idyllic life in Mother Africa. A heroic but dead Malcolm took the place of the living Jesus. Huey P. Newton (minister of defense for the Black Panther Party), *Fred Hampton,* * *Mark Clark,* * *the New York 13* * and others were substituted for the persecuted saints and the martyrs. The ideal society after the revolution was substituted for heaven. Though Christianity was condemned as too otherworldly and naive, some of the revolutionaries turned out to be far more naive. The revolution they were talking about was just as impossible as overthrowing the slave system. Only this time the impossibility was in ourselves.

Theologian William E. Pannell beautifully summed up this impossibility in a conversation with me in 1972. When I asked him if he thought there would be a revolution, he said, "No, because the revolution can't get past Saturday night!"

Malcolm X, as far back as May 1964, recognized this inertia when he said, "Nowadays, as our people begin to wake up, they're going to realize, they've been *talking* about . . . revolution. You can't talk that stuff to me unless you're really for one. I don't even want to hear it unless you're really for one. And most [of] you *aren't*. When the deal goes down, [you'll] back out."[42]

The revolution turned out to be only a flash in the pan. Many of those who had been involved in the quest for freedom and dignity dropped out. They concluded that the goals of the revolution were unattainable, so they settled for fulfilling some limited personal goals.

Why didn't the revolution materialize? Partly because its goal, liberation, had never been defined. Under humanism the definition of liberation was left up to the individual. For example, a brother might consider himself "liberated" when he was able to shack up with his girlfriend without the disapproval of his peers. Once he had achieved his personal goal, he would drop out of the revolutionary cause.

Definitions of liberation not drawn from the Word of God will always fall short of true liberation. With the definition left up to the humanistic revolutionaries, the failure of the revolution was assured.

When the revolution failed to materialize, however, it was more than a missed shot at progress. It was a step backward. As would-be revolutionaries dropped out of the cause to do their own thing, they killed the possibility of a new Black unity. The massive dropout rate produced a huge number of contradictory do-your-own-thing-isms.

The early optimistic thinkers had not anticipated this because they did not have a functioning biblical understanding of sin's effect on a people. They did not realize that achieving justice required a total, radical change in us as well as in our environment. We could not have a revolution without divine help. We found that the failure we criticized in White humanism showed up in Black humanism too. This failure meant falling short of our revolutionary goal because of unrighteousness (Romans 3:23).

### Salvage Attempts

Some tried to stop the hemorrhage, to salvage the dying revolution. I call these people Neo-Black revolutionaries. Basically they equated revolution with mere change and said, "Since we have had a *change* in our consciousness, we have had a revolution." But this linguistic sleight of hand only served as further justification for pursuing counterrevolutionary personal goals.

The erosion of Neo-Black revolutionism wiped out almost all the remnant still in the secular quest for freedom and dignity. The few who were left embraced Neo-Pan-Africanism. Ironically, the Pan-African idea had originated with the African-American church in the antebellum North.[43] Under the banner of Pan-Africanism, the fourteenth and fifteenth episcopal districts of the African Methodist Episcopal Church were formed in western and southern Africa.[44] The aim was the "uplift" of our African "motherland."

Pan-Africanism affirmed the oneness of all people of African descent. Neo-Pan-Africanism, on the other hand, was secularized and infused with Marxist ideology. For Black America, secular Neo-Pan-Africanism was too little too late. It never became a consensus. However, the movement reminded us that we as a people have an important role to play among other African peoples and as part of the *Two-Thirds World.**

### A Secular Gamble

By the mid-eighties, the Black movement had seriously disintegrated, a testimony to the inadequacy of secularism. As early as 1968 its inadequacy had become visible to some Black thinkers. Black unity, which had been the basis of all the optimism, was on the verge of collapse. Secularism was beginning to show its self-destructive nature.

The Black movement had long disqualified the historic Black church and accused its theology of being invalid. Yet the church's theological dynamic remarkably survived the torrents of criticism that came from the militants. Indeed, the theological dynamic still had a powerful influence on Black consciousness—so resilient that even *Nikki Giovanni,** a leading poet of secularism and de-Christianization, could not bypass it.

The title of her first album, *Truth Is on Its Way,* expressed the prevailing sentiment that we did not yet have the truth but somehow we would succeed in finding and consolidating it.[45] Giovanni needed a medium that would capture her verbal power and intensify her ability to preach her message of Black secularism. She chose one of the most powerful elements of Black culture—*gospel music.** (Ironically, the Black militants had earlier considered gospel music—a part of the oral tradition of the Black church—to be an expression of the White man's religion.)

To lead off *Truth Is on Its Way,* Giovanni juxtaposed a gospel music arrangement of "Peace, Be Still" to her poem *"The Great Pax Whitie."** Here was gospel music, the very fruit of the African-American church, being used for its spiritual and cultural power. For Nikki Giovanni, gospel music functioned merely as a preamble for her secular ideology—an ideology based on the view that "Christianity" was the very core of the White man's past atrocities.

Such use of gospel music was not a phenomenon restricted to Giovanni. It was indicative of what was going on among Black thinkers in general. During the late sixties and early seventies it became apparent that absolute secularism was faltering. Secular humanism would never dislodge the theological dynamic as a base, even though the African-American church had, up to that time, been largely left out of the Black movement. Across the country, militants were reluctantly conceding to the church a minor role in the movement. For example, during "Black Week" on many university campuses the Black church was given a piece of the action.

In using the oral tradition of the church, the Black thinkers were taking a gamble. Would Black unity have the desired secular character or a Christian one? Secularists had no choice. Their only hope lay in a synthesis between secularism and the Black church (figure 9). Humanism needed some theological "propping up on its leaning side."

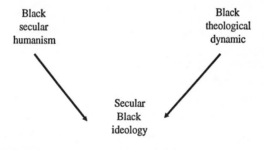

**Figure 9.**   Proposed Black ideology

Those days saw the emergence of new Black theologians like Albert Cleage. For many of them the ultimate reference point was the Black experience itself, not the Word of God. Even Huey P. Newton was beginning to talk about returning to the church. But this new Black theology was largely ignored by the African-American church, which even now has hardly budged from its traditional stance.

So the seventies witnessed the results of Black ungodliness. Secularism succeeded only in producing cultural confusion. Black humanism degenerated into do-your-own-thing-ism, and that in turn has led to libertarianism (looking-out-for-number-one-ism) and hedonism (if-it-feels-good-do-it-ism). There was even a new Black bourgeoisie-ism (materialism), hanging on to the same false values we used to condemn in White society. Although some leftover splinter groups remained, trying to reestablish the momentum of the militant Black movement, the dynamic and the cultural consensus of the sixties were gone (figure 10).

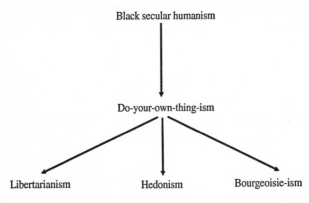

**Figure 10.**   Degeneration of Black ideology

## Oil and Water
The church did lose some of the influence it had enjoyed before the Black movement, but it survived in relative health and even made a significant comeback. With the disintegration of Black humanism, the remainder of the Black movement was in danger of reversing its secular development. Many thought the movement was drifting back in the unthinkable direction of Christianity.

The militants realized that if a non-Christian ethnic identity was going to be developed, they would have to find another crutch to buttress Black humanism.

## The Black Phase: A Religious Approach
For many who followed the religious approach to liberation, the

alternative by the early to mid-seventies became Islam. *The Nation of Islam\** had been with us through the sixties, but the Black militants had not taken it too seriously because of their commitment to secularism. However, with the deterioration of secularism they took a hard second look. Perhaps they began to remember when Malcolm said, "I am and always will be a Muslim. My religion is Islam. . . . I am going to organize and head a new mosque in New York City, known as Muslim Mosque, Inc. This gives us a religious base and the spiritual force necessary to rid our people of the vices that destroy the moral fiber of our community."[46]

Through Islam the militants hoped to salvage and revitalize the ailing dream of a de-Christianized Black culture. They also wanted to develop a Black Islamic theological dynamic. This, however, posed some serious problems because—contrary to the popular myth that Islam is indigenous to Africa—the very essence of Islam is rooted in and tied to a language and culture that are neither African-American nor African, but Arab. Thus Islam cannot take on itself the identity of a non-Arab culture. Islam and Black culture would have to function in an "oil and water" relationship, the oil layer of supraculture being Islam and the water layer of culture being Black humanism. They cannot blend.

Islam

---

Black Humanism

The Black Muslims eventually wanted to replace this unstable dualism with a solid theological and cultural unity. Some tried. But to do this, they had to either absolutize Islam, thereby wiping out secularism, or absolutize secularism, thereby wiping out Islam. Neither method brought success.

Because of its exclusively Arab orientation, Islam as a religious motif fails. It cannot foster the desired cohesion in African-American culture. Black adherents of orthodox Islam have tended to develop not an appreciation for legitimate African-American culture but a disdain and suspicion of it.

After all, how can a Muslim say "Black is beautiful" when the Qur'an says,

> On the Day when
> Some faces will be (lit up
> With) white, and some faces
> Will be (in the gloom of) black:
> To those whose faces
> Will be black, (will be said):
> "Did ye reject Faith
> After accepting it?
> Taste then Chastisement
> For rejecting Faith."
> But those whose faces
> Will be white,
> They will be in
> Allah's mercy: therein
> To dwell (for ever). (SURAT Al-Imran, 3:106-7)[47]

Those who attempt to be authentically African-American and Muslim face a dilemma. Many still speak Black English and still like jazz; yet in Islam you can neither worship Allah with jazz nor pray to him in Black English. One way out of this dilemma is to develop a Black Islamic heresy, as Elijah Muhammad did. But then this would not be Islam.

African-American advocates of Islam seem to have forgotten that historically wherever Islam has spread beyond its original geo-ethnic cradle (the Arabian peninsula) to become the absolute religion, it has done so primarily by the sword: "There is no God but Allah, and Muhammad is his prophet. Convert to Islam, submit to Islamic hegemony [and become a second-, third- or fourth-class citizen], or die." Needless to say, this meant the rupture of the non-Arab culture and usually its replacement by the Arab Islamic culture. In Africa, where the spread of Islam was not accompanied by total cultural rupture and replacement, Islam has become merely an oil layer over the water layer of a native belief system, producing an unstable syncretism.

Some call this "folk Islam."

Among African-Americans, Islamic believers chose an evangelistic strategy for the spread of Islam. They knew that the rupture and replacement strategy would be counterproductive, to say the least. Besides, it was logistically impossible. So through evangelism they produced an "oil and water" cultural dualism or folk Islam, just as in many parts of Africa.

Islam

---

Native Belief System

**A General Belief System?**

In the mid-seventies some Islamic thinkers saw this dualistic folly and took the approach of Imam *Warith Deen Muhammad*,* son of the late Elijah Muhammad and leader of the American Muslim Mission. Imam Muhammad probably saw that Islam would never dislodge the African-American church. He began to reluctantly concede to the church a minor role as part of a general Black belief system. He was moving toward a Black religious synthesis—a far cry from his father's position.

The late Elijah Muhammad had recoiled at White Christianity-ism and built its mirror image, a Black Islam-ism. What Elijah Muhammad saw was a White man's religion, a Christian heresy that denied that it had anything to do with the *physical* world. What he attempted to create was a Black man's religion, an Islamic heresy that denied that it had anything to do with the *spiritual* world. The substance of the White Christianity-ism was a set of unbiblical myths that had justified the oppression of Black people in America. The substance of the Nation of Islam was a set of non-Qur'anic myths that justified our total separation (by choice) from White society and the establishment of our own Islamic state in America.

When Warith Muhammad inherited the reins of leadership after his father's death, he inaugurated sweeping changes in the life and racial policy of the sect, signified by its name changes.[48] Many in the church were pleasantly surprised when Muslims went from being belligerent to being gracious toward them.

In Warith Muhammad's view, neither the theology of the African-American church (expressed in the theological dynamic) nor the beliefs of the Nation of Islam (expressed in doctrinaire ideology) were key to understanding African-American history or culture. Rather, both were merely products of our history and culture. As such they could merge. This is why, at Mosque No. 2 in Chicago, gospel choirs were invited to sing some of their songs after the Islamic services. Imam Muhammad knew that if Islam was to be successful among our people, it would need cultural "propping up on the leaning side." At that time this combination was the only hope Islamic believers had to establish a place in the African-American cultural fabric. By appealing to the proposed general belief system, Muslims attempted to win our people to Islam.

Imam Muhammad appeared to have solved the oil and water problem, but a difficulty remained. A syncretism of Christianity and Islam can never be true to both. It will be either primarily Christian in form and belief or primarily Islamic. To ensure that the combination would not become predominantly Christian, Warith Muhammad added a layer of Islamic doctrine. This only served to reintroduce the oil and water problem.

Another problem remained as well. According to the principle of parsimony (in this instance, the economy of thought), why make things more complicated than they have to be? In other words, why bother with this cumbersome combination or this irrelevant Islamic supraculture at all? We had done fine without them—who needed them now? The soul dynamic had sufficiently carried and inspired our people.

This was a question asked not by skeptics but by the African-American church itself. It was a question already answered by the church in its oral tradition. Someone has said,

We've come this far by faith
leaning on the Lord,
trusting in his Holy Word.

He's never failed me yet.

Oh, Oh, Oh . . . can't turn around.

We've come this far by faith.

And another:

As long as I've got King Jesus

I don't need nobody else!

Since oil and water didn't blend, the Islamic thinkers were unable to develop an adequate non-Christian theological foundation for the Black movement. The anti-Christian/pro-Islamic orientation of many of today's militants will eventually confront them also with the same oil and water problem.

Warith Muhammad eventually gave up on the idea of a religious synthesis. He ended up leading the American Muslim Mission into the Sunni Muslim orbit. By the mid-seventies, however, Minister *Louis Abdul Farrakhan*\* had grown dissatisfied with this move toward orthodox Islam. To him the former Nation of Islam had departed from the faith. He therefore broke with Warith Muhammad in 1977 and founded the "Original Nation of Islam" (now known as the Nation of Islam). He reinstated and revised Elijah Muhammad's doctrines and myths.

In the minds of many, Minister Farrakhan has eclipsed Warith Muhammad, capturing considerable media attention with his controversial statements. By the early 1990s Farrakhan himself was appealing to the old concept of a general belief system. Farrakhan's ideology was most clearly articulated at the *Million Man March*\* in Washington, D.C., on October 16, 1995. In his concept, the "water layer" consists of a mystical mingling of the theological dynamic, the doctrine of the old Nation of Islam, orthodox Islam and ancestor worship. The "oil layer" is a Neo-Nation of Islam—an Islamism embodied by Farrakhan as its fulfillment. (See figure on page 126.)

Thus far, however, Farrakhanistic Islam-ism has proven inadequately persuasive. In his speeches Farrakhan continues to quote the Bible far more than the Qur'an. Thus in reality it is not his brand of Islam-ism or his proposed general belief system that makes his mes-

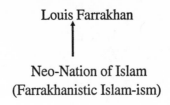

Louis Farrakhan

Neo-Nation of Islam
(Farrakhanistic Islam-ism)

oil layer

water layer

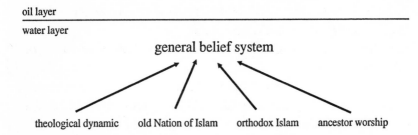

general belief system

theological dynamic    old Nation of Islam    orthodox Islam    ancestor worship

sage so alluring to so many. It is essentially "borrowed capital" from biblical truth—truth that the church has largely neglected for the past one hundred years.

Clearly, the emerging African-American militant movement is at a crossroads. For oil and water still won't blend.

## Post-Black Blues

The original goals of the post-Malcolm Black movement were the liberation of the Black community from oppression and exploitation, and the development of a new Black culture that pulled together all its diverse elements. Sadly, both goals were lost in a dualistic sauce. The de-Christianization of the Black movement was supposed to be an essential part of the first goal. However, with secularization came do-your-own-thing-ism. The result of Islamization was legalism and a preoccupation with works-righteousness (that 51 percent that would tip the scale to let one enter Paradise).

Gone were social concern and activism on behalf of the poor and oppressed. Gone was the ethical "oughtness" for this concern and activism. Gone was the cultural unity that many had assumed was achievable. Gone, in short, was all warrant for the optimism of the mid-sixties. Black secularism and Islam—whether one was absolutized or both juxtaposed in an unwanted dualism—gutted the very soul of the militant Black movement. Malcolm's legacy was betrayed, and the hope of developing a positive Black ethnicity was on the critical list.

Thus far the historic African-American church has produced the only unified soul dynamic in the African-American community. In fact, history shows us that no Black movement has survived for long apart from the Black theological dynamic. The secular and Islamic Black intellectuals failed to produce it, and no African-American cultural identity has been possible without it.

But it is not enough for the African-American church to rest on its past success. We must realize that being the strongest institution in the African-American community does not prevent the church from being in a state of decline as it is today.

A de-Christianized Black culture will always lack theological and cultural unity. Black people will simply never achieve this unity without the theological dynamic. Yet for some the theological dynamic is still "Christianity," and "Christianity" is still the White man's religion. This, then, was the post-Black crisis. This is why many had the post-Black blues.

### Becoming

The Black militants who pronounced the death of the Civil Rights Movement never saw that the theological dynamic was an application of the scriptural message and not an extension of White Christianity-ism. The doctrine of White supremacy (a fruit of Euro-American ethnocentrism) had never infected Black theology. Not seeing this, the militant Black thinkers rejected the theological dynamic and with it the power of God's Word. This is why the Black secular and religious approaches both failed.

About Malcolm X there was nothing static. In the end he was in a state of flux. But what was Brother Malcolm heading toward? In

January 1965 he confessed to Alex Haley, "The so-called 'moderate' civil-rights organizations regard me as 'too militant' and the so-called 'militant' organizations avoid me as 'too moderate.' They won't let me turn the corner."[49] Even Malcolm himself could not yet define this philosophical corner. On the Thursday before he died, he told a reporter, "I'm man enough to tell you that I can't put my finger on exactly what my philosophy is now, but I am flexible."[50]

For this reason many of Brother Malcolm's Black militant contemporaries turned their backs on him. They began to criticize him openly for being too "confused to be seriously followed any longer." The word in Harlem was that "he doesn't know what he believes in." Some even accused him of being all talk, a con man, while Dr. Martin Luther King and others were getting "beat over the head" for the cause.[51]

But Malcolm simply pursued truth and freedom for our people wherever they led. Those who harshly criticized him for his new flexibility only revealed their shortsightedness. They did not understand the real significance of Brother Malcolm.

Some have suggested that Brother Malcolm was headed in a biblical direction. If this is true, and if the integrity he showed in the pursuit of truth was as real as it appears to have been, then surely on his arrival he would have acknowledged the Lord of the Scriptures as "Lord of all." But given the mood of the Black community and the sorry condition of institutional Christianity at that time, if he had arrived at this conclusion I wonder if the church would have known what to do with a Christian Malcolm. I wonder if those who followed him would still have accepted and respected him. Would he have been rejected as a cultural prophet and branded a traitor by those who still confused Christianity with White Christianity-ism?

Only God knows the answers to the riddle of Malcolm X, and it is with God alone that our questions must rest. Those who have tried to extrapolate the direction of his life to a particular ideological, philosophical or religious destination have, in my judgment, missed the mark. In any case, they should have noted the extreme tentativeness of human life. Whatever our desires, however lofty our dreams, we as a people must be about our Father's business "while it is still day."

Furthermore, the issue of Brother Malcolm's destination was not the most important contribution of his life. We lost him while he was in a state of "becoming," and it was the *becoming* itself that made Malcolm X "our living Black manhood."

True humanity is to be in a perpetual state of becoming (Romans 1:17; 12:2; 2 Corinthians 3:17-18; Philippians 1:6; 3:12-14). It is this dynamic process that holds the key to freedom and dignity. This manifestation of becoming, like the ongoing pursuit of the kingdom of God and his righteousness (Matthew 6:33), makes the contribution of Malcolm X so valuable to us. And we can be thankful for it.

# 9
# A Great Legacy

When the apostle Paul spoke to the intellectuals of Athens he used a remarkable poetic quotation from Epimenides, a sixth-century B.C. Cretan poet (Acts 17:23, 28). In Titus 1:12 Paul again quotes from Epimenides, calling him a prophet. I'd call him a *cultural prophet*. The Bible thus suggests that all nations, including the African-American nation, may have had cultural prophets. Whether they are Christian is not necessarily the issue. Since God is Lord of all, the real issue is whether they were witnesses to God's Word in what they did and said.

## Streams in Stereo
As we have seen, the Southern quest for freedom and dignity started with the Colored phase and has gone through the Neo-Colored and Neo-Negro phases. This Southern stream has generally been oriented to church culture.

The Northern quest involved the Negro phase and has gone through

Black awareness, Black power and Black revolutionism. This Northern stream has generally been oriented to nonchurch culture.

Of course the two streams have overlapped and benefited from each other. Put together, what we learned from them is similar to some things the Old Testament teaches. Let's look at these streams in stereo. From the Southern stream we learned the following:

1. *Racism is deeper than slavery or segregation.* The end of slavery was not the beginning of freedom and dignity for our people. Slavery, though an expression of racism, was not the total picture of racism. In the absence of slavery, racism reemerged in Jim Crowism, segregation, disenfranchisement and exploitative economics. Even when segregation was defeated by the law of the land, racism itself was not erased, because segregation was not the total picture of racism either. Racism survived in the hearts of many, ready to be applied in new ways. The survival of racism reveals the farce of White humanism, since racism is a form of oppression, and oppression is a form of human unrighteousness.

2. *The melting pot is not the answer.* Desegregation, though a fruit of liberation, is not the total picture of liberation. While it is better to have access to the melting-pot lifestyle than to be excluded from it, gaining entrance is not worth being stripped of our cultural identity. True desegregation should never mean assimilation; the melting-pot system is unable to produce freedom and dignity for African-Americans.

3. *The Bible is our basis for freedom and dignity.* The parallels between Hebrew history and African-American history reveal that life cannot be lived only on an otherworldly basis. Freedom and dignity for our people, like the Promised Land for the Hebrews, have as much to do with this life as with the next. The theological dynamic that emerged from the message of the Bible can give us wisdom to see through the phony nature of White Christianity-ism as we embrace and apply the truths of Christianity.

4. *We must develop the resources we already have and unite around them.* This is essential if we are going to achieve the goals of our quest.

The soul dynamic is one such resource, and we can be proud of it. When applied properly, it can have a profound effect on African-Americans and on America at large.

From the Northern stream we learned the following:

1. *White humanism is bankrupt, and any African-American strategy that depends on it is doomed to fail.* When we tried to be acceptable in White society by imitating the melting-pot lifestyle, we only gave in to White standards and imitated White racism. Besides, we never were able to imitate White folks acceptably, because we were still Black. The result of this was complexion consciousness, self-hatred, feelings of inferiority and economic stress among our people. The only ones who seemed to succeed were those who "passed" for White, but they lived their lives in bondage to a lie. Any strategy based on genetics and environment is unworkable and reinforces oppression.

2. *There is dignity in Black humanness and beauty in Black culture.* Our culture and consciousness, therefore, are worth affirming and preserving. The best way to do this is through "body life"—an active, caring concern for each other, especially for those who suffer most from oppression. Without body life there is no guarantee that Black power will not just end up substituting a "hateful honky" for a "nasty nigger."

3. *We need a radical change if we want justice.* Such a change must be revolutionary, transforming us and our environment. This is impossible without God's help. Without God's truth and power at the root of our quest for justice, we are left with Black humanism; and Black humanism is guaranteed to fail because of human unrighteousness.

4. *If our community functions as a nation, we can move toward freedom and dignity.* Dealing with racism on an individual basis will prove impossible because, along with other sins, racism is institutionalized in American society. Functioning as a cultural nation will help equip us to deal with racism from a position of strength. We need to control the politics of our community and, where appropriate, make coalitions with other groups at points of agreement—but not as allies. We also need to control the economics of our community. But we must

remember that while African-American economic power is important, it is not the final solution, because ultimately it is tied up with the American economic system. In short, we need new institutions on which to build a new cultural nationalism. We have an important role to play among other African and *Two-Thirds World\** peoples, and functioning as a nation will help us fulfill that role.

## Prophets in Parallel

Dr. Martin Luther King Jr. was the culminating cultural prophet of the Southern stream, while Malcolm X was the culminating cultural prophet of the Northern stream. The perspectives of these two prophets, from a humanistic standpoint, apparently contradict each other. But a God-centered perspective shows a complementary relationship between the two. The relationship between the contributions of these two men has been one of the greatest riddles in African-American history. Part of the problem has arisen from a failure to see them in terms of the Northern stream/Southern stream mode.

Let's take a look at these two prophets in parallel.

1. Martin was a prophet from the *South;* Malcolm was a prophet from the *North.*

2. Martin exposed the sin of *omission* of American Bible-believing Christianity (what they did not do); Malcolm exposed the sin of *commission* of American Christianity-ism (what they did do—racism).

3. Martin exposed *relational* racism; Malcolm exposed *institutional* racism.

4. Martin was against *segregation;* Malcolm was against losing our identity through *phony integration.*

5. Martin advocated *gracious love;* Malcolm advocated *raw truth.*

6. Martin worked for *moral and spiritual power;* Malcolm worked for *political and economic power.*

7. Martin was a prophet for *nonviolence,* the Southern strategy; Malcolm was a prophet of *militancy,* the Northern strategy.

8. Martin came from an African-American *church,* and church-ori-

ented people followed him because he provided recognizable leadership as he called America to repent; Malcolm came from the *streets,* and street people followed him because he crystallized and articulated their hurts as he exposed systematic oppression.

9. When Martin went *north* to Chicago to improve the economic condition of the masses trapped in the ghetto, his strategy had little success; when Malcolm went *south* to address the participants in the Selma-to-Montgomery march, his strategy was less acceptable to the leaders of the march.

10. Toward the end of his life Martin began moving toward a *more militant* position; toward the end of his life Malcolm began moving toward a *more conciliatory* position.

11. Martin expressed the *theological* side of soul dynamic; Malcolm expressed the *cultural* side of soul dynamic.

12. Martin predicted his death shortly before it happened; so did Malcolm.

13. Martin had a vision of a great opportunity for our people but was assassinated before he was able to articulate it; Malcolm experienced the same fate.

14. Martin died at age thirty-nine; so did Malcolm.

Both Martin's and Malcolm's lives were parallel, in a sense, to Moses' life; they brought us to the brink of an opportunity, but they themselves never entered it. What opportunity did they see? The answer to that question could be the key to why God in his sovereignty brought us forth as a cultural nation out of the horrors of slavery.

**Kingdoms and Streams**

One of the clearest notions in the soul dynamic is the idea that we are in this land for a special purpose. Since the deaths of Malcolm and Martin we have balked at the River Jordan, and we can't seem to agree where to go from here. Perhaps looking at the biblical kingdom of Israel at a later stage in its history can shed new light on our situation.

Israel had divided into a southern kingdom and a northern kingdom. The southern kingdom stayed within the pattern of Yahwism, the true worship of God, but it became an empty tradition. The result of their indifference was the Babylonian conquest. The northern kingdom tried to replace Yahwism with paganism. The result was instability, apostasy, splintering, violent disputes between factions, assassinations, the Assyrian conquest and, finally, obliteration.

In the historic African-American quest the Southern stream stayed within the pattern of the church, but it has become a formal tradition. The result has been indifference toward God and the loss of the prophetic power we had discovered in the Civil Rights Movement. The Northern stream tried to replace the theological dynamic with an alien religious base (Islam, secularism and the like). The result has been instability, apostasy, splintering, violent disputes between factions, assassinations and the loss of the African-American culture as a unified force.

We can thank the Southern stream for showing us that freedom and dignity are not found in the melting pot. We can thank the Northern stream for showing us that freedom and dignity are not found within ourselves.

### The Law and the Quest

If we look at how God used the law in the Old Testament to disciple the people of Israel, we may find further parallels with the African-American experience to instruct us.

Paul asks, "What, then, was the purpose of the law? It was added *because of transgressions* until the Seed to whom the promise referred had come" (Galatians 3:19). The Israelites' ordeal of slavery and their consequent social problems were going to keep them from surviving as a nation—and keep them from receiving the promised Seed (Christ). Without the law they would never have survived to fulfill their destiny as the nation through whom the Messiah of the world would come.

What then is the purpose of the soul dynamic? It was added *because of transgressions* until the Joshua generation should come in which our destiny would be fulfilled. The African-American ordeal of slavery and its consequent social problems would have kept us from surviving to see the Joshua generation. Without the soul dynamic we would never fulfill our destiny as a cultural nation.

What was the function of the law? "The law was our *schoolmaster* to bring us unto Christ" (Galatians 3:24 KJV). Through the law, Israel learned about the One whom God would send and what God was going to do through their people.

What was the comparable function of our "inheritance," the knowledge we gained from the phases of our quest? The inheritance was our *schoolmaster* to bring us to the Joshua phase. Through our inheritance we learned much about the Joshua phase and what it can do through us.

What was the result of the law? "We know that whatever the law says, it says to those who are under the law, so that *every mouth may be silenced* and the whole world held accountable to God" (Romans 3:19). "Indeed it is the straight-edge of the Law that shows us how crooked we are" (Romans 3:20 Phillips). Failure to keep the law made Israel shut up when they began to brag about their own righteousness before God.

What was the result of our quest for freedom and dignity? Whatever the quest means, it communicates to those who are aware so that *every mouth may be silenced.* Indeed, it is the high ideal of liberation that shows us how unliberated we are! The failure of the Black revolution, for example, illustrates the effect of sin.

Scripture pictures sin as "missing the mark" or "falling short." Understanding how our sin and ungodliness affect us in our pursuit of freedom and dignity can be key to understanding the significance and necessity of a Joshua generation of leadership. Our African-American heritage is a great legacy, and we should be proud of it. But it has given us only a glimpse of our potential. It should be boldly proclaimed that a Joshua phase is the only way to fulfill that potential. We must step over into our cultural destiny.

The law *never succeeded in producing righteousness,* because sinful human nature was weak (Romans 8:3). Freedom alone will also *never succeed in producing righteousness,* because our sinful human nature is still weak. The liberation of our ungodliness has taught us that we can never live up to all our aspirations as a beautiful people apart from God's grace.

# Part III

# Roots and Fruits
of Consciousness

# 10

# A Little "White" Lie in the Name of Black Truth

*T*he militants of the sixties and today were right to challenge the way we think. They were right to point out that if we are going to have a culture and a movement with any kind of integrity at all, we must root it in African-American history and experience.

It is true that we could not afford to buy into a toxic belief system, nor could we afford to accept the inferiority arising from it. Many still assume that Christianity is for Whites and Islam is for Blacks. The Black thinkers of the seventies and eighties generally considered themselves religiously neutral, because by then Islam was no longer an exotic novelty. Among today's militants, however, there is another rising tide of Islamic orientation. Christianity is once again dubbed "the White man's religion."

If Christianity is the White man's religion, then surely it must be rejected in spite of our historic theological dynamic. But *is* Christianity the White man's religion?

To answer that question we will have to take a closer look at the nature of an ethnic religion. To be ethnic, a religion must have two characteristics. First, it must arise out of the historical experience of a people and take on itself their cultural identity. Second, its assumptions must be the basic commitment of the vast majority of that people. It must be woven into the fabric of the culture to such an extent that it seeps into the minds of the people without needing conscious acceptance.

## The Roots of Christianity

Although Western Christianity is somewhat expressed through Euro-American culture, Christianity itself did not arise in Europe or America. It grew up in the Middle East, among the people known as Hebrews. Its roots can be traced to Abraham. These roots continue back to a time when all people were monotheistic and approached God through animal sacrifice. Ultimately, the roots of Christianity will lead us back to Adam and his response to God's salvation promises.

In Genesis 3:15 God tells a fallen Adam and Eve that a savior will come (the woman's "offspring"). This savior will conquer Satan (crushing the serpent's head), but the salvation will come through the suffering of the savior: "his heel will be bruised." This is a primitive but accurate description of what Christ accomplished on the cross. Thus Christianity is disqualified as the "White man's religion" in the first sense, for its roots precede the White race by a long shot.

## A European Dialectic

White society may appear to be Christian at a superficial glance, but on closer examination the picture radically changes. We must remember that as Western thinking grew and developed, it was heavily influenced by Greek philosophy in the early stages and by secular science in the later. Although Christianity played a major role in this development, and although many Europeans were indeed true to the Scriptures, the history of European thought in general has been one of rejecting the biblical world-and-life-view and replacing it with the White man's religion. This rejection came about through a series of distortions of Christian theology on the part of Western philosophers.

Let's take a brief look at what happened. Again and again Christian thought would be opposed by some nonbiblical perspective, which modified it sufficiently to create, in time, a new religion. G. W. F. Hegel called such a process of change a *dialectic,* and the two opposing forces the *thesis* and *antithesis;* the new "product" emerging from the struggle he called the *synthesis.* This synthesis would become a new thesis, inducing a new antithesis, and so forth.

Western thought finds its roots in Greece. Prior to the emergence of New Testament Christianity, Greek thought was already going through its own dialectical process. By the seventh century B.C. Greek religion had degenerated into decadent polytheism. Myths proliferated, and many of the priests were corrupt and ruthless.

Among the discontented were men known as the Sophists. They attempted to develop an alternative comprehensive account of reality so as to render superfluous the myths and gods of the priests. This could have been accomplished later if the Greeks had taken the advice of Epimenides and returned to the worship of the one true God. But it was not to be.

The father of Sophism was Thales of Miletus (640-546 B.C.). Other Sophists arose in the fifth century B.C. They included Protagoras of Abdera (481-411) and Gorgias of Leontini (483-375). Protagoras based his thinking on the premise that "man is the measure of all things." Apparently his theory of man was defined by the image of Greek-man. Doubtless Africans and Asians were not included in his concept. Sound familiar?

Due to the Sophists' lack of moral and ethical power, they never succeeded in overcoming the influence of the corrupt priests in Greece.

In Persia, however, there was a similar problem of religious corruption in the sixth century B.C. There the power of the corrupt priests was broken by the ethical teaching of *Zoroaster*\* (630-553 B.C.).

A pre-Christian synthesis in Greece came when the influence of Zoroaster met the influence of the Sophists. The result was the Socratic school of thought, with its *cerebral* approach to knowledge. The father of this movement was Socrates (470-399 B.C.). He is best known for the statement "Know yourself." He believed that (1) no person is really sinful and (2) the basis of sin is ignorance. Ironically, much later these same concepts were incorporated in Elijah Muhammad's doctrines regarding African-Americans. The best-known disciples of the Socratic school were Plato (428-348 B.C.) and Aristotle (384-322 B.C.). They would have a major influence on the European dialectic.

When New Testament Christianity arrived on the scene, it was dominated by the Hebrew mind and its *practical* approach to knowledge. Thus the first post-Christian synthesis came when the Hebrew mind met the Socratic way of thinking as it reflected on the Scriptures. The result was a scientific theology, an analytic and rational approach to Christian thought.

Augustine of Hippo (A.D. 354-430) was able to synthesize scientific theology with some of Plato's philosophy. In Plato's concept, reality was divided between forms (the world of unchanging ideas) and matter (the world of changing, unstable substance). Augustine expressed Plato's bifurcation of reality in part in his pivotal work *The City of God,*[1] where he compares the heavenly city, whose God is the Lord Jesus Christ, to the earthly city, whose citizens worship their own gods.

Now Augustine contributed many good things to the development of Christian theology, and for these we can praise God; but he did have a weakness in his framework. And, unfortunately, the European rejection of the scriptural worldview focused on this weak point, transforming it into a major problem.

In Augustine's concept, the city of God was too closely identified with the church as an institution. This might at first appear to be harmless. However, it leaves room for a dichotomy between a *secular* realm, which is thought to be independent of God and his revelation, and a *sacred* realm—the institutional church as "the peculiar instrument of God's gracious dealings with men." Such a dichotomy would not arise from a truly biblical worldview. Scripture distinguishes between the church as the kingdom of God in a narrow or special sense and creation as the kingdom of God in the broad, general sense. In the Bible, God reveals that his lordship is not limited to the scope of the institutional church. Indeed, he exercises his lordship over the whole creation in his plan of redemption.[2]

Because Augustine did not recognize that philosophical thought has its root in religious commitment, he was never able to develop a comprehensive Christian worldview. He saw pagan philosophy and Christian theology as two unrelated fields. But this kind of dualistic structure is unscriptural.[3]

After Augustine, European theology evolved into medieval scholasticism, where theology was considered "the queen of the sciences," and the doctrine of the institutional church set the agenda for all learning. Scholasticism came out of a synthesis of Augustine's framework with the work of Thomas Aquinas. Aquinas is best known for his work *Summa Theologica,* a synthesis between Aristotle's philosophy and Roman Catholic theology.

The Augustine/Aquinas synthesis "set into motion . . . the pattern of thought that was to dominate the Middle Ages, a pattern of 'nature' and 'grace' featuring a dichotomy between the natural, earthly powers and the supernatural powers of the institutional church."[4] Augustine's ideas were gradually replaced by Thomas Aquinas's concepts, and the motif of "nature" and "grace" "made its entrance into [European] Christian thought."[5] Now the sphere of "nature" was considered to be independent from "grace," and the dualism in European thought grew even more acute.

With human reason elevated to a status equivalent with "grace," some thinkers began to consider "grace" irrelevant or unnecessary. Thus the "Age of Reason" began. Since that time European thought has looked to humankind as the final judge for all truth. Remember Protagoras?

A completely mechanical view of "nature," with no room for personhood, resulted. In various ways European thinkers recognized this view as dangerous. To keep things from getting worse, a desperate search began for a substitute for the lost concept of "grace." Jean-Jacques Rousseau, Immanuel Kant and G. W. F. Hegel all came up with alternatives. By this time European thinking had completely cut itself off from God's Word. The result was rationalism, which considered human reason alone as the final authority for establishing truth. Remember the Flatlanders?

Next in this development of thought came the synthesis between rationalism and the Reformation. Their offspring was deism, a secular Christianity-ism. The deistic notion that God started the great machine of the universe and then stood back and did nothing about its inner workings was a cornerstone in the thinking of John Locke (1632-1704). Locke was an English philosopher whose influence was felt in Europe. He was a major influence on Thomas Jefferson (1743-1826), a deist who had a major influence on American thinking.

Deism provided fertile soil for European ethnocentrism, which saw the world revolving around Europe. It is true that Europe did not have an exclusive hold on ethnocentrism. Every group, whether tribal, racial, cultural, political or geographical, has a strand of ethnocentricity. It comes from unrighteousness. European ethnocentricity was especially devastating, however, because through colonialism it asserted its negative influence far beyond the boundaries of Europe.

We must remember that science, itself the result of a biblical view of our environment, had also been ripped from its biblical framework and secularized, and was thought to be independent from God. Such was the trend of almost everything in European thought by now. Secularized science yielded a blind technology gutted of all ethical restraints. It functioned as an ideal tool for European ethnocentric ambitions of expansion. This is what Nikki Giovanni identified in "The Great Pax Whitie." For her, this technology without ethics is what released destructive forces on the world—in the name of "peace"/"Christianity."

With the lordship of God thrown out of the arena of European thought, the way was paved for a synthesis between deism and European ethnocentrism. The result was White secular humanism, the view that White humanity is the source of truth and value. Behold the White man's religion: obviously it was not Christianity (figure 11).

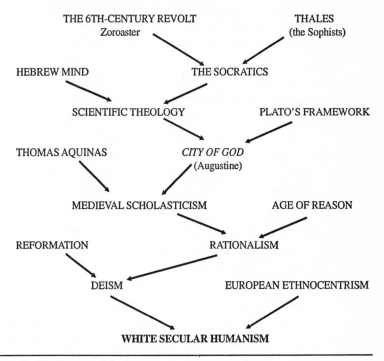

Figure 11.    The European dialectic

### Ramifications of the White Man's Religion

The "ungospel" of White secular humanism spread to the entire world as its domination was established and maintained by a prostituted technology. Every aspect of life was touched by this ethnic religion in its global expansion.

1. Applied politically (outside Europe), White secularism became *colonialism.* As colonies were established around the world, their political structures and geographical boundaries were determined by

the politics of Europe. The colonialists had little or no concern for the natural ethnic groupings in those foreign lands. For example, sub-Saharan Africa was carved up by the colonial powers at the Congress of Berlin (1878) and the Conference of Berlin (1884-1885). No Africans were present. The political boundaries that were fixed split some tribes and caused power struggles among others. Though most of these colonies are now independent nations, much of their political and tribal turmoil is due to the arbitrary boundaries that were dictated in the colonial era.

2. Applied economically, secularism became *mercantilism.* What colonialism did politically, mercantilism did economically. Though it did not work well for all European nations, mercantilism did serve the economic interests of the elite class in countries such as Spain, Portugal and France. Economic development for the benefit of the indigenous population was never very high on the agenda.

3. Applied biologically, secularism became *evolutionism.* Contrary to popular myth, evolution is not a proven scientific fact. It is a basic assumption forming a framework by which many biologists interpret and classify the differences in life forms. Creation is also a framework. Not all that passes for creationism is true to the creation framework; the same can be said for evolution.

Unlike evolution, however, the theory of creation derives from God's Word. God was there at the beginning, and humankind was not. An explanation of the origin of race consistent with creation will lead to human equality, because we are all in God's image. Thus if creationists are racist, they are being inconsistent with their framework.

An evolutionary account of biological variety assumes that differences within groupings reflect the fact that some are "higher" on the evolutionary scale than others. Thus if evolutionists are racist, they are consistent with their framework.

4. Applied philosophically, secularism became *materialism.* When Thomas Aquinas developed his "nature" and "grace" framework, he opened the door to materialism: secularized "nature" became the preoccupation of the European thinker, and materialism emerged without a ripple. Once secularism was firmly established, self-grati-

fication through the accumulation of wealth became a substitute for spiritual values. Often materialism turned into greed as it tried to fill the spiritual emptiness left by the rejection of "grace."

5. Applied sociologically (outside Europe), secularism became *racism.* The roots of racism can be traced all the way back to Adam and Eve and their rebellion against God. When they set themselves up as final judges in all matters of good and evil, they were judging the Creator by the standards of the creature. In essence they were guilty of "creaturism." Creaturism today manifests itself as me-ism. Individuals set their selfish desires up as the standard for determining the worth of other people. A collective manifestation of the same creaturism is racism, a simple extension of me-ism: one race sets itself up as the standard of judgment for all races.

6. Applied culturally, secularism became *imperialism.* If Western culture had kept the Word of God as the source of its values, imperialism would have been avoided. But the Bible had lost its central role in the West. Western culture itself became the standard by which to judge other cultures. Like racism and me-ism, cultural imperialism has led to a disrespect for other cultures and a failure to see truth—the grace of God at work in other cultures. Cultural imperialism was the root of the White bias that Black militants pointed out.

7. Finally, applied as a cult (in America), secularism became *White Christianity-ism.* This I have already discussed.

When the advocates of Black militancy identified "Christianity" as the White man's religion, they were in fact identifying a cultic mutation of White secular humanism. This heresy originated as a justification of American slavery, which was itself a byproduct of racism. The militants neither saw secularism as the basis of White Christianity-ism nor recognized unrighteousness as its root. Their analysis of racism, radical as it was, was not radical enough. It never dealt with the real root of racism (figure 12).

**Built-In Racism**
By and large, the Bible-believing community had been blinded to the

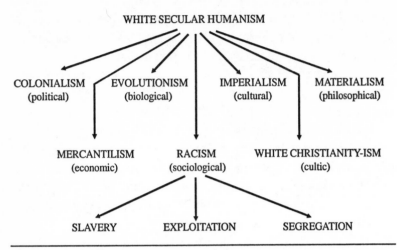

**Figure 12.**   Applications of White secular humanism

institutional evils in American society. This blindness is somewhat understandable. For example, how can one understand institutional sin like racism when the scope of sin has been limited to personal issues such as drinking, smoking and chewing? Furthermore, most members of the Bible-believing community belonged to the middle class, and middle-class life is highly individualistic. How can you see evil in a system that delivered the goods so efficiently? In his essay "The Web of Urban Racism," Harold M. Baron wrote:

> Maintenance of the basic racial controls is now less dependent upon specific discriminatory decisions and acts. Such behavior has become so well institutionalized that the individual generally does not have to exercise a choice to operate in a racist manner. The rules and procedures of the large organizations have already prestructured the choice. The individual only has to conform to the operating norms of the organization, and the institution will do the discrimination for him.[6]

This unthought-out racism explains in part the social ineptitude of the Bible-believing community when it came to racial justice in the twentieth century. It justified Malcolm X's condemnation:

> If the so-called "Christianity" now being practiced in America

displays the best that world Christianity has left to offer—no one in his right mind should need any much greater proof that very close at hand is the *end* of Christianity.

Are you aware that some Protestant theologians, in their writings, are using the phrase "post-Christian era"—and they mean *now?*

And what is the greatest single reason for this Christian church's failure? It is its failure to combat racism. It is the old "You sow, you reap" story. The Christian church sowed racism—blasphemously; now it reaps racism.[7]

It is White Christianity-ism that was bitterly denounced in the militant movements of the sixties and is still denounced today—and rightfully so.

But if Christianity is the White man's religion, why has it been thrown out of the life of so many institutions in White society, such as the public school system? What is the real, underlying religion in today's American society? It is not Christianity; it is secular humanism. This notion of human independence from God has enjoyed an increasing position of authority in Western thinking since the Renaissance. The secular framework has left absolutely no room for the God of the Scriptures. Yet, unfortunately, Western society is still called Christian.

**A Black Dilemma**
The soul dynamic that emerged from our experience never developed such a notion of independence from God. The survival of our theological dynamic is a real testimony to the grace of God. It is worth noting that the theology of the African-American church is oriented to the Old Testament. Part of the reason for this is the close similarity between the Hebrew and the African-American experience. Both developed a *covenant consciousness.*

Biblical Christianity is, by God's plan, universal in nature; it can take on itself the identity of any culture. We see this universality of the gospel in the book of Acts. The day of Pentecost, when the gospel was preached in every language of the world, is clear proof that the Christian gospel is not locked into a particular culture or language. We see its universality as it was communicated and absorbed in Jewish and Greek cultures in the first century. The call of the church was to penetrate every nation, every culture, with the message of salvation, that all peoples might submit to God in their ethnicity. So in Christianity, if I do not worship God in my own culture, I am being inconsistent with my faith.

Notice how unlike an ethnic religion Christianity is. In Islam if I try to worship Allah in my own culture, I am being inconsistent with my faith! According to Muslim teaching, the Qur'an is in Arabic only (Suras12:2; 20:112; 39:28, 41; 42:7). If it is translated into another language, it is no longer Qur'an. It becomes merely a commentary or a paraphrase.

Given that biblical Christianity intends us to worship God in our culture, we can see that the African-American theological dynamic is a legitimate expression of the biblical message. It fully qualifies as African-American, having historical and cultural continuity in the Black experience. This satisfies our need to be African-American. Yet it does not have merely ethnic origins; it is rooted in the universal Word of God. This satisfies our need to transcend Blackness. One thing is clear: the theological dynamic does not qualify as the White man's religion.

It is a shame that the militant figures of the sixties failed to make this obvious distinction. Ironically, when they searched for a replacement for Christianity in their movement, instead of escaping the White man's religion they fell right into its trap. These Black militants tended to have more formal education than what had been historically attainable for our people, but that education was founded on Western thought, which by that time had infected even the predominantly Black colleges. Thus they chose the alternative supplied them: secular humanism.

In essence, then, the Black militants turned away from a valid expression of the universal Word of God. As a result they turned away from the only valid basis for the Black ethnicity they were trying to develop. They turned to secular humanism, a little "White" lie in the name of Black truth. And the Black movement degenerated from there into contradictory do-your-own-thing-isms.

Today's Islamic-oriented militants believe they have avoided the inadequacies of secularism. But like their counterparts in the seventies they will once again discover the inadequacies of Islam. As long as they insist on ignoring the lessons of the recent past, the collapse of the new militant movement will be inevitable.

## Too Small

Absolutized Blackness at first appeared to give fresh new meaning to our experience and culture, but the limitations of Blackness soon became visible.

Blackness became a particular type of abstraction, and like other such abstractions, it could not give a complete account of reality. Blackness as a symbol of oppression in White society and a symbol of pride in the African-American community gave us valid understandings of history, sociology, psychology, economics and so on. But it could not give us, for example, an alternative understanding of math, physics or chemistry.

This presented a dilemma, because the ideal of Blackness was supposed to be a universally valid absolute for our emerging cultural identity. Many went so far as to say that what could not be completely contained within Blackness was by definition White.

At first the Black ideal was liberating. But after it had been absolutized, it became a restricting Black box—a box unable to contain all the humanity to which the Black movement had sensitized us. Later we discovered that even where Black consciousness had given us new insights, those insights were not comprehensive but perspectival; that is, they represented not objective truths, but the truth seen from where we stood.

Likewise, if the advocates of today's Afrocentrism recognize its perspectival nature, it will be the source of many valid and valuable insights. But as an absolutized ideal, Afrocentrism, like absolutized Blackness, will turn out to be another restrictive box.

When we discovered that Blackness, as a limited ideal, was not big enough to be an absolute, the quest was on for a transcendent non-White absolute to buttress Blackness. Hence the turn to Islam. Others "bit the bullet" and gave up on Blackness as an ideal, settling merely for a Black style as they opted for materialism. Hence the emerging narcissism. Secularists and Muslims had accused Christians of being dualistic and self-centered, but now they were opting for dualistic and self-centered structures.

Black is truly beautiful, but it is not beautiful as a god. As a god it is too small.

Afrocentrism is truly magnificent, but it is not magnificent as an absolute. As an absolute, it will infect us with the kind of bigotry we've struggled against in others for centuries.

**God's Gift**
Ethnicity has beauty only as it derives from understanding that we are in God's image. Absolute ethnicity, like every other finite concept that is absolutized and cut off from God's revelation, will always end up crashing on the rocks of meaninglessness and chaos. African-American identity will have its real fulfillment only when it is seen in light of how God is active in the world. Historic Black theology has always affirmed this truth. It is the power of this truth that has accounted for Black theology's remarkable survival.

The Word of God embraced in the Black theological dynamic has always given us a transcendent reference point for reflection on ourselves and our situation. Whenever we seek to understand our situation without this transcendent reference point, we fail to find an answer to our crisis. The White man's religion has failed us. The Black version of the White man's religion has failed us. The Arab ethnic religion has failed us and will fail us again.

True ethnic identity will be impossible if it is based on ethnic identity itself. It is God who gave us the basis of the Black consciousness of the sixties and the African-American consciousness of today. It was not a human invention. Yet as we have seen, the Scriptures will show us the true significance of the African-American consciousness. The theological dynamic is God's gift to our people, and it will lead us to develop a true ethnic identity.

# 11

# "Busting Out"

*B*asic to a reconstruction of African-American culture must be a more radical understanding of God's assessment of why we do what we do. We need God's assessment of our basic religious commitment, which is the root of culture itself. Not religious commitment in the sectarian sense of belonging to a particular organization, but in the *generic** sense of the basic human attempts to solve problems in our relationship with the Creator. To find God's assessment of our condition, we must go to the Word of God.

## The Knowledge of the Nations

When our first parents began to experience the result of their rebellion against God, they did not run toward God and ask forgiveness; instead they ran and hid (Genesis 3:7-8). This vain attempt to get away from God was itself a religious act. In one way or another all people have been acting out this same religious tradition ever since. Religion can be defined as *the basic commitment to seek or avoid God and his revelation in every area of life.* Let's begin the discussion of our basic religious commitment by seeing what Scripture says about it.

> Why do the nations conspire
> and the peoples plot in vain?
> The kings of the earth take their stand
> and the rulers gather together
> against the LORD
> and against his Anointed One.
> "Let us break their chains," they say,
> "and throw off their fetters."
> The One enthroned in heaven laughs;
> the Lord scoffs at them. (Psalm 2:1-4)

Here the nations of the world are seen involved in a futile conspiracy to rid themselves of God's authority, control and presence. Although these nations, by and large, do not have the Scriptures, they know enough about God to plot rebellion against him and his "Anointed One." How do they know this?

It is often forgotten that according to Scripture, people without the Bible are not without God's revelation. A pervasive assumption in Scripture is that the nations without Scripture still have extensive knowledge of God.

> The wrath of God is being revealed from heaven against all the godlessness and wickedness of men who suppress the truth by their wickedness, since what may be known about God is plain to them, because God has made it plain to them. For since the creation of the world God's invisible qualities—his eternal power and divine nature—have been clearly seen, being understood from what has been made, so that men are without excuse.
>
> For although they knew God, they neither glorified him as God nor gave thanks to him, but their thinking became futile and their foolish hearts were darkened. (Romans 1:18-21)

According to this passage, not only is God's character plain in our environment, but God himself is present in reality, making it plain. Therefore all people perceive and understand God's "eternal power and divine nature." So no human being can claim ignorance about God. But the passage does not stop there; not only do all nations know *about* God, but they know God himself.

Thus in Psalm 2:1-4, along with trying to extricate themselves from God's authority and control, the nations are vainly trying to avoid the presence of God. This is quite a serious indictment against humanity and its basic religious commitment.

Just how extensive is human knowledge of God? To know that we will have to take a closer look at the content of God's revelation that comes to all people.

1. *God is.* Moses must have been somewhat startled when God revealed his name as "I AM" (Exodus 3:14). God was saying that his existence is the most obvious and fundamental thing in human experience. There can be no *is* without God's *is;* and since *is* is, God is, because God is *is.* God here introduces himself as the very bedrock of all existence. Since all people experience existence itself, all people automatically experience God's existence.

The only way anyone can declare that God "ain't" is to declare that *is* ain't. And if *is* ain't, there never was a "God ain't" declaration in the first place. Without God even the atheist could not say "God ain't." He would not exist to say it. Without *is* there would be *nothing.* "The fool says in his heart, 'There is no God' " (Psalm 14:1); he is a fool because the only way he could say "there is no God" is on the basis of God himself. This dilemma is an aspect of what the theologians call "the ontological problem." (Ontology is the study of existence and being.) Duke Ellington, though not a theologian in the classical sense, beautifully communicated this in his song "Something About Believing" when he said, "The silliest thing ever read was that somebody said 'God is dead'; the mere mention of the first word automatically eliminates the second and the third."[1]

If we accept the existence of a building, we automatically accept the existence of its foundation, because all buildings sit on something. This is so obvious that we don't have to think about it. There simply would be no building in the first place without some kind of foundation.

God? The humanist has therefore left himself with nothing as the basis of existence. But all that is based on nothing is nothing.

Therefore if our humanist appeals to "nothing" (or himself) as a higher authority than God, he is in deep trouble. As we saw from "the ontological problem," without God there would be no secular humanist in the first place. Oh, well! Back to nothingness.

All this reasoning is an aspect of what theologians call "the epistemological problem." (Epistemology is the study of how we know what we know.) The epistemological problem flies in the face of those who say that there is no absolute truth anywhere. If we deny the possibility of absolutes, our only alternative is to say that everything is relative. But this, of course, would mean that we have failed to escape from absolutes, for to say that all is relative makes relativism the absolute! It becomes the basis of do-your-own-thing-ism.

How does this understanding affect us in our quest for freedom and dignity? It reminds us that if we want a sound basis for a reconstructed African-American culture, we had better start with what God says and work our way through our task, "reflecting back" on God's revelation in Scripture and in our own environment. Since Scripture teaches that God speaks through the creation, Scripture should serve as the key to rediscovering what God says in our culture.

Having said that God *is* and that Scripture is our best source of revelation about God, we will use it now to see what we can know about God.

2. *God is the Creator.* Genesis 1:3-26 is pregnant with the phrase "And God said . . ." What does God say in the creative act? He says things like "light" (v. 3), "atmosphere" (v. 6), "water and land" (v. 9), "plants" (v. 11), "sun, moon and stars" (vv. 14-16), "sea creatures and birds" (v. 20), "land animals" (v. 24), "man—male and female—in God's image" (vv. 26-27). These words are the obvious environmental realities that all human beings have in common. Since they are all expressions of God's creational word, they all say, "God is the Creator." "Long ago by God's word the heavens existed and the earth was formed" (2 Peter 3:5).

But God has not left us only knowledge of his existen[ce ...]
gone beyond that to communicate the characteristics of his [...]
the nature of reality, and the Scriptures provide the key for di[...]
this natural revelation. They testify that they are the Wor[d ...]
(2 Timothy 3:16-17; 2 Peter 1:20-21), and in them we learn [...]
speaks both through Scripture and through the environment ([...]
1:20).

A person, let's say a humanist, may accept the fact that th[e ...]
foundation to all existence and yet deny that the God of the Scr[ipture]
is that foundation. He would be denying that the Scriptures a[re the]
Word of God. Or he may take another tack in his search for a [...]
from God's authority: he may accept some aspects of scrip[...]
teaching of a revelational environment but reject the Script[ural]
testimony that Scripture is revelation. He may even accept som[e of]
the scriptural self-testimony and reject the rest of it. No matter [how]
he slices the cake, his decision as to which parts of Scripture are t[rue]
and which are false rests on the notion that he himself is the high[est]
authority in determining truth. But if God is not the highest authori[ty]
then God is not God, by definition. The secular humanist has mad[e]
himself the god, the reference point of existence.

I have argued already that if we deny God, we deny existence itsel[f]
and end up with nothing. But we cannot talk about nothing, because
nothing is *nothing*. If we can talk about nothing, then nothing becomes
*something*—but who or what is it? However, if we deny God, we deny
existence itself, and we end up with nothing, and so on. The secular
humanist has already eliminated the Scriptures as the means of divine
communication by his original denial that the Scriptures are God's
Word. If he also eliminates the environment as revelation, he has
eliminated the very possibility of revelation itself, because by definition people never leave their environment. Our environment is always
where we are. And if there is no revelation of God in our context, there
is no other place to see him. This brings us back to the nothingness of
nothing.

Now since nothing is nothing, how can it be a higher authority than

John 1:1-5 follows this line of reasoning.

In the beginning was the Word, and the Word was with God, and the Word was God. He was with God in the beginning.

Through him all things were made; without him nothing was made that has been made. In him was life, and that life was the light of men. The light shines in the darkness, but the darkness has never put it out. (NIV/TEV)

Here the Word of God is pictured as being present with God from the beginning. It is God himself. John goes on to say that nothing came into creation that was not an expression of God's Word, and that all life and knowledge are derived from God's Word. The knowledge of God through his Word in creation (the light) has survived all attempts to snuff it out (the darkness).

Thus every aspect of our environment, including ourselves, relentlessly cries out, "God is Creator!" Even for the oppressed, whose environment has been corrupted by the oppressor, the message is "God is Creator, but he did not create things this way." Why? Because the light still shines in the darkness, and this light undergirds the oppressed's resistance to oppression.

3. *God is the Sustainer.* "The Son is the radiance of God's glory and the exact representation of his being, *sustaining all things by his powerful word*" (Hebrews 1:3). "In [the Son] all things hold together" (Colossians 1:17).

The power of God's Word, his Son, sustains the whole creation. The fact that the creation holds together testifies that God is the Sustainer.

4. *God is glorious.* According to Scripture, every time anyone looks up, he or she sees the *glory* of God, his brilliance.

The heavens declare the glory of God;
　the skies proclaim the work of his hands.
Day after day they pour forth speech;
　night after night they display knowledge.
There is no speech or language
　where their voice is not heard.

Their voice goes out into all the earth,
   their words to the ends of the world. (Psalm 19:1-4)
With an inaudible voice God reveals his glory in plain and understandable language.

5. *God is infinite and eternal.* "For since the creation of the world
God's invisible qualities—his eternal power and divine nature—have
been clearly seen, being understood from what has been made"
(Romans 1:20).

It is clear to all, says Scripture, that the nature of God puts him in
a class all by himself. There is a sharp distinction between Creator and
creature. God is divine and we are human; God is infinite and we are
finite; God is unlimited and we are limited. God himself is "invisible"
because he is too glorious, too bright, too vast, too perfect, too
righteous to be seen with our limited and fallen sight.

6. *God is a righteous Judge.* "The heavens proclaim his righteousness, for God himself is judge" (Psalm 50:6). Anybody who sees the
sky sees God's righteousness and his unique, divine qualification to
be the ultimate Judge of right and wrong.

7. *Human existence has eternal significance.* God's revelation to
all peoples, even those without the Scriptures, extends beyond a
knowledge of himself to an understanding of our human place before
him. "He has . . . set eternity in the hearts of men; yet they cannot
fathom what God has done from beginning to end" (Ecclesiastes 3:11).

All people know at the core of their being that they must deal with
eternity. This is a function of being in the image of God. Though we
have eternal existence in common with God, we remain different from
God, because he is infinite and we are finite. The real issue we wrestle
with is not *if* we will exist forever, but *how.* Will it be eternal life or
eternal death?

8. *We are unrighteous, and God's wrath hangs over our heads.* "The
wrath of God is being revealed from heaven against all the godlessness
and wickedness of men" (Romans 1:18). Since God reveals his wrath
from heaven, all people know they are guilty before him, the righteous
Judge.

9. *We cannot save ourselves from God's wrath.* The Scriptures teach that people without the Scriptures (the law) know what God requires.

All who sin apart from the law will also perish apart from the law. ... (Indeed, when [nations], who do not have the law, do by nature things required by the law, they are a law for themselves, even though they do not have the law, since they show that the requirements of the law are written on their hearts, their consciences also bearing witness, and their thoughts now accusing, now even defending them.) ...

"There is no one righteous, not even one;
    there is no one who understands,
    no one who seeks God.
All have turned away,
    they have together become worthless;
there is no one who does good,
    not even one." (Romans 2:12, 14-15; 3:10-12)

We know that we are guilty of not meeting our obligations. We know this by the light of God's Word shining in us. Is there anyone who is not guilty? No, "not even one!" Since there is no righteousness among fallen humanity, we have no hope of salvation—even in our best efforts—from the wrath and judgment of God. Without God's help we would be totally hopeless.

10. *God has shown us favor that we in no way deserve.* He revealed his grace in creating the nations and giving them a chance to search for him, being close so they could find him and sustaining them in spite of their sinful condition.

From one man he made every nation of men, that they should inhabit the whole earth; and he determined the times set for them and the exact places where they should live. God did this so that men would seek him and perhaps reach out for him and find him, though he is not far from each one of us. "For in him we live and move and have our being." (Acts 17:26-28)

God reveals his grace in his patience toward all the nations. He has yet to execute the full wrathful judgment we deserve: "God ... made heaven and earth and sea and everything in them. In the past, he let all nations go their own way. Yet he has not left himself without testimony" (Acts 14:15-17). God reveals his grace by meeting all our basic life needs: "He has shown kindness by giving you rain from heaven and crops in their seasons; he provides you with plenty of food and fills your hearts with joy" (Acts 14:17).

Since, according to the Scriptures, God's truth in creation is plain for all to see and God has ensured that all people will understand what his revelation says, all people who have their five senses have a knowledge of God. They know that God is, that he is the Creator and Sustainer, that he is glorious, infinite and eternal, the righteous Judge. They know of humanity that our existence has eternal significance, that we are unrighteous, having God's wrath hanging over our heads, and that we cannot save ourselves from that deserved wrath. But they also know that God has shown humankind favor that is not in any way deserved.

### Prisons of Paganism

All people in the world have extensive knowledge of God. It is plain, however, that this knowledge is not universally acknowledged in all cultures. Why? The Bible implies the answer when it states that God's wrath is aimed at those "who suppress the truth by their wickedness" (Romans 1:18).

The Greek word *katecho,* translated "suppress," has both a positive and a negative meaning. On the positive side it means to hold fast or lay hold of. But Paul uses the word here in its negative sense, meaning to hold back, to restrain. Here it means "holding in prison."[2]

Thus the Word of God is not universally acknowledged in the world's cultures not because the truth is not there, but because the truth of God is incarcerated in prisons of paganism. "Although they knew God, they neither glorified him as God nor gave thanks to him, but their thinking became futile and their foolish hearts were darkened" (Romans 1:21). They know God himself. God has shown them that he is a God of grace and that he is a God who deserves to be glorified

(Acts 14:16-17). In spite of this, they do not give him that glory or thank him for the grace. People refuse to take advantage of God's grace and therefore refuse to seek him (Romans 3:11-12).

Even though all knowledge is derived from God's Word, human-kind tries to hold the truth of God's natural revelation hostage in anti-God frameworks. The result is anti-God "knowledge" that denies the revelation of God, the very source of knowledge itself. "Their thinking became futile and their foolish hearts were darkened. Although they claimed to be wise, they became fools and exchanged the glory of the immortal God for images made to look like mortal man" (Romans 1:21-23).

As I look around at our world, I see four basic anti-God frameworks, four prisons of paganism.

*Suicidal religion:* an attempt to solve the human problem with God by denying reality. People do this by seeking either to eliminate their own existence or to radically alter it. The goal here is to come to an end so that we will no longer have to deal with God's wrath. The foundation of this religious prison is a refusal to acknowledge that human existence has eternal significance.

Suicidal religion is primarily found in the East, but it is also seen in our part of the world. Some Western examples are suicide, various Eastern-style mysticisms, drug and alcohol abuse (or just the attempt to get high), and militant shallowness (refusing to relate to others on a truly human level).

*God-bribing religion:* human attempts to solve our problem with God by trying to earn God's favor. Since God's wrath is revealed from heaven, this religious motif is in essence an attempt to bribe God into looking the other way when we come before him for judgment. The foundation of this religious prison is refusal to acknowledge that God is a righteous Judge and that we cannot save ourselves from his wrath. This religion is also based on a refusal to acknowledge the consequences of unrighteousness.

God-bribing religion is primarily found in the Middle East, but it is also seen in our part of the world in religions such as Islam, which promote reliance on works for righteousness, and in the widely held belief that "God helps those who help themselves."

*Peekaboo religion:* human attempts to solve our problem with God by trying to hide from God. The goal here is to shield ourselves from the wrath of God behind little gods, other human beings or some form of ritualism. Undergirding this religious prison is a refusal to acknowledge that God's wrath is inescapable.

Peekaboo religion is primarily found in Africa, South America and elsewhere in the Southern Hemisphere, but it is also seen in our part of the world. Some examples of it are animism, ancestor worship, idol worship, voodoo, astrology and "bureaucratic monotheism." Bureaucratic monotheism, an expression of African religious experience, has been described in Osadolor Imasogie's essay on traditional African religion:

> While Africans accord prominence to the divinities, the divinities are regarded as having been created and appointed ministers by the Supreme Being. However, the place given these divinities is so conspicuous that monotheism must be qualified in such a way that this prominence is maintained while the underlying monotheistic motif is not obscured. . . . This author, however, is convinced that the phrase "bureaucratic monotheism" best describes the African traditional religion. . . .
>
> It is common knowledge that in any bureaucratic system . . . the average citizen is more familiar with the officials who regulate his day-to-day activities than the king whom he seldom sees. Even though the ministers and officials derive their authority from the king, the ordinary citizen looks up to these officials rather than to the king for his needs. My contention is that this socio-cultural pattern of the African society becomes the paradigm by means of which the African expresses his religious experience.[3]

Originating in Africa, bureaucratic monotheism could be considered the Black man's religion. It is seen in our community among those who submit themselves totally to authoritarian religious figures.

*Theicidal (God-killing) religion:* human attempts to solve our problem with God by trying to eliminate God's existence or by "de-deifying" him in some way. The rationale is, if we can get rid of God, we will get rid of God's wrath. This religious prison is based on a refusal to acknowledge that God *is*.

Theicidal religion is primarily found in Europe and North America. We have met this character before in the White man's religion. Other examples of this religion are atheism, materialism and civil religion. This last occurs when people blur the distinction between God and country; for example, some in our country wrap God up in the American flag and present him as an American, supporting the American system.

A final religious view belonging to this category is love-is-god-ism. Here we find those who accept the love of God but totally ignore his wrath and those who equate contentless love with God. I shall discuss this theicidal religion in chapter thirteen.

### Anti-God Christianity-isms

All four of these anti-God religions show up as forms of Christianity-ism. Let's look at each again in this light.

Suicidal Christianity-ism includes people who strictly forbid the mind to enter into their Christian walk. The goal of this distortion is to eliminate all thinking out of fear of being "intellectual." It results in a kind of liver-quiver religiosity. People in this camp confuse human-centered thinking with thinking itself. Biblically speaking, there is nothing wrong with being intellectual. The mind is no more sinful than any other aspect of a human being, and to negate the mind is to negate a part of our humanity. The same could be said about denying emotions.

God-bribing Christianity-ism includes those who think they obligate God to show them favor because of the good things they have done. They think that because they go to church so many times, pray so many prayers and so on, God will do something for them in return. It results in a doctrine of works-righteousness. By this they do violence to the grace of God. God's grace is not a response to our goodness;

we have none (Isaiah 64:6). We can only respond to God's grace (Titus 3:5). It's not that we first loved God, but that God first loved us (1 John 4:19).

Peekaboo Christianity-ism is the category for those who submit to the dictates of a religious tyrant. They see him or her as a substitute Christ. They let the tyrant do all their thinking and explain away his or her shortcomings. The result is a spectator-sport religion. The *Jonestown tragedy** exemplifies this heresy at its worst. Peekaboo-ism is characteristic of Black Christianity-ism too. It is one thing to respect people in authority; it is another to hide from God behind them.

Theicidal Christianity-ism includes those who try to squeeze God into a mold or reduce him to some kind of system. For them, God can be manipulated. Those who identify God with only one race of people are also guilty of this distortion. White Christianity-ism is one of several theicidal manifestations. During the days of legal apartheid, segments of the Dutch Reformed Church in South Africa were guilty of this. In such instances the people worship Baal, not God, for Baal is the local or ethnic lord.

### Application or Pollution?

When the gospel is applied to a particular culture, the result is Christianity. There can be as many varieties of Christianity as there are cultures, but these cultural Christianities will not contradict one another. They will have a complementary relationship as they focus on God's gracious deliverance accomplished in Christ. Hence it is not necessarily wrong to have a White Christianity or a Black Christianity.

Christianity-ism, on the other hand, is a Christianity that has been polluted by the paganisms of its culture. It attempts to hold the gospel hostage. Every culture where Christianity functions has a tendency to drift toward Christianity-ism.

The White man's religion is not a unique pagan prison. All cultures of the world, including African-American culture, have their own variation of paganism. Secular humanism did not fail us just because it was the White man's religion. It failed because it is a vain attempt to deny that God is. Islam is not failing us merely because it is the Arab ethnic religion. It is failing us because it refuses to acknowledge our inability to save ourselves apart from the grace of God. Islam is failing because all our righteousness is a total failure. And peekaboo religion is not failing us merely because it is the "Black man's religion." It is failing us because it refuses to acknowledge the inescapability of God's wrath.

How can we prevent this pagan pollution? The various Christianities must balance between spiritual unity and cultural diversity, just as different cultures interact, borrow from each other and blend. We cannot allow cultural variation to become walls of cultural isolation, as it did in the United States and South Africa. In an atmosphere of crosscultural fellowship, the pollutions of Christianity-ism in my culture will often be more clearly seen by someone of another culture; we all have blind spots.

Our soul dynamic, for example, has aspects that have survived from Africa. Some of these are positive, but not all of them. We must build our culture by selecting those Africanisms that are compliant to the Word of God. On the other hand, we must not be afraid to contextualize the gospel. Jesus himself should be our example. He was a Jew, but he did not come in the name of Judaism. He came in the name of the Father. If we are Christian, we should be active in our cultures, not in the name of Christianity-ism or Christianity, but in the name of Christ.

### God's Success

The only basic religious commitment that will not fail us is to seek God rather than avoid him, and that is possible only on the basis of God's grace. We live as God's guests on God's turf. God is Lord, and he simply will not let humanity's sinful plots frustrate his ultimate purposes in the world. In fact, God does and will frustrate every negative conspiracy that humankind tries to implement. God's revelation is always "busting out" of the human prisons of paganism. This is why God laughs and scoffs at these plots, because it's like a gnat trying to take on an elephant in a wrestling match. For God has decreed that even "the wrath of men shall praise [him]" (Psalm 76:10 RSV).

> The God who made the world and everything in it is the Lord of heaven and earth. . . . He himself gives all men life and breath and everything else. From one man he made every nation of men, that they should inhabit the whole earth; and he determined the times set for them and the exact places where they should live. God did this so that men would seek him and perhaps reach out for him and find him, though he is not far from each one of us. "For in him we live and move and have our being." (Acts 17:24-28)

Against the backdrop of a totally negative religious commitment, a commitment to avoid God, this is an astonishing statement in Scripture. It seems to go against the stream of what is clearly set forth in Romans 1 and 3. The book of Acts says that the nations were created by God so that they would seek him and find him, in spite of their universal practice of paganism. It says further that God is not far from any of us, because we live our whole lives in him.

If all the nations try to hold God's truth hostage, how can they be seeking God? The statement that God still gives us "life and breath and everything else" (Acts 17:25) should give us a clue. This is alluded to in Acts 14:16-17: the answer is *God's grace*, which he showers on all people. It is by God's grace that we seek God. He sends rain on the just and the unjust (Matthew 5:45).

### Good News

If we are going to succeed in rebuilding our culture, our commitment must be based entirely on the consciousness that God, by his grace, is active in the world today. Solely because of God's active grace, many people are able to commit themselves to seek God and his revelation. These are the people who, by God's power, will confess to him their lost and hopeless condition and throw themselves on God's grace as their only hope of deliverance from wrath.

As we have noted, the driving force that gives rise to every culture is religious in nature. But for fallen humankind, apart from God's grace, this religious commitment is always negative, an effort to avoid

God. However, because God graciously frustrates evil, those who practice negative religion will never succeed in avoiding God's Word in any area of life (Psalm 139:7-8, 11-12). Because of God's grace, we can have a positive religious commitment. However, because God's gracious work is not yet complete, we do not yet consistently seek God in every area of life (Philippians 3:12). Those who seek God by his grace are the ones in whom the history and destiny of a nation will ultimately be fulfilled (Revelation 7:9-10). Jesus called them the salt of the earth and the light of the world (Matthew 5:13-14). They are the hope of the nations.

We can now see what causes culture to well up in the life of the nations. It is the dynamic interplay between these positive and negative religious undercurrents, over which God exercises his gracious lordship. Knowing this, we will understand why a culture's noble aspirations are due to the grace of God. With this knowledge we will understand that it is because of their unrighteousness that people betray and fall short of their noble aspirations (Romans 3:23).

The unique message of Scripture is that God has indeed provided the solution to our problem with God. This message is stated throughout the Scriptures. In the Old Testament the message was that God *would* accomplish deliverance for his people. In the New Testament the message is that God in Christ has accomplished deliverance now. This is *good news* to all who by God's grace seek him.

# 12

# "That Boy Sho' Can Preach!"

*T*hus far I have only touched on the soul dynamic. In this chapter I want to explore its characteristics further by comparing it with what we think of as formal theology. I would like to look at new roles the dynamic can play as we reconstruct African-American culture.

Because music is key to the theological dynamic, music will be the basis of this discussion.

## Tone and Rhythm

Much of God's Word came to us through singing—the Psalms, the Song of Songs, the lyrics of Deborah, Moses, Hannah and Mary, the hosannas sung by the crowd when Jesus triumphantly entered Jerusalem. Like the Israelites of the exodus, who sang when they saw the hand of God at work in their midst, our people also sang about God's work among them during slavery. I have noted that many Black spirituals, with their double message about the kingdom of God and freedom from slavery, communicated the slaves' understanding of how God would deliver them from bondage.

But not only the words reflect our theology; the music itself mirrors our understanding of God's divinity and the world's future. Music is a function of theology, and to do theology is to apply God's Word to all areas of life. Theology—formal, systematic theology and our own casual-as-an-old-pair-of-sneakers beliefs—finds expression in our music. And the songs that we moan and groan shape our ideas of God and his world.

The two main components of music are tone and rhythm. These have always been part of our revelational environment. God created us to express beauty and truth musically to his glory. Song can serve as a parable of reality. We cannot, however, compose or perform music employing all the possible combinations of tone and rhythm in all possible modes of unity and diversity, form and freedom, any more than we can know all the mind of God. We are finite. Only the infinite, triune God of the Scriptures can create perfect music.

In God's music, form and freedom are conterminous, each being the ultimate fulfillment of the other; but in our music they are not. Either form serves freedom, or freedom serves form. We have retained our musical ability since the Fall, but like the image of God in us, our music is marred by sin. Sin brings no music, only noise, with unity and diversity subject to chance. It is only by God's grace that even though we are fallen, we have true music rather than mere noise. In our music we catch glimpses of God's creative image in us and of our original potential.

As we saw in chapters ten and eleven, when people submit themselves to God's lordship, they have dignity. But when they attempt to set themselves up as the absolute, their humanity breaks down. Likewise, as long as music remains an expression of the glory of God, of truth and beauty, it retains its dignity. But when music is absolutized, becoming its own end, it breaks down into noise.

## Two Approaches

There are essentially two approaches to music, the formal and the dynamic. We call them *classical* and *jazz.* We know what classical music is—the little dots, circles and lines of Beethoven and Brahms that come to life when a conductor stabs the air with a baton. These sounds that fill the air are not the conductor's or the violinists'. They belong to Beethoven and Brahms. The beauty of a classical piece is found in the mind of the composer, in the music as it is *written.* Thus the goal of the classical musician is to reproduce as faithfully as possible the sounds the great composers imagined. Only in rare moments and clearly marked cadenzas do classical musicians improvise. Their main task is not to improvise but to imitate.

Jazz is different. The beauty of jazz is found in the soul of the musician and in the music as it is *performed.* Jazz is improvisational. Just as classical music has developed musical composition into a fine art, jazz has cultivated musical improvisation into a fine art. The notes that fill the air do not belong to a deceased composer; they issue from the vibrant souls of great performers like "Diz,"[1] "Byrd"[2] and "Lady Day."[3]

Theology bears analogy with music in that it too can be approached as formal or dynamic. The two modes reflect two aspects of God's nature. Like classical music, the classical approach to theology comprises the formal methods of arranging what we know about God and his world into a reasoned, cogent and consistent system. Classical theology interacts in critical dialogue with the philosophies of the world. It investigates the attributes of God and communicates primarily through a written tradition.

If the classical approach to theology has been called "the queen of the sciences," the jazz approach to theology could be called "the queen of the arts." The latter investigates God's dealing with people in the joys and trials of daily life. This improvisational approach is illustrated in the soul dynamic. The jazz approach is not so much concerned with the status of theological propositions as with the hurts of oppressed people. It is communicated not so much by a literary tradition as by an oral tradition. And it is not so much concerned with facts as it is with life skills: knowing *how* rather than knowing *that.*

Jazz theology is a participation in the basic patterns revealed in biblical life situations. It inquires not only *what* God did and said but *how* he said and did it. Furthermore, it expects him to do it again in a similar way in our lives: "Didn't my Lord deliver Daniel? Well, I know he'll deliver me." Effective Black preachers respond to current situations by theologizing creatively on their feet, just as jazz musicians improvise new music and enliven old songs in response to the feeling and needs of the moment.

Classical theology and classical music reflect God's oneness. The unity of God's purpose and providence is reflected in the consistent explanations and consonant harmonies of classical music and classical theology. The genius of classical theology is in theology *as it was formulated.*

But God is not just classical. *God is jazz.* Not only does he have an eternal and unchanging purpose, but he is intimately involved with the difficulties of sparrows and slaves. Within the dynamic of his eternal will, he improvises. God's providential jazz liberates slaves and weeps over cities. Jazz can be robustly exultant or blue; God has been triumphant and also sad. Jazz portrays the diversity, freedom and eternal freshness of God. The genius of jazz theology is in the theology *as it is done.*

Even the divine name, I AM, carries aspects of both classical and jazz theology. To the classical theologian, God's name means "I HAVE BEEN WHAT I HAVE BEEN." To the jazz theologian he is "I WILL BE WHAT I WILL BE."

## Let's Have Chu'ch

Jesus was a master jazz theologian. The Bible says that the crowds were amazed at his teaching (Matthew 7:28). The emphasis here, as can be seen from the context, is not on the substance or content of his teaching *(didaskalia)* but the act or skill of the teaching method *(didachē).* Jesus brilliantly transformed historic scriptural teaching into living contemporary parables. He used the art forms of the Scriptures themselves. He evoked in the hearts of his hearers an intuitive knowledge of God—a knowledge that God placed in them by grace. In his delivery of the Father's precious truths, he artfully appealed to the people's common sense and experience. "His words had the ring of authority" (Matthew 7:29 Phillips). "It ain't just what he said but the way how he said it."

The best African-American preaching is analogous to Jesus' use of short phrases and parallelisms, as we see in the Sermon on the Mount (Matthew 5—7). This jazz approach sweeps listeners into verbal and emotional responses. I can imagine that many folks said of Jesus, "That boy sho' can preach!" Jesus' conceal-to-reveal technique with parables enticed listeners to listen with their hearts and to participate in the teaching. In other words, "they had chu'ch." So powerful was Jesus' skill that even the police sent by the Pharisees to "bust" him returned empty-handed, explaining, "No one ever spoke the way this man does" (John 7:46).

I am not saying that the *content* of Jesus' teaching had nothing to do with his power as a teacher. Indeed, his teaching was unique in that his content and skill were both equal and ultimate. For a rabbi in the first century, the development of one memorable parable—which was considered the pinnacle of achievement—demanded many years of academic sweat. Jesus, with his jazz approach, came along and delivered over sixty such parables!

Jesus' jazz teaching maintained a constant variety of fresh, picturesque imagery; he didn't let the culture or people numb the teaching. Culture tends to respond to truth the way we respond to a joke. A good joke is hilarious when first heard, but its repeated telling elicits only boredom. Likewise, a parable's initial effectiveness decreases with successive hearings: a culture numbs itself to truth. Jesus flooded culture with his parables. People could not escape the implications. Truly out of his belly flowed living water (John 4:14).

Jesus' use of parables shows one way his teaching style was like jazz music. It was experiential and improvisational in nature. But it was jazzlike in other ways too.

## What You Know Is What You Do

The dynamic concept of knowledge, as the word is used in Scripture, also parallels the jazz-classical distinction. Jesus criticized the scribes, saying, "You err because you don't know the Scripture!" Certainly they knew the Scriptures in great detail. But they knew them in a detached manner. Jesus spoke of knowledge in terms of intercourse. You can see, then, said Jesus, how "every scribe who has been trained for the kingdom of heaven is like a householder who brings out of his treasure what is new and what is old" (Matthew 13:52 RSV).

At the height of the Festival of Booths, Jesus went to the temple and began teaching (John 7:14-15). The Jews were amazed and remarked. "How does this boy know all this? He has never been to seminary." Jesus was not a "doctor of the law," yet by his teaching he showed himself to be a doctor in his own right—a person with knowledge unattainable in the seminaries.

For years the African-American church has conferred on its outstanding preachers the title *doctor.* This is a recognition, consistent with a biblical concept, that knowledge is not just something that must be attained at school. It can be found in life. While the facts of classical theology are formally taught, the skills of jazz theology are dynamically "caught."

The great advantage of the jazz approach to theology is its requirement that people be *involved* with Truth. "If anyone wants to do God's will, he will *know* . . . my teaching is from God" (John 7:17 Phillips). Jesus delivered to his disciples all that the Father had given him. But he did not give his disciples a course outline and a lecture. Instead he began portraying truth in his own life. He did not give his inquirers a bibliography; he said, "Follow, imitate and be involved with me" (see Matthew 9:9; Mark 1:17; 8:34; Luke 5:27; John 1:43). Choosing twelve men to play out the drama of discipleship, he told them that the ultimate goal of being taught was to be like the teacher (Luke 6:40). This concept of knowledge-as-lived is demonstrated in Jesus' life. It shows a second way jazz theology illuminates Christian experience.

## More Than Music

The jazz approach can also illuminate how we understand the inspiration of Scripture. It is sometimes difficult to understand how, for instance, the four Gospels can all be inspired when each of them is unique, incorporating certain traits of its author. But when the Holy Spirit breathes the gospel through Matthew, Mark, Luke and John, it is like Dexter Gordon playing the same tune on his sax on four different occasions. Every time he played it, he made changes in his riffs. Does that mean that any one playing was not musically superb and consistent with the other performances? Does it mean that he had not played the same piece four times—that he had, in fact, played four different pieces?

In a similar way there is complete "harmony" between the musicians in a jazz combo. The performance of "On Green Dolphin Street"[4] by the Miles Davis Sextet serves as an excellent illustration of the jazz harmony among the Gospels. In this renowned performance, harmony was based on (1) the underlying chord progressions, (2) a specific rhythm and (3) the musicians' quest for excellence. Among the four Gospels, harmony is based on (1) the person of Christ as the content and meaning of the Gospels, (2) the Holy Spirit as the agent of inspiration and (3) our quest for God's fullness as he transforms us, and our culture through us.

The improvisations of Miles Davis on trumpet, Cannonball Adderley on alto sax, John Coltrane on tenor sax and Bill Evans on piano did not break the rules of musical harmony. On the contrary, these musicians, "carried along" by rhythm, fulfilled the rules in an open, lucid and dynamic way. They were "inspired" *within* the chord progressions. Similarly, the unique arrangement of events in Matthew, Mark, Luke and John did not break the rules of historic harmony. On the contrary, these Evangelists, inspired by the Holy Spirit, fulfilled the rules in an open, lucid and dynamic way. They were *carried along* within the bounds of infallibility and inerrancy.

In "On Green Dolphin Street" Bill Evans's piano introduces and develops the theme. Miles, Trane (John Coltrane) and Cannonball also improvise from their stylistic perspectives. Among the four Gospels, John introduces and develops the theme from "the beginning." Matthew, Mark and Luke reveal Christ from their cultural and theological perspectives. Where the four Gospels share the same narratives, there are relatively few differences in the texts. But like jazz musicians who have distinctive differences in their solos, the Evangelists have distinctive differences in their arrangement of the facts when they do not share the same narratives.

The instruments of Miles, Trane and Cannonball are monotonic, and in a sense they could be considered synoptic because of their similarity. Each of their instruments, however, has a distinctive range: soprano (trumpet), alto sax and tenor sax. When these men improvise they add dimension and beauty to the performance *because* of their differences.

The books of Matthew, Mark and Luke are called Synoptic Gospels because their texts are similar. However, Matthew addresses himself to Jewish readers, Mark to Romans and Luke to Greeks; the distinctive perspectives of the audience show up in the presentations of the life of Christ. Since these three Evangelists also wrote from their own perspectives, they added further dimension to the revelation of Jesus because of their differences.

The rhythm line also illustrates the relationship between inspiration and revelation. Paul Chambers on bass provides rhythm at various levels of tone, while Jimmie Cobb on drums provides rhythm where tone remains relatively constant. The Holy Spirit reveals Christ at various levels of revelation while he provides us with inspiration that remains constant.

Bill Evans on piano demonstrates unique capabilities as he plays chords. With one stroke he is able to cover as much ground as Miles, Cannonball and Trane do in the flow of their riffs. Similarly, John's Gospel has multiple levels of theological depth; it is simple yet profoundly sophisticated. Though John gives several levels of understanding of Jesus, his Gospel weaves the body of Christ together in spiritual union. John gives "chords" of depth to our understanding of Jesus.

The New Testament writers have, like jazz musicians, demonstrated something positive—"soul"! Jazz is more than music. It's a way of *doing*. Through jazz theology, African-American preachers participate in a basic pattern set by God in the act of revelation. Jazz theology helps us apply God's Word to every area of life and culture.

# 13
# Cultural Seeding

*J*azz theology and classical theology are not mutually exclusive. Just as George Gershwin and the Modern Jazz Quartet wed the freedoms of jazz to the forms of classical music, so biblical scholars may marry the intuitive spirit of jazz theology to the rational principles of classical theology.

Solid, classical orthodoxy provides limits within which we may improvise, even as musical keys and chord progressions guide jazz musicians. It tells us what God is like and what he is not like. It keeps us from error and excess. However, it does not keep us awake, because it does not have the power to blast us out of the "paralysis of analysis."

You may sleep through a symphony, but most people will pay attention to a jazz riff. Jesus calls us to stay awake and be involved in the movements of the times. That is what jazz theology does. It involves us where the "nitty" meets the "gritty." It tells us that God is on the move, that the kingdom is coming. And since the kingdom is coming, it tells us how to get ready. We need to get ready. Our culture is in trouble. Jazz theology can equip us to revive it.

Dr. King's application of the theological dynamic to desegregation provided the jazz-theological basis for the Southern Black church to play the key role in the Civil Rights Movement. The Northern church had nothing comparable in its fight against institutional racism. It had no theological base for involvement in the Black Consciousness Movement. The Northern church's involvement tended to be sociological, not theological. Jazz theology could have made the difference for the Northern church.

In turning to Islam, Northern thinkers choked off the very possibility of a jazz theology for the faithful. Islam is strictly classical; it does not allow for improvisation. All non-Arabic cultures and languages are excluded from Islam. Even within Arab culture, Islam frowns on nontraditional phraseology, leaving the Muslim with doctrinaire repetition and cold orthodoxy. There is no room for soul.

### Song of the Soul

African-American music expressed our spiritual life in the days of slavery. It still does, but now it paints a bleak picture. The music of our day has been shaped by the soul dynamic, but it does not have the hope of the spirituals. Our popular songs no longer speak of the Promised Land, the deep river or the sweet chariot. Our music once reflected a life lived from Sunday to Sunday, looking expectantly toward the everlasting Sunday of freedom and dignity. But with the secularization of African-American culture, our music has come to portray anger or a life stretched thin between one brief romance and the next. The spirituals have become the *blues.**

*Rhythm and blues (R & B)** and *rap** are the most influential fountainheads of the cultural dynamic. Millions of young people live by this music. They carry their boom boxes all day long. They skate to the solitary music of their headphones and cruise to the pulsating rhythms of their ground-shaker car stereos. What they hear shapes their lives and ours. What does the music say to them?

Though the African-American church no longer sets musical

trends, theological phrases are woven into the lyrics of recent African-American music. A couple of major trends in R & B developed in the 1970s. The first trend considered God as the source and lord of love. I call this God-is-love-ism. In his 1971 album *What's Goin' On?* Marvin Gaye expressed a seemingly genuine turn toward God.[1] The album was rich in Christian themes. Selections such as "Wholly Holy" and "God Is Love" had lines like "Jesus left a long time ago. / He left us a book to believe in / and in it we've got a lot to learn," and "Don't go talking about my father, / God is my friend." The album became a hit.

Other artists, such as Stevie Wonder, Eddy Kendricks and Earth, Wind and Fire began recording albums with similar themes. Stevie Wonder became by far the most influential artist of this trend with his albums *Music of My Mind, Talking Book, Inner Visions, Fulfillingness First Finale* and *Songs in the Key of Life.*[2]

A second trend in R & B might be called love-is-God-ism. Songs of this trend used spiritual terms as code words for secular love. In a perverse, inverted manner, *born again* and *moving with the spirit* (along with the soul dynamic these terms reflect) were given sensual overtones. They came to mean "having a new lover" or "engaging in sex outside marriage." These phrases have become familiar in our culture, but it was their secular meanings that influenced and undercut our culture, not their spiritual meanings. In his later album *Let's Get It On* (1973) Marvin Gaye picked up on these secular meanings.[3] His title selection concludes with the line "[Let's] get sanctified." Here a theological term refers to sexual arousal.

The jazz theologian must affirm and fulfill the positive aspirations of God-is-love-ism while counteracting love-is-God-ism. The apostle Paul did this on Mars Hill. He affirmed the truths of Epimenides while exposing the pagan nature of Greek philosophy and religion (Acts 17:22-34).

Rap music has emerged as a potent message carrier. But what message is coming across to those who listen to rap? Is it positive or negative, constructive or destructive? So far it seems that many of the leading rappers are verbalizing rage or propagating the message of the *Five Percenters.**

Response to our culture demands more than simply reprising "The Old Rugged Cross." What we need is an injection of the biblical worldview into our culture. I call this *cultural seeding.* Simple, basic, fundamental truth must be planted in our culture before the fruit of the gospel can ripen. This is what Jesus did with his jazz parables. This is also what Martin Luther King Jr. did with his ethics dramatizations. Today rap and rhythm and blues are key cultural fountainheads into which seeds of God's truth must be planted.

A simple return to the old music—even the old spirituals—would be merely in the classical mode. We need to return not to the spirituals but to the *spirit* of the spirituals. In that spirit theologians and musicians can craft an artistic and creative response to the needs and crises of our age. Through cultural seeding in R & B and rap we can begin to revive the soul dynamic and reconstruct African-American culture.

Even though I referred to the blues negatively, we may also see the blues in a positive light. The blues remains one of the most influential phenomena in the development of our culture. Where other American musical forms have gone through radical changes, the blues themes in our music have been consistent. Many blues descriptions of the relationship between a man and a woman are parallel to the covenantal themes found in the Prophets, such as Jeremiah, Ezekiel and Hosea. Here God plays the role of a husband speaking to his unfaithful wife (God's people). Because we are a "blues people," we have great potential of response to God, who in the Old Testament preceded us in singing the blues.

### Involved Obedience

We need to reexamine Jesus as a jazz theologian and use the Scriptures as he did. He lived portraying his teaching. If we can do this, we will fulfill the aspirations of the historic theological dynamic and lay the foundation for a Joshua generation of African-American leadership to emerge. Through jazz theology we can become equipped to enter culture at all levels and to portray God's truth in the living, dynamic style of Jesus.

We now go to Hillside Baptist Synagogue, where the sermon of Dr. Joshua X. Davidson[4] is already in progress.

| Dr. Davidson: | And what's the use . . . |
| People: | Yeah! |
| Dr. Davidson: | *in calling me, Lord, Lord . . .* |
| People: | Well! |
| Dr. Davidson: | *if you don't do what I say?* |
| One man: | Look out, Preacher! |
| People: | (laughter) |
| Dr. Davidson: | *Let me show you what a man is like . . .* |
| People: | Uh-huh! |
| Dr. Davidson: | *who only hears what I say . . .* |
| People: | Come on now! |
| Dr. Davidson: | *and doesn't do it.* |
| One man: | Better leave that one alone, Doc! |
| People: | (laughter) |
| Dr. Davidson: | *He's like a man who built his house . . .* |
| People: | Talk to me! |
| Dr. Davidson: | *and laid his foundation . . .* |
| People: | Uh-huh! |
| Dr. Davidson: | *on soft earth.* |
| One man: | I know you gone to meddlin' now, Doc. |
| People: | (laughter) |
| Dr. Davidson: | *When the storm came . . .* |
| People: | Say that! |
| Dr. Davidson: | *down came the rain . . .* |
| People: | Yeah! |
| Dr. Davidson: | *up came the flood . . .* |
| People: | Yes suh! |
| Dr. Davidson: | *and the house fell in . . .* |
| People: | My lawd! |
| Dr. Davidson: | *in a great noise.* |

| People: | Mercy! |
| Dr. Davidson: | *But the man who does what I say . . .* |
| One man: | Go 'head. |
| Dr. Davidson: | *is like a man building a house . . .* |
| People: | Whatcha say! |
| Dr. Davidson: | *who dug down to rock bottom . . .* |
| People: | Help yo'self. |
| Dr. Davidson: | *and laid the foundation on it.* |
| People: | Yes suh! |
| Dr. Davidson: | *And when the storm came . . .* |
| People: | Well! Well! |
| Dr. Davidson: | *down came the rain . . .* |
| People: | Take yo' time. |
| Dr. Davidson: | *up came the flood.* |
| People: | Preach it! |
| Dr. Davidson: | *But the house was like a tree . . .* |
| One man: | Talk to me, Doc. |
| Dr. Davidson: | *planted by the water.* |
| People: | My lawd! |
| Dr. Davidson: | *It could not be moved.* |
| People: | Ooooh! Thank you, Jesus! |
| One man: | It's all right to preach. |
| People: | Good God a'mighty! |

A'nt Jane and Miss Sally walk away from the meeting after the service.

| Miss Sally: | Honey, that boy sho' 'nough came through to-day! |
| A'nt Jane: | Yeah, honey chil', them scribes and folks ain't never preached like that! Mmmm glory! We sho' had chu'ch today. |

(Luke 6:46-49, contextualized)

# Part IV

# Toward
# a New Agenda

# 14

# New Vistas

*M*any of us have achieved a greater degree of freedom than our people have ever had, but are we truly "free at last"? We saw in chapter three that the closer a people get to liberation, the more their own ungodliness and God's judgment will show.

This point is often overlooked by advocates of liberation. Liberation is insufficient if it is not accompanied by the empowerment that results from a quest for godliness in every area of life. Liberation alone will lead to self-oppression, because a liberated ungodliness will always do its thing, and that thing is sure to bring death (Romans 6:23).

But this should not excuse us to give up the fight for freedom. We should fight for liberation *because* it is not enough. We should seek it in order to see our own need for godly empowerment.

Human freedom is an aspect of justice. Justice and godliness are two sides of the same coin; the coin is the kingdom of God and his righteousness (figure 13). This is why Jesus said we should seek the kingdom "first" and "all these things [freedom and dignity] will be

added." Liberation, as a perspective on God's justice, is the freedom
and dignity we have pursued in our historic quest. Godly empowerment as a perspective on God's justice is the fulfillment of African-
American economic development and cultural awareness. Godliness
involves doing theology with a commitment to seek God.

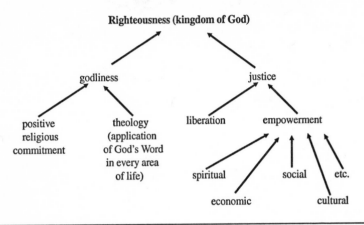

**Figure 13.**   The kingdom of God

## Not a Right But a Power

Righteousness includes liberation. Righteousness will never liberate
ungodliness to do its thing. Righteousness, both collective and individual, will lift a people above the frustrating effects of ungodliness
and give them the will and power to realize their loftiest aspirations
(Matthew 5:6). The quest for righteousness in every area of life must
be on the top of the African-American agenda if we are to become the
people God created us to be (Matthew 6:33).

The more an oppressed people seek to construct their resistance to
oppression around the Word of God,

☐ the stronger will be the cultural power generated by their struggle

☐ the greater will be the likelihood that the oppression will be broken

☐ the smaller will be the likelihood that the resistance movement will
be destroyed by the ungodliness of those involved in it

☐ the smaller will be the likelihood that they will lose their cultural cohesion and compassion for fellow human beings

This was the dynamic that gave Dr. Martin Luther King Jr.'s leadership of the Civil Rights Movement such cultural power.

The *less* an oppressed people seek to construct their resistance to oppression around the Word of God,

☐ the weaker will be the cultural power generated by their struggle

☐ the smaller will be the likelihood that the oppression will be broken

☐ the greater will be the likelihood that the resistance movement will be destroyed by the ungodliness of those involved in it

☐ the greater will be the likelihood that they will lose their cultural cohesion and compassion for fellow human beings

I believe that the secular Black Consciousness Movement splintered into many fragments because it sought to do away with God and his revelation. This also explains why when some of our people began to "make it," they became wrapped up in me-ism. Because their own ungodliness was never challenged when it resurfaced, they lost their compassion for those who remained in the underclass.

True "freedom is not the right to do what I want, it is the *power* to do what is *right*."[1] If we are going to achieve the freedom of our historical quest, we must go *beyond freedom* to righteousness—God's righteousness. Not the "holier than thou" brand of self-righteousness, nor religiosity, but an applied righteousness lived out in all aspects of culture.

**Where Do We Go from Here?**

Part II discussed several phases of our historic quest for freedom and dignity: Colored, Neo-Colored, Negro, Neo-Negro and Black. The fulfillment of these phases, I said, could be called the Joshua phase. There has never been a more critical time in our history than *now* for the emergence of a Joshua generation. But what shape should the Joshua phase take? If Malcolm and Martin were like Moses in pointing us toward the promised land, who will be like Joshua to lead us in?

First of all, our entry into the promised land must involve both our collective and individual identities. The biblical world-and-life-view, expressed through an expanded and revitalized soul dynamic, can make this possible.

The Old Testament covenants could not produce righteousness, because the Righteous One had not yet been revealed. Yet the concept of the covenant was valid. It foreshadowed the coming of the Messiah. Where Adam, Seth, Noah, Abraham, Moses and David failed, Jesus succeeded.

The historic phases in our quest could not produce true freedom and human dignity. Yet the soul dynamic that came from them is valid. African-American history is not over yet. Where the Colored, Neo-Colored, Negro, Neo-Negro and Black phases fell short, the Joshua phase can succeed.

Southern-stream desegregation was not the ultimate answer for Black America. But the application of the soul dynamic is key for providing the *basis* of life in the promised land. Northern-stream nationalism was not the ultimate answer for Black America. But cultural nationalism is key for providing the *shape* of life in the promised land. "Christ is the end of the law" (Romans 10:4). Jesus said that the whole Old Testament pointed to him (John 5:39-40). So the Joshua phase will be the fulfillment of our historic quest. Our whole inheritance points to it.

The Joshua generation must apply the soul dynamic to the issues now confronting us. We may enter into the Promised Land with dignity and surefootedness if we enter with Jesus—if we let his Spirit lead us in righteousness.

### A Renewed Dynamic

Northern-stream thinkers were concerned not just with justice but with power, not just with desegregation but with nationalism. The theological dynamic could have been applied in the Northern situation, but the militants feared that a theological approach would mean accommodating to racism. So instead of taking advantage of this powerful, God-given resource, Northern thinkers were left fighting over the crumbs that fell from the barren tables of secular humanism (the White man's religion) and Islam (the Arab man's religion). The Northern stream can be reconstructed only through the principles God showed us in Brother Martin's example.

To apply the theological dynamic to our contemporary situation, two things must happen: we must *revitalize* the fading soul dynamic with a fresh injection of biblical illumination, and we must *expand* the dynamic by addressing it to *all* our cultural concerns and issues. This is the challenge and opportunity especially for African-American followers of Christ. But what characteristics must they have to bring forth this renewed soul dynamic?

In Israel there was a tradition of Spirit-filled "ecstatic" prophets, men like Samuel, Elijah, Jehu, Gad, Nathan and Obadiah. Their usual method of prophecy was singing, backed up with musical instruments (2 Kings 3:15-19). These prophets lived on the love offerings of the people. The tradition was eventually corrupted, and prophet "unions" were formed to legislate standardized prophets' fees. These later official prophets were merely trying to milk the ecstatic prophetic tradition for all they could get.

God raised up a new prophetic movement, referred to as the "poetic" prophets, which included Isaiah, Jeremiah, Ezekiel, Daniel and Amos. Often these new prophets were not a part of the official prophetic clergy (Amos 7:13-14). Their prophecies employed poetry and puns, and they often pronounced God's judgment on the unionized prophets (Jeremiah 23:9-40).

African-American history has included an antebellum tradition of Spirit-filled preachers. Their usual method of preaching has been *toning** and *whooping** with an organ or piano, while a toning congregation backs them up as they interact with each other. These preachers were often the only ones able to keep our people going from week to week. They lived on the love offerings of the church. Today, in some cases, the tradition has been corrupted. Some preachers are merely milking the tradition for themselves (me-ism). Fortunately there is a righteous remnant of uncorrupted whooping preachers.

God may be raising up a new movement of jazz theologians to stand beside the traditional preachers who have not been corrupted. Together they will be equipped to disciple the African-American culture in new and creative ways.

### Restoration and Expansion

Unlike the northern Israelite kingdom whose people were obliterated, the southern kingdom saw a remnant restored to the land of Canaan. To that restored kingdom Jesus came and began his harvest of the righteous remnant of Israel.

Unlike our Northern stream, whose power has disintegrated, our Southern stream is still with us—because the African-American church is still with us. Inspired by a renewed and expanded concept of the church, Spirit-filled jazz theologians can begin a harvest of new cultural prophets more powerful than Malcolm and Martin. These prophets will point our people toward new vistas of righteousness.

In earlier times the church pulled in the majority of our people. Today it involves a plurality. While the church is still our single most powerful institution, there are now significant groups of people who would be involved in our historic quest but are beyond the theological reach of the traditional church. These include people who are primarily concerned with broad cultural issues (such as poverty and justice) and those who focus on personal disciplines (such as diet and self-control). The first group has been left stranded by secularism, while the second group has been marooned by Islam.

It would be inappropriate to attempt to bring both these groups into the culture of the traditional church. And we need not try to transplant existing Black Christianity into either subculture. We need instead to develop a fresh approach to applying the good news to these contexts. We need a new mode of African-American Christianity—a mode that, among other things, would include new models of the church to correspond to these subcultures.

Such new manifestations of the church, incidentally, would not necessarily be all African-American. Certainly we should not want to replace the traditional church. But with the addition of new models of the church, the cultural range of the church at large would be greatly expanded to involve a majority of our people once again. Thus we would be in a better position to expand the theological dynamic.

Jazz theologians will be the ones who revitalize the theological dynamic. Those who have had theological training on the classical side need to transfer that knowledge to the jazz side. In doing that, we gain a new appreciation for the wisdom of A'nt Jane. We also need to reestablish the relationship between the nuggets of the theological dynamic and their corresponding passages of Scripture. Revitalized, the dynamic could be more effectively passed on to succeeding generations. Its survival would be ensured.

# 15

# The Fields Are *Black* unto Harvest

*T*he jazz theologian must actualize what we have learned from both streams of our history as well as what we will learn through an ongoing process of revitalization, expansion and application of the soul dynamic. The renewed dynamic will provide the reason for doing it. The renewed dynamic will provide the ethical basis for doing it. And the renewed dynamic will provide the means for identifying and resisting unrighteousness.

As the jazz theologian begins to apply the revitalized and expanded theological dynamic to all aspects of our culture, a practical righteousness will begin to emerge—an *intra*cultural righteousness to overcome our ungodliness, and an *extra*cultural righteousness to overcome oppression. This must be the task of the Joshua generation of leadership.

How can we facilitate the emergence of this Joshua generation? Where do we begin? Whatever the shape of the Joshua phase, it must be undergirded by an ongoing process of education and realization.

## Education: To Know Who We Are and Who We Should Be

In the first edition of this book, *Beyond Liberation* (1983), I made the following observations.

> Rootlessness is one of the great problems of today's generation. In spite of the great renaissance begun in the '60s, the youth of Black America lack a working knowledge of our history.
>
> The optimism of the '60s is partially at fault here. It assumed that the succeeding generations would carry on the struggle with our same sense of urgency. Those who made this assumption forgot that each generation's response to its situation is based on its *own* perception of what is and what should be. With many of the superficial manifestations of racism gone, the new generations have no appreciation for what it took to remove them. Do-your-own-thing-ism and me-ism thwart any attempt to motivate our people to move forward. While education will not fully instill in them our old sense of urgency, it will help to prevent each generation from seeing itself in historical isolation.[1]

The new militancy has seen the restoration of this "sense of urgency." But like the old apathy, today's urgency is still disconnected from our historical quest. We still lack an adequate framework in which to view and understand the facts of our cultural history. Secular humanism proved inadequate because of its finite reference point, and Islam proved inadequate because it excludes all non-Arab culture and does not acknowledge our need for God's grace. Because the lesson of Islam's failure has been lost by many of today's militants, they have ensured their eventual demise.

Only the soul dynamic can provide an authentic framework for self-understanding. It is indigenous to the African-American experience, yet it is derived from God's Word, which speaks to every cultural and historical situation.

We saw in chapter twelve that while education involves knowledge, knowledge involves not just facts but also skills. Education must not only teach the facts of our history, consciousness and destiny from a scriptural perspective. It must also teach the skills to analyze and actualize this knowledge in terms of God's Word.

Cultural unrighteousness assaults us from all sides. It especially overwhelms the young and impressionable. Countless children are raised in the church only to be lost to the pagan practices of secularism or the futile works-righteousness of Islam. This is unacceptable. We must equip our children both with a biblical world-and-life-view and with the skills to outthink their counterparts with sound reasons for the hope that is within them (1 Peter 3:15). We must also equip them with the wisdom to influence their culture through such avenues as rhythm and blues, rap and the media. Otherwise we have little hope of saving our youth from the erosion of secularism and Islam.

To prevent this erosion and to help develop a Joshua generation of leadership, we need to commit ourselves to the task and invest in alternative models of schooling. The public school system, as it stands, reeks with humanism. Not only that, but it functions primarily not to educate or inform, but to *conform* our youth to a secular value system that serves only the interests of the elite who call the educational shots. Neither the long-term nor the short-term interests of our community are served by these schools. As long as we depend on the public school system (in its present condition) as our primary means of education, we will not get far in establishing or implementing an agenda for righteousness. Without alternative schooling and a substantial commitment to change things in the public schools, we will continue to see the erosion of the positive values that made us strong.

In some cases we will have to leave behind the public schools and establish full-time alternative schools, both large ones and home-based models. In other cases we will have to develop supplemental educational programs for those who remain in the public school system. These would be biblically based workshops to teach such skills as reading, math, critical thinking and computer literacy, and to engage students in such studies as African-American history, jazz theology, economics, Bible, community development and contemporary cultural issues.

While churches may want to form coalitions to develop full-time alternative schools, most individual churches already have the facilities necessary for supplemental schools. If they have Sunday schools, why not also have Saturday or after-school workshops? Why not borrow a page from the book of Jewish synagogues, involving young people on Saturdays as they do in "sabbath schools"?

Whatever the case, we must avoid duplicating the fiasco of what often passes for Christian education today. In too many cases it consists of secular education with a bit of private salvation squeezed in the gaps. In too many cases Christian education has merely been a smoke screen used to maintain segregation in the classroom.

To develop effective alternative schools, we must completely rethink the learning process itself and develop innovative curricula that truly reflect a wholistic, scriptural world-and-life-view. Also, because there is more to education than schooling, we must develop, recognize and affirm alternative ways of doing education—modes like community projects, guided study and apprenticeships.

Both traditional and new-model churches could develop these modes of learning and encourage mentors. Joining forces, churches with vision could sponsor symposiums, consultations and conferences to bring together educators who share the vision of a Joshua generation. Once an educational agenda has been worked out, we could seek the cooperation of Christian colleges and other educational institutions that can help actualize our educational agenda. They could implement programs to develop new mentors and enrich our pastors.

Jesus taught us that what you know is what you do. Whatever modes of education we choose, one of our central goals must be to instill in the next generation commitment to righteousness, to goal orientation and to excellence.

*Commitment to righteousness.* As we have already seen, a dedication to righteousness is key to the fulfillment of the historic quest for freedom and dignity. Not only so, but the intensity of a people's commitment to righteousness is directly related to the effectiveness and wisdom of their leadership.

The enormous turnout for the *Million Man March** on Washington

(October 16, 1995) could be an indication that the Spirit of God has moved upon African-American men across this country to take a stand for righteousness. When they discover their human weakness and inability to be righteous on their own, will jazz theologians be available to point these brothers to God's strong grace in Christ (Philippians 4:13)? Or will we just watch them flounder in the futility of Islamistic works-righteousness?

*Commitment to goal orientation.* In 1983 I stated:

Since losing the momentum of the '60s, no cultural goals any longer capture the imaginations of our people. We wander in circles because we are not setting and pursuing righteous goals. Given the lingering effects of the slave experience, this is understandable. The veto power of slavemasters rendered goal setting absurd at best. Somehow we have never fully overcome the "present orientation" that slavery precipitated. Though we are no longer in physical chains, in some ways we are still in cultural chains. If we do not form the habit of setting and pursuing righteous goals, we will condemn ourselves to a treadmill of merely reacting to unexpected oppressions.[2]

Many would argue that we no longer "wander in circles." This does not mean, however, that confusion has subsided. Today's cacophony of conflicting voices indicate that too many of us are not "setting and pursuing righteous goals." We are still "reacting to unexpected oppressions."

When the desegregation of the South became our goal, it caught the imagination of millions, both Black and White, across the country. It became a powerful demonstration of the kingdom of God and his righteousness before the watching world. We need the vision of new, righteous goals now more than ever.

*Commitment to excellence.* Many programs today try to instill in our young people a sense of excellence. They are to be commended. However, excellence for its own sake will prove an inadequate stimulus for the required discipline. Only in the diligent pursuit of righteous goals can a quest for excellence and self-discipline be fulfilled.

Because so many people accepted the goals of the Civil Rights Movement as their heartfelt convictions, they had the discipline to remain nonviolent in the face of vicious police dogs and bone-crushing fire hoses.

### Realization: Renewed Institutions

Having begun to lay the foundation of righteousness through biblically based education, we can complete the foundation by rebuilding our cultural institutions. We need to revitalize cultural life from the basic family unit through the political sphere.

*Family life.* The breakdown of the family is the greatest tragedy of our contemporary experience. From the creation, the family unit has been the main institution by which culture is instilled in succeeding generations. Reconstruction of African-American culture will be impossible without the encouragement and restoration of strong family units. The family must be the root of goal orientation and commitment to righteousness and excellence. I have been impressed with the strong sense of family I see in Asian-American communities. We need to learn from our Asian friends and emulate their example of family life where appropriate.

The intracultural aspect of the Joshua phase must involve a rediscovery and application of the scriptural teaching on manhood, womanhood, the marriage relationship, fatherhood and motherhood. We also need to overcome the disastrous effects of me-ism and do-your-own-thing-ism with regard to sex. We must teach the beauty and fulfillment of sex within the context of God-centered marriage. Every goal we set as well as everything we do in pursuit of these goals must place a premium on strengthening family units.

*Body life.* Truly the African-American church body has played a key role in our history. Though we need to develop additional models of the church, we must also broaden the ministry of the traditional church. While Black preaching has been a priceless resource, traditional preaching alone is not adequate to prepare our people to meet the challenges of our day.

Our churches must function as extended families. They must bring families together and help them prepare each new generation for the responsibilities of marriage and parenthood. In 1983 I noted that there were "far too many fatherless children among us." Today we continue to see an alarming rise in parentless children. They are raising themselves without significant input from either parent, and the results are disastrous! In some cases, our girls are in danger of losing their sense of worth, and our boys are in danger of extinction. The renewed church as an extended family could play a crucial role in providing models of manhood, womanhood and parenthood for our children at risk.

The church must once again play a prominent role in education and realization. The new models of the African-American church must take the lead, helping the traditional church to do the same. Then the church will be not only the bearer of good news; it will *be* that good news for individuals and families.

*Economic development.* The oppression we face today is less racially based than economically based. Since the sixties we have seen the bifurcation of the African-American community into the middle class and the underclass. During the sixties the "White flight" from changing city neighborhoods was a symbol of racism. Today we are seeing a Black flight. The new classism is rooted in economics.

Me-ism among many in the African-American middle class has led to the pursuit of opulence and a corresponding lack of concern or compassion for those locked into the underclass. As the church expands its prophetic role in our community, it must address this economic problem. But where do we begin?

We are a nation of consumers, and so consumer economics should be our starting point. We must develop strategies to stretch our consumer dollar and increase our consumer power. We can do it through such basic things as using sale items and generics, forming buyer co-ops and organizing selective boycotts aimed at changing the policies of businesses whose practices hinder our pursuit of righteousness. We also need to develop and patronize businesses committed to building an African-American economic base in and around our cities.

But it is not enough for us to remain a community of consumers. We must also become producers. To do this we must borrow a page from Booker T. Washington and "cast down the bucket where we are." We need to match our cultural resources to our economic opportunities. With proper education and a keen sense of economics, we can build strategic employee-owned businesses. Toward the end of the nineteenth century, the world's leading economies began to shift from an agricultural base to an industrial base. Today we are in the midst of another significant economic shift, from an industrial base to a communications/information base. It is imperative that we develop appropriate economic enterprises that take advantage of these trends. This will involve development of new and creative businesses in the areas of service, information, communication, media and so forth.

Whatever the economic directions we choose, our goals must be to do cultural seeding, to improve the quality of life in the African-American nation and to soften the blow of institutional classism. This task will indeed require wisdom and insight. It can be done if we can develop economists who will help us develop an economic base. Without a solid economic and righteous base, the resources that come to us will dissipate without benefiting those who really need them. This is what happened to the Great Society programs of the sixties. If the proper economic institutions had been in place, we would not be as vulnerable as we are to the whims of the federal government.

*Political cohesion.* While the exercise of cultural power has far greater effect on society than political power, a little political savvy is crucial if we want to eliminate the institutional oppressions of today. We can truly be thankful for the work of the Congressional Black Caucus. But as noted in chapter seven, we need to do this kind of work at state and local levels of government also.

We must never let our cultural goals become allied with political liberalism or conservatism, Republicans or Democrats. The real issue for us is whether those who hold political office have a commitment to social justice and a righteous compassion for the oppressed—

whether the public policy they advocate has a strengthening effect or a destructive effect on our key institutions, especially the family. At those points we can form coalitions with them regardless of their broader stance.

We can't wait to see if sympathetic political leadership will emerge by coincidence. We must do all we can to develop and elect this kind of leadership. This means, among other things, massive voter registration, voter education and voter facilitation. We must also follow Brother Martin's example in finding new, creative ways to apply the theological dynamic to raising politicians' consciousness to issues concerning the righteous liberation of the oppressed.

**Lift Every Voice**

The infrastructure that would grow out of doing theology in the areas of cultural education and realization would put us in a position to meet the cultural challenges we face. It would lay the foundation for the emergence of the Joshua generation. But what would a fully functioning Joshua phase be like? Certainly not a static state of existence, but a dynamic state of becoming. It would be a process of pursuing God's righteousness—a pursuit made possible only by grace and a deep love for God. This is why the Joshua phase must be theological. The state of becoming is the fulfillment of what Brother Malcolm illustrated by his life.

The Joshua generation should not be limited to African-Americans only. It should transcend African-American culture as it has a redemptive effect on America at large. The crosscultural aspects of the Joshua phase would help keep it from being spoiled by Christianity-ism.

The Joshua phase may have worldwide implications. In my international travels I have been struck by the tremendous cultural influence African-Americans have had through music (R & B, jazz, blues, gospel and so on). It has amazed me to see how people all over the world seem to have positive feelings toward our people. For example, when the *Iranian hostage crisis*\* was at its height, the Ayatollah Khomeini ordered the release of African-American hostages. I believe the influence and favor we have with Two-Thirds World nations is

God-given. It is also worth noting that most cultures of the Two-Thirds World are jazz-sided like ours. This gives us a distinct advantage in communicating the good news to the world. African-American culture embodies a dynamic system of language. And the African-American experience has enabled our people to more easily establish rapport with Two-Thirds World and oppressed people. Recognizing these facts, mission organizations such as Wycliffe Bible Translators have been asking especially for African-American recruits.

Given the current shift from Western missionaries to Two-Thirds World church leaders, African-American jazz theologians may be the only ones who can still go into the whole world without creating hostilities. A Black man was the last one to carry the cross of Christ (Matthew 27:32). Black Christians may be the last ones to carry the banner of worldwide cultural discipleship.

Not all African-Americans will be part of the Joshua generation. Only two Israelite men who left Egypt made it to the Promised Land. The Joshua phase is an opportunity for those of our people who are willing to pursue the kingdom of God and his righteousness.

These are the last days of the lull before the second wave of the Black quest. We are in the eye of a hurricane. Will the foundation of the second wave be a framework of righteousness to maximize its effectiveness? Or will we just do nothing, and watch Black frustration increase?[3]

Such was my perspective in 1983. Today the post-Black lull is giving way. The eye of the hurricane has passed. The African-American phase is upon us. What is the nature of its foundation and framework? Have we once more missed an opportunity to actualize the Joshua phase? Are we witnessing an increase in frustration? Have we ignored the warnings from the rage of the rappers? Have we failed to be alarmed by the *trial of O. J. Simpson*\* and what it revealed about the racial polarization of American society? The riots that followed the *Rodney King incident*\* speak for themselves.

We still stand at a fork in our historic path. We can fulfill our historic aspirations through the righteousness of the Joshua phase or betray these aspirations through unrighteousness, frustration-overflow and terrorism. We can follow Christ as Lord and realize our cultural destiny or reject Christ and face judgment. *Which way will it be?*

Being part of the Joshua generation will be no cakewalk. If it is actualized, many people, Black and White alike, will see it as dangerous and subversive. As we go forward, we must be prepared for an avalanche of harassment and sabotage, so severe as to make all previous anti-Black persecution pale in comparison. For our ultimate adversaries will not be human (Ephesians 6:12).

Still I say, "Let us move toward the Joshua phase! If we do, we will be empowered to participate in a great harvest as we proclaim the full counsel of God with a clarity and power never seen before (Acts 20:27)."[4] "For God has allowed us to know the secret of his plan, and it is this: he purposed long ago in his sovereign will that all human history [including African-American history] should be consummated in Christ, that everything that exists in Heaven or earth should find its perfection and fulfilment in him" (Ephesians 1:9-10 Phillips).

O the depth of the riches and wisdom and knowledge of God! How unsearchable are his judgments and how inscrutable his ways!

"For who has known the mind of the Lord,
or who has been his counselor?"
"Or who has given a gift to him
that he might be repaid?"

For from him and through him and to him are all things. To him be glory for ever. Amen. (Romans 11:33-36 RSV)

Maybe it was a vision of the Joshua generation that inspired James Weldon Johnson to pen the words of our Black national anthem:

Lift ev'ry voice and sing
Till earth and heaven ring,
Ring with the harmonies of Liberty.
Let our rejoicing rise
High as the list'ning skies,
Let it resound loud as the rolling seas.

Sing a song full of the faith that the dark past has taught us,
Sing a song full of the hope that the present has brought us.
Facing the rising sun of our new day begun,
Let us march on till victory is won.

Stony the road we trod
Bitter the chast'ning rod
Felt in the days when hope, unborn, had died.
Yet with a steady beat
Have not our weary feet
Come to the place for which our fathers sighed?
We have come over a way that with tears has been watered,
We have come treading our path through the blood of the slaugh-
tered.
Out from the gloomy past,
Till now we stand at last
Where the white gleam of our bright star is cast.

God of our weary years,
God of our silent tears,
Thou who hast brought us thus far on the way;
Thou who hast by Thy might
Led us into the light,
Keep us forever in the path, we pray:
Lest our feet stray from the places, our God, where we met Thee,
Lest our hearts, drunk with the wine of the world, forget Thee.
Shadowed beneath Thy hand,
May we forever stand
True to our God,
True to our native land.[5]

The fields are *Black* unto harvest!

## Glossary of People, Events and Terms

**A'nt Jane**  Aunt Jane and/or Miss Sally, usually the oldest or one of the oldest "mothers of the church." She has little or no formal education, but she knows the Lord and has a homespun, God-given wisdom from life experience. She cannot articulate her *faith*\* intellectually, but she has discernment to know when ideas are not scriptural. Every traditional African-American church has an A'nt Jane or a Miss Sally.

**apologetics**  The application of God's Word to controversy.

**Battle of Selma**  The "Battle of Selma" involved a massive voter registration drive conducted by the *Student Non-violent Coordinating Committee (SNCC)*\* in 1964-1965 among African-Americans in Dallas County, Alabama. Selma was the county seat. Sheriff Jim Clark did all he could to thwart the effort. When SNCC exhausted its resources, an appeal went out to the *Southern Christian Leadership Conference (SCLC)*\* for help.

The campaign began to get national attention after a confrontation between the Reverend C. T. Vivian of SCLC and Sheriff Clark on the steps of the Selma courthouse. When the Reverend Vivian tried to lead some African-American citizens of Dallas County into the courthouse to register to vote, the sheriff physically blocked the entrance. As Vivian spoke out against the injustice of the situation, Sheriff Clark struck out at him in a fit of violent rage. The Reverend Vivian remained nonviolent. The incident was covered in all the news media.

The most notorious incident of the campaign came early in the winter of 1965. While a young man named Jimmy Jackson was trying to protect his mother from being violently attacked by angry Whites, he was shot to death by a state trooper. This incident filled campaign participants with anger and outrage. To channel the anger, the SCLC organized a march to Montgomery, Alabama (the state capital, fifty-four miles [eighty-six kilometers] away), in honor of Jimmy Jackson.

The first attempt to march came on March 7. But Governor George Wallace was determined to block the march. The marchers left Selma by way of the Edmund Pettus Bridge. On the far side of the bridge they were turned back by an army of Alabama state troopers wielding clubs and shooting tear gas. Many marchers were injured. This police brutality got extensive coverage in the national news.

The leaders sent out an appeal across the country for others to join them in a second attempt at the march two days later (March 9). People converged on Selma by the hundreds. However, a judge in the federal district court in Montgomery imposed an injunction on the march until a hearing could be held.

The second attempt at the march was blocked by state troopers at the same spot the first march was turned back. This time the leaders of the SCLC led the marchers to kneel and pray. Martin Luther King Jr. and other leaders believed that if they defied the federal court injunction, the state troopers would assume their violence was justified, and brutality would be unrestrained. Thus the leaders of the march elected to return to Selma. This decision disillusioned *Eldridge Cleaver*\* and other militant Black thinkers.

It was events surrounding the "Battle of Selma" that prompted President Lyndon Johnson to propose that Congress pass a comprehensive voting rights bill.

Eventually the court injunction was lifted, clearing the way for the march to Montgomery. To protect the marchers, President Johnson federalized and mobilized the Alabama National Guard. The Selma to Montgomery March culminated with Dr. King's famous "How Long? Not Long" speech.

The Voting Rights Act was passed by Congress and signed into law by the president in August 1965.

**Black humanism**  A belief that Black people and Black cultural standards are the final authority of all truth, or that Blacks are not really affected by unrighteousness.

**Black Panther Party**  Full name: the Black Panther Party for Self-Defense. This group was founded in Oakland, California, in October 1966. Among the national leaders were *Bobby Seale\** (chairman), *Huey P. Newton\** (minister of defense) and *Eldridge Cleaver\** (minister of information). The Panthers were known for strongly advocating Black control of Black communities and the use of force if necessary in self-defense. They also called for a Black revolution. Their slogan was "All power to the people."

They saw the police as an occupying force in the African-American community and assumed the role of protectors of the community. They were often seen monitoring the activities of the Oakland police while carrying loaded guns. They conducted these activities in accord with their constitutional rights. They stirred up great controversy on May 2, 1967, when thirty Panthers carried these weapons into the California State Assembly House in Sacramento to lobby against a bill pending in the legislature.

Chapters of the Black Panther Party sprang up in many major U.S. cities. In reactionary paranoia, J. Edgar Hoover (then head of the FBI) dubbed the Black Panthers "the number one threat to the internal security of the United States." Thus the party came under extensive FBI surveillance and sabotage. In time they were linked to several fatal shootouts.

Eventually, after Seale left the party, a major ideological rift developed between Cleaver and Newton. The party fractured into the "Cleaverites" and the "Newtonists." This conflict degenerated into open warfare. With several leaders incarcerated, murdered or exiled, the party eventually fell apart.

**Blackness** A perspective on reality based on the cultural *consciousness** (including sense of *history** and *destiny**) of African-American people.

**blues** This music emerged in the Delta region of Mississippi (northeast corner). It soon became popular in Southern cities including New Orleans, Memphis and St. Louis. Blues songs focus on the male-female relationship—its joys, trials and sorrows. Its roots are in the *spirituals** and work songs sung by slaves in the South.

Classical blues is based on a twelve-bar pattern, divided into three stanzas of four bars each. When the blues is sung it follows the AAB pattern. That is, the first stanza makes a statement. The second stanza repeats the statement. The third stanza brings the first and second stanzas to a rhyming, punchy conclusion.

**Brown, H. "Rap"** In 1967, when the Civil Rights Movement was giving way to the Black Consciousness Movement, H. "Rap" Brown burst upon the scene because of a fiery speech he delivered to an angry crowd of African-American youth in Cambridge, Maryland—a speech that triggered a rampage of arson. Brown had been crisscrossing the United States, calling on African-Americans to launch an armed rebellion against racist oppression.

He was born Hubert Gerald Brown to Eddy and Thelma Brown on October 4, 1943, in Baton Rouge, Louisiana. Raised Roman Catholic, Brown was enraged by the oppression he witnessed in his formative years. In high school and college he was full of impatience with these institutions for failing to combat racism. After receiving his B.A. in sociology from Southern University in Baton Rouge, he worked to improve the lives of African-Americans through government-funded antipoverty programs. He soon became disillusioned with what he saw as the American system's attempt to assimilate African-Americans, usurping their culture and identity. Brown was one of those who became disenchanted with the nonviolent tactics of Dr. Martin Luther King Jr.

In 1966 Brown got involved with the *Student Non-violent Coordi-*

*nating Committee (SNCC)** as an organizer in the Greene County, Alabama, voter registration drive. Later that year he was named Alabama state project director. At the age of twenty-four Brown succeeded *Stokely Carmichael** as chairman of SNCC. As the new spokesman, Brown called for an armed struggle against police brutality. He blasted Black leaders who opposed riots. He also verbally attacked President Lyndon B. Johnson, both for his Vietnam policies and for not going far enough to eliminate racism in the United States. Brown was also a strong advocate for the *Black Panther Party** and in 1968 was appointed the party's minister of justice. It was his blazing rhetoric which earned Hubert Gerald Brown his identity as H. "Rap" Brown.

In 1969 Brown published his autobiography, *Die, Nigger, Die!* In April 1970, as his trial over charges stemming from the Cambridge incident approached, Brown went into hiding. During his time as a fugitive, he was on the FBI's "Most Wanted" list, yet he stayed out of sight for a year and five months. In September 1971 Brown was wounded by police in a gun battle and arrested in connection with a holdup at a New York City saloon. Brown and three fellow Black militants were charged with armed robbery and attempted murder.

During his pretrial incarceration, Brown became a Sunni Muslim and changed his name to Jamil Abdullah Al-Amin. His trial was held in 1973. In spite of his appeal to a "higher authority"—that is, "ultimate law"—the court found Al-Amin guilty as charged.

After Al-Amin was paroled in 1976, he moved to Atlanta and opened a small grocery store. Eventually he became the imam of a small mosque in a poverty-stricken neighborhood in southeast Atlanta.

**Carmichael, Stokely** Among the civil rights activists who grew impatient with nonviolence was Stokely Carmichael, whose advocacy of Black power catapulted him to national prominence. He was born in Port-of-Spain, Trinidad, on June 29, 1941. His father, Adolphus, was a dedicated activist in the Trinidadian independence movement. When Stokely was two years old, his family immigrated to the United States. Eventually Stokely Carmichael settled in New York City, living in Harlem, then in the Bronx. Carmichael displayed a keen interest in politics at an early age. He was especially inspired by Bayard Rustin, an African-American socialist. By the time he was ready for college the Civil Rights Movement in the South had aroused his interest.

In 1960 he enrolled at Howard University, a predominantly African-American institution in Washington, D.C. In his freshman year he participated in the *Freedom Rides\** sponsored by the *Congress of Racial Equality (CORE).\** Carmichael received his B.A. in philosophy in 1964 and headed south to be involved in various efforts of the *Student Non-violent Coordinating Committee (SNCC).\**

As an organizer for SNCC, he participated in the Lowndes County, Alabama, voter registration drive. He also helped establish the Lowndes County Freedom Association, a political party for African-Americans and others who were locked out of the electoral process. The police brutality he witnessed against his fellow civil rights workers led him to reconsider Martin Luther King Jr.'s tactic of nonviolence. Carmichael began to emphasize the need for empowerment for Blacks and deemphasize the need for civil rights.

In 1966, armed with his more militant philosophy, Carmichael succeeded *John Lewis\** as head of SNCC. Carmichael articulated his new philosophy in a 1967 book he wrote with Charles V. Hamilton, *Black Power: The Politics of Liberation in America.* In 1967 *H. "Rap" Brown\** took over the leadership of SNCC, freeing Carmichael to travel the world, denouncing U.S. foreign policy and American involvement in the Vietnam War. During this time the *Black Panther Party\** named him "honorary prime minister."

When Carmichael returned to the United States, federal agents seized his passport. He settled in Washington and continued to be an outspoken critic of U.S. foreign policy throughout the country.

In 1968 Carmichael married Miriam Makebe, a popular activist singer from South Africa. The Carmichaels moved to the Republic of New Guinea in West Africa. There Carmichael worked to restore Kuame Nkrumah, the deposed president of Ghana, to power. In New Guinea he changed his name to Kuame Ture. He continued to be a strong advocate of revolution as the means to deal with problems of injustice and racism.

**chickens roost** In the midst of national grief over the tragic death of John F. Kennedy (November 22, 1963), Malcolm X was asked for his reaction. He answered, "It is a case of the chickens coming home to roost." Malcolm was pointing out that the atmosphere of violence permeating American society (brought to light by the Civil Rights Movement) had reached the presidency.

The American news media offered a twisted interpretation, implying that Malcolm rejoiced in the death of the president. Believing this distorted version of the statement, *Elijah Muhammad\** suspended Malcolm from the Nation of Islam and quickly issued a moderate "official" statement.

**Christianity** The *gospel\** applied in a cultural context, involving both its expression and the response of its adherents. These cultural manifestations do not contradict or undercut the gospel itself. On the contrary, a properly functioning cultural Christianity can bring out insights on the gospel not seen in other cultural contexts.

**Christianity-ism; "Christianity"** This ugly term is most fitting, because of its ugliness, to refer to negative or unchristian religious practices expressed in the language of *Christianity.\** Christianity-ism consists of making Christianity itself the object of *faith\** rather than an expression of faith in God's solution to the problem of human unrighteousness and God's revealed wrath on humankind. In essence Christianity-ism is a subtle form of idol worship—the idol being institutional Christianity, and the form often being associated with racism.

**Clark, Mark** *See* Hampton, Fred, and Mark Clark

**Cleaver, Eldridge** Leroy Eldridge Cleaver was born to Thelma and Leroy Cleaver on August 3, 1935, in Wabbaska, Arkansas. His family soon moved to Phoenix, Arizona, and then to Los Angeles, California. They settled in the Watts neighborhood, where Thelma and Leroy separated.

When Eldridge began junior high school, he began to get into trouble with the law. By 1955 Cleaver had spent time in several

California correctional institutions for crimes ranging from bicycle theft to dealing in marijuana. In fact, most of his teenage years were spent behind bars. Cleaver earned his high-school diploma at Soledad State Prison and became an avid reader of works by such writers as Richard Wright, Karl Marx, Thomas Paine and *W. E. B. Du Bois.**

Soon after his release from prison Cleaver resumed his life of crime—selling marijuana and committing rape and other assorted acts of violence. In 1957 he was convicted of assault with intent to murder. During his time in the California State Prison at San Quentin and at Folsom State Prison, Cleaver began writing essays in an attempt to articulate and understand the rage that filled him. He also joined the *Nation of Islam** under the leadership of *Elijah Muhammad.** Thereafter he was often placed in solitary confinement for proselytizing for the Nation of Islam. He used these times of solitude to write and to study the Bible.

One year prior to his parole in 1966, *Ramparts* magazine published several of Cleaver's essays. These well-written pieces attracted the attention of notable authors such as Maxwell Geisman and Norman Mailer. After his release from prison, Cleaver served as a contributing editor to *Ramparts.* In 1967 he married Kathleen Neal and was instrumental in starting Black House, an African-American youth cultural center in San Francisco. It was at Black House that Cleaver met *Bobby Seale** and *Huey Newton,** founders of the *Black Panther Party.** Cleaver became the party's minister of information.

On April 6, 1968, the Black Panthers were involved in a shootout with the San Francisco police. The police had overwhelming fire-power; Cleaver was wounded, and Bobby Hutton, treasurer of the party, was shot and killed while trying to surrender. Cleaver was arrested but later was released because a local court ruled the charges against him to be politically motivated. At the time, Cleaver was running for U.S. president as the nominee of the Peace and Freedom Party, a coalition of several radical groups.

Toward the end of 1968, a higher court ruled that Cleaver had violated his parole. This court ordered Cleaver to be returned to prison and face charges related to the San Francisco shootout. Cleaver fled to Canada and then to Cuba (under the communist rule of Fidel Castro), where he was warmly welcomed as a revolutionary hero. Later in 1968 *Soul on Ice* was published. This bestselling book won the 1970 Martin Luther King Memorial Prize. From Cuba, Cleaver went to Algeria.

His time in the communist world opened his eyes to a form of racism and oppression far worse than anything he had witnessed in America. He realized that because the Marxist-Leninist ideology lacked humanity and love, it was unworkable. He also saw that the tactics of the Black Panther Party were inadequate means for Black progress.

Eventually the Cleavers, with their son Maceo and daughter Joju, moved to Paris. During his time in France Eldridge Cleaver had an apparent conversion to Christ. In time he also adopted a conservative political philosophy. When Cleaver returned to the United States in 1976, he was incarcerated. But all charges against him were cleared by 1978, and he was set free. His book *Soul on Fire* was published that year.

In 1980 Cleaver settled in Berkeley, California, where he unsuccessfully sought seats on various political boards including city council (1984), U.S. Senate (1986) and San Francisco Regional Transit Board (1992). His marriage ended in divorce in 1987. Around that time Cleaver became involved in the ceramic pottery business and the recycling business.

**Cleveland riot** The most destructive of the 1966 riots broke out in the Hough section of Cleveland, Ohio (July 18-23). It was triggered when a Black woman was refused a glass of water and ejected from the White-owned neighborhood bar. News of the incident spread rapidly, and soon there was a wave of arson and gunfire. Four people were killed, fifty were injured, and there was widespread destruction.

**Congress of Racial Equality (CORE)** The roots of CORE go back to the late 1930s and an organization called the Fellowship of Reconciliation (FOR). FOR was a pacifist group advocating nonviolent social change.

In 1942 *James Farmer,** an activist for FOR from about 1940, began planning for a mass movement against racial segregation based on Mahatma Gandhi's principles of nonviolence. As race relations secretary of FOR, Farmer wrote his "Provisional Plan for Brotherhood and Mobilization." The movement he envisioned would not be strictly pacifist, yet it would have a broad theological base. The nonviolent direct action strategy would include various methods of civil disobedience including picketing, boycotts, sit-ins and noncooperation. The movement would include all races and faiths in a disciplined community committed to the elimination of racism in America. Farmer and his colleagues began to implement these principles in Chicago, where they lived.

The group called itself the Committee of Racial Equality, and its nonviolent direct action tactics electrified civil rights activists across the United States. In June 1943 the Committee of Racial Equality became a national organization called the National Federation of Committees of Racial Equality. Farmer became national chairman. In 1944 the name of the organization was changed to the Congress of Racial Equality (CORE). As civil rights activity throughout the South increased in the late 1950s, CORE was on the vanguard with its nonviolent direct action strategy.

In 1961 Farmer became national director of CORE. Under his leadership the group organized and sponsored the *Freedom Rides** to challenge segregation in interstate travel. After this CORE partnered with other civil rights groups in organizing "Freedom Schools" and voter registration drives in the South and urban projects in the North.

In 1966 *Floyd McKissick** succeeded James Farmer as national director of CORE. Under McKissick's leadership CORE's philosophy shifted from a *moral* base to a *power* base. With its more militant stance, the organization became Black Power-oriented. Eventually, as the Black Consciousness movement disintegrated, so did CORE.

**consciousness; collective consciousness** That which a people uses to understand its world. Consciousness determines what people do and how they do it in every area of life. It also gives rise to a people's *history** and *destiny** as well as their sociology, psychology and anthropology.

**cultural dynamic** *See* soul dynamic

**culture** The cumulative effect of *history,** *consciousness** and *destiny** on the life of a collective body of people. Culture is made up of commitments, values and beliefs about the world and the people in it. The radical root of culture is the dynamic interplay between positive religious commitments (which are the result of God's *grace**) and negative religious commitments (which are the result of human un-righteousness). Culture results in the patterned way people do things together.

**"curse on Ham" myth** Many who claim that *Christianity** is "the White man's religion" cite the "curse on Ham" myth as proof. Others see this myth as a reason for advocating the conversion of African-Americans to Islam.

Ironically, this myth originated in the Islamic world to justify the enslavement of Black Africans by Arab Muslims. Wahb Ibn Munab-bih, a leading ninth-century Muslim apologist, stated the following:

Ham the son of Noah was a white man, with a handsome face and figure, and the Almighty God changed his color and the color of his descendants in response to his father's curse. He went away, followed by his sons, and they settled by the shore, where God increased and multiplied them. They are the blacks. . . . Ham begat Kush ibn Ham, Kan'an ibn Ham, and Fut ibn Ham. . . . Kush and Kan'an's descendants are the various races of blacks: Nubians, Zonj, Qaran, Zaghawa, Ethiopians, Copts, and Berbers. (source: Ibn Qutayba, *Kitab Al-Ma'arif,* p. 26)[1]

Eventually this myth found its way into the fabric of White *Christianity-ism** and was used to justify American slavery.

**"Daddy" Grace** (1882-1960) Bishop Charles Emmanuel "Daddy" Grace was a wealthy cult leader, mostly known on the Eastern seaboard of the United States. Of Portuguese and Black descent, he came to America in 1920 and began to preach in 1925. As the absolute head of the United House of Prayer for All People, he controlled all its finances. (This was how he acquired his wealth.) Because he played the role of a father figure, his followers referred to him as "Daddy."

Bishop Grace was able to elicit the worship of his followers through wordplays using his names. For example, "salvation by grace" meant salvation by Daddy Grace; "Immanuel," meaning God with us (Matthew 1:23), also referred to the bishop, whose middle name was Emmanuel; "the throne of grace" (Hebrews 4:16) was the throne of Daddy Grace (every House of Prayer had a throne).

To allay the suspicions that led to the demise of the *Garvey**movement (whose colors were red, black and green), Bishop Grace adopted red, white and blue as the official colors of his sect. Its worship services were characterized by loud, pulsating band music dominated by trombones and frenzied, ecstatic dancing. In the United House of Prayer for All People, the God of the Bible was relegated to obscurity. After all, according to Grace's followers, "this is the age of [Daddy] 'Grace' and only [Daddy] 'Grace' can save you from your sins against God. But God cannot save you if you sin against his [Daddy] 'Grace.' "

After the death of Daddy Grace, Bishop McCollough took over the leadership of the cult and assumed the title "Daddy Grace."

**death blow to the Reconstruction** As the 1876 presidential election approached, President Ulysses S. Grant (whose administration was riddled with corruption) became increasingly concerned about the political prospects of his party. Grant was a Republican, but the U.S. House of Representatives was controlled by the Democrats. In order to gain more support for the Republican Party in the North, Grant dispatched federal troops to the South (a stronghold of the Democrats). Their initial mission was to protect the recently freed slaves from the increasing terrorist attacks from the *Ku Klux Klan.**

The 1876 election pitted Rutherford B. Hayes (a Republican) against Samuel J. Tilden (a Democrat). Tilden won the popular vote by a margin of 461,035 votes.

Both candidates ended up claiming electoral college victories in

Florida, South Carolina and Louisiana. Congress established a commission to settle the dispute, but it was unable to agree on a solution. Just prior to Inauguration Day it looked as if the country would be without a president. So Democrat and Republican leaders struck a last-minute bargain: the Democrats agreed to concede the election to Hayes, and the Republicans agreed to withdraw federal troops from the South.

By April 20, 1877, the federal troops were gone and Reconstruction was over. Soon after that, Blacks were denied civil and voting rights. By then the Democratic Party had reestablished White supremacy in the South.

**destiny** A people's sense of the direction and ultimate fulfillment of their *history.**

**Detroit riot** The riot in Detroit, Michigan, July 23-30, 1967, eclipsed the 1965 *Watts riot** both in death toll and in property damage. It was triggered by a 4:00 a.m. police raid on an after-hours drinking club on the West Side. Seventy-three Blacks were arrested, and a crowd gathered. Tempers flared as rumors spread that a Black man had been beaten and a Black woman kicked by police. Enraged, the crowd began to throw rocks at the police and set fires. Soon an all-out riot erupted. In the wake of this riot forty were dead (thirty-three Blacks and seven Whites), more than two thousand were injured, at least five thousand were left homeless, and $500 million worth of property was destroyed.

**Divine** *See* Father Divine

**Douglass, Frederick** (c. 1818-1895) Frederick Douglass was born a slave in Tukahoe, Maryland. His birth name was Frederick Augustus Washington Bailey. At the age of eight he was sent to Baltimore to work for a relative of his master. There he began an extensive program of self-education. In 1838 he fled to freedom in New Bedford, Massachusetts. He changed his name to Frederick Douglass to avoid capture.

In 1841 Douglass spoke to the Massachusetts Anti-slavery Society about what freedom meant to him. His speech impressed the society so much that they hired him as a lecturer. During the early 1840s he actively protested the patterns of segregation and discrimination that surrounded him.

The year he published his autobiography (1845) he went to England, concerned that his identity as a runaway slave would be revealed. In England he continued to speak against slavery and was able to raise enough money to buy his freedom.

In 1847 Douglass returned to the United States and founded an antislavery newspaper, the *North Star*, in Rochester, New York. It was Douglass who first pointed out the systematic elimination of African-Americans from the skilled labor force in favor of European immigrants. He was also instrumental in desegregating the public schools in Rochester, facilitating the Underground Railroad (see *Harriet Tubman\**) and recruiting Blacks to fight in the Union Army.

**Du Bois, William Edward Burghardt** (1868-1963) W. E. B. Du Bois was a significant leader in the cause of justice in the early twentieth century. He was born in Great Barrington, Massachusetts, and in 1888 he graduated from Fisk University (Nashville, Tennessee). In 1895 he became the first African-American to earn a Ph.D. from Harvard University.

Du Bois was an important historian, and he pioneered the study of sociology. As a strong advocate of African-American civil and political rights, he made countless contributions to our advancement.

In 1900 he stated that the "color line" would be the number-one problem facing the world in the twentieth century. An advocate of Pan-Africanism, Du Bois organized several Pan-African conferences, both in the United States and in Europe. His views on the means of African-American progress were at loggerheads with those of *Booker T. Washington.\**

He was professor of history and economics at Atlanta University from 1897 to 1910. He left the university to become editor of *The Crisis* (magazine of the *National Association for the Advancement of Colored People,\** or NAACP). He held this position till 1934. Ten years later (1944) he resumed his faculty position at Atlanta University. In 1948 he once again took up his work with the NAACP.

Eventually Du Bois became disillusioned by the slow progress of African-Americans toward first-class citizenship. To him, entrenched American racism seemed impervious to the heroic battles waged against it. In the end he embraced the empty promises of communism. He later moved to Ghana (West Africa), where he died.

Among his outstanding literary works are *The Souls of Black Folks* (1903), *Black Reconstruction in America* (1935) and *The Autobiography of W. E. B. Du Bois* (1968).

**Emancipation** When the American Civil War broke out, many in the North (the Union) put great pressure on President Abraham Lincoln to free the slaves in the South (the Confederacy). However, Lincoln repeatedly insisted that the war was to "save the Union," not to free the slaves. He opposed slavery in the new western territories but had no intention of altering the situation where slavery was already established.

As the war dragged on, the Union suffered many setbacks. It was in desperate need of more soldiers. Blacks wanted to fight for the Union, but since captured slaves were considered "contraband," they had to be freed if they were to fight.

Also, there was a distinct possibility that Britain would intervene on the side of the Confederacy. Through the work of courageous committed Christians like William Wilberforce (1759-1833) and others, slavery had recently been abolished in the British Empire. Lincoln knew that Britain would not intervene if the Union made the abolition of slavery a major objective.

Therefore President Lincoln was coerced into declaring the end of slavery. However, to prevent it from appearing to be an act of desperation, Lincoln decided to make this proclamation after a major military victory for the Union. That victory came at the Battle of Antietam (September 17, 1862), the bloodiest battle of the war. Five days later, on September 22, Lincoln issued an initial proclamation: if the Confederate states did not return to the Union by January 1, 1863, he would proclaim the slaves "forever free."

The Confederacy did not comply, and the Emancipation Proclamation was issued as promised on January 1. Because Lincoln did not have the peacetime power to make this proclamation, he did it "as a fit and necessary war measure." Slavery continued in many areas, however, until the ratification of the *Thirteenth Amendment** on December 18, 1865.

**ethics** The study of how we are to obey God. Ethics is not a branch of theology but is equivalent to theology, because all theology answers ethical questions.

**evangelicals** People who, like *fundamentalists,** are associated with a belief in the so-called fundamentals of the faith. But unlike the fundamentalists, evangelicals generally have a broader view of *culture** and are a little more involved in cultural issues.

**existential** (not existentialism) Dealing with the application of truth to the needs of the moment; understanding what it means in terms of the present situation.

**faith** The proper response to the *gospel,** for which God holds every individual who hears it responsible. Faith is a reliance on God's *grace** alone for the solution to the human problem of unrighteousness and God's revealed wrath on humankind—a grace that is rooted in Christ. True faith is more than mere belief. It also includes (1) a complete turning away (repentance) from unrighteousness and all attempts to solve our problem with God by human means and (2) a complete submission to Christ as supreme Lord and ultimate authority. In essence, faith is the root of *righteousness.**

**Farmer, James** James Farmer is one of the great pioneers of the Civil Rights Movement. Born on January 12, 1920, in Marshall, Texas, Farmer showed great promise as a child. He was four years old when he entered first grade and fourteen when he entered Wiley College in his hometown. Initially intending to become a physician, he majored in chemistry. But he found that the sight of blood made him ill, and eventually he decided to enter the ministry. Farmer had a great concern for racial justice, and he saw the ministry as the best way to pursue this cause.

Having received his B.A. in the spring of 1938, he entered Howard

University (in Washington, D.C.) as a religion major in the fall of that year. Among his professors were Carter G. Woodson, Ralph Bunch and Howard Thurman. Thurman introduced Farmer to Mahatma Gandhi and his nonviolent strategies for freeing India from British colonial rule. During this time Farmer worked with the Fellowship of Reconciliation (FOR). Toward the end of his studies at Howard, Farmer began to despair about the grip of *White Christianity-ism** on large segments of the American church. He received his B.D. in 1941 but did not seek ordination as a Methodist minister. Instead he moved to Chicago and continued to work with FOR. Farmer's vision was to develop a national movement to combat racism based on Gandhi's principles of nonviolence.

Soon after his arrival in Chicago, Farmer organized the first "sit-in" demonstrations to end discrimination at a local restaurant. As his group continued to develop its nonviolent direct action strategy, it gained the attention of groups like the *National Urban League** and the *National Association for the Advancement of Colored People (NAACP).** There was such a widespread and enthusiastic response to this new weapon against racism that in 1943 a national organization was launched which became the *Congress of Racial Equality (CORE).** Farmer was elected national chairman.

When the Civil Rights Movement erupted onto the national scene with the Montgomery Bus Boycott in 1955-1956, Farmer was in great demand as an expert on the Gandhian nonviolent strategy. In 1961 Farmer planned and participated in the *Freedom Rides,** which ended segregation in buses and facilities used in interstate travel. During the height of the Civil Rights Movement he was the target of numerous death threats. He was unable to be at the 1963 March on Washington because he was in jail for his courageous civil rights activities.

Though Farmer was committed to nonviolence, he realized the implications of and need for Black consciousness; his close friendship with Malcolm X doubtless contributed to this awareness. However, for the growing numbers of militants in CORE, Farmer was not militant enough. His book *In Freedom—When?* was published in

1965. Eventually, under pressure Farmer resigned from CORE. He was succeeded by *Floyd McKissick.*\* Farmer then developed and headed a federally funded literacy program. But because of Farmer's opposition to American policy in the Vietnam War, President Lyndon B. Johnson sabotaged the program, blocking its funding.

In 1966, after a period of unemployment, Farmer accepted a teaching post at Lincoln University, a predominantly African-American institution near Philadelphia. In 1968 he ran for U.S. Congress in the twelfth district of Brooklyn, New York, as a candidate of both the Liberal and Republican parties. However, Farmer was defeated in the general election by Shirley Chisholm. Soon after the election, Farmer accepted a position in the Nixon administration as assistant secretary of administration in the Department of Health, Education and Welfare (HEW). By 1970, finding himself at odds with many of Richard M. Nixon's policies, he resigned.

Since then Farmer has been a much sought-after lecturer. He has campaigned tirelessly for racial justice, labor relations and senior citizens issues. In 1985 Farmer published his powerful autobiography, *Lay Bare the Heart.*

**Farrakhan, Louis** Louis Abdul Farrakhan was born Louis Eugene Walcott on May 11, 1933, in New York City. As a young man he became an accomplished musician, learning the guitar and the violin. He also displayed outstanding skills as an orator. In the early 1950s he enrolled at Winston-Salem Teachers College in North Carolina, but he did not graduate. Because he was a gifted preacher, his studies faded into the background as the demand for his ministry increased. Walcott eventually moved to Boston, where he became a guitar-playing calypso singer, calling himself "Calypso Gene." His lyrics were more concerned with politics and social issues than with love and relationships.

During his days as an entertainer, Walcott was recruited into the *Nation of Islam*\* by Malcolm X. After his conversion to Islam he adopted the name Louis X. Later *Elijah Muhammad*\* gave him the name Louis Farrakhan.

Farrakhan worked closely with Elijah Muhammad and quickly rose through the ranks. By 1963 Farrakhan had become chief minister of the Muslim temple in Boston. When Malcolm X broke with Elijah Muhammad and left the Nation of Islam, Farrakhan succeeded him as chief minister of Temple no. 7 in New York City. In 1972 Elijah Muhammad named Farrakhan national spokesman, another position once held by Malcolm X.

*Warith Deen Muhammad,*\* son of Elijah Muhammad, had left the Nation of Islam along with Malcolm X. But Warith Muhammad returned to the Nation of Islam in 1969, and his father restored him to the ministry in 1974. On February 25, 1975, Elijah Muhammad died of congestive heart failure. The following day the Nation of Islam pronounced Warith D. Muhammad the new leader.

Under the leadership of Warith Muhammad, the former Nation of Islam has become an orthodox community of American Sunni Muslims. In response to his restructuring, four reactionary factions broke off from the former Nation of Islam. They resisted the changes and held to the doctrines of Elijah Muhammad. Farrakhan was the leader of one of these factions. He broke with Warith Muhammad in December 1977 and founded the "Original Nation of Islam" (now known as the Nation of Islam).

Farrakhan has received a great deal of media attention for his inflammatory statements. Reporters continue to ask him about his alleged anti-Semitism. In reality, the doctrine Farrakhan subscribes to classifies all White people—Jews and Gentiles alike—as devils.

**Father Divine** (c. 1880-1965) As founder of the Peace Mission Movement, Father Divine aimed to end racial discrimination, stop war and abolish poverty. His real name was George Baker. Apart from the fact that he was born in Georgia, not much is known about his early life. He opened his first church in New York City in 1915 and soon took the name Major J. Divine, but his followers began to call him "Father Divine." In 1919 he bought a house in Sayville, New Jersey, and opened a free employment bureau. As he began to feed the poor, people came to his house in great numbers. Father Divine was known for serving great feasts and also gained a reputation for having healing powers.

Eventually he was arrested in New York for being a public nuisance (mainly because he had many well-educated White followers). When his case came before Justice Lewis J. Smith of the Supreme Court of Nassau County, he refused to cooperate with the trial. Father Divine was found guilty and sentenced to jail. Within one week, Justice Smith died of a sudden heart attack. Divine's sentence was later overturned by the appellate court.

This incident gave Father Divine the reputation of being omnipotent. He grew in popularity and triumphantly returned to Harlem in 1932. During the Great Depression he provided inexpensive food and clothing to the poor through a chain of stores and other businesses.

In 1942 he fled Harlem to avoid several embarrassing lawsuits and set up his headquarters in Philadelphia. After his death, however, the Peace Mission Movement lost much of its popularity.

**Five Percenters** Also known as the Five Percent Nation of Islam and the Five Percent Nation, this group traces its roots directly back to a man named Clarence 13X (Clarence Jowars Smith), a member of the Nation of Islam's Mosque No. 7 in Harlem. Clarence 13X taught that the Black man was the God of the universe and had his origins in Mecca. His iconoclastic teachings resulted in his suspension from the Nation of Islam in 1964. Subsequently he was the target of assassination attempts. He died under mysterious circumstances in 1969, at the age of forty. Those who followed 13X referred to him as "Father Allah." This group became the Five Percenters.

The Five Percenters agree with *Elijah Muhammad*'s* teaching that the White man is the devil, but they include all unscrupulous and deceitful people in this category, regardless of color. They also believe that the Black race was the original race and the creator of civilization.

For the Five Percenters the demographics of the African-American community break down as follows: the masses who are ignorant of their true "divine self," 85 percent; the corrupt rulers over the masses, 10 percent; and the truly righteous who are the followers of Father Allah, 5 percent.

Among rappers who propagated the doctrine of the Five Percenters in the late eighties and early nineties were King Sun, the Supreme Team, Lakim Shabazz, Rakim Allah, Brand Nubian and the Poor Righteous Teachers.

**Freedom Rides** Soon after the end of the post-Civil War Reconstruction (see *death blow to the Reconstruction**) in 1877, Southern state legislatures passed a series of laws called the "black codes" (see *Jim Crow backlash**). These statutes firmly established racial segregation throughout the Southern United States. In the early days of the *Congress of Racial Equality (CORE),** nonviolent direct action became a powerful weapon in the struggle against segregation. In 1946 discrimination in interstate transportation was declared unconstitutional; in the South, however, African-Americans were still subject to the humiliating practices of segregation. To call attention to the plight of African-American travelers, CORE, under the leadership of *James Farmer,** organized and sponsored a "Journey of Reconciliation," an integrated bus ride through the South. One of those who joined Farmer's group of protesters was *Floyd McKissick,** who would eventually become CORE's national director. Despite their nonviolence, the demonstrators experienced physical violence at the hands of angry Whites.

In 1961 CORE once again challenged racial segregation in interstate travel. On May 4, Farmer and twelve other Black and White demonstrators called "Freedom Riders" departed from Washington, D.C.; *Stokely Carmichael** and *John Lewis** were among them. The protesters encountered minor unpleasant incidents as they passed through Virginia, North Carolina, South Carolina and Georgia. In Alabama several of them were brutally beaten and their bus was firebombed. After this incident made front-page news around the world, over three hundred more joined in the demonstration. They were trained in the methods of nonviolent direct action and sent through Mississippi and Alabama on buses. In Jackson, Mississippi, many of the demonstrators were brutalized by the police, and many more were arrested. Farmer himself was incarcerated in the dreaded

Parchman State Penitentiary in Mississippi.

The Freedom Rides were successful. Soon afterward U.S. attorney general Robert F. Kennedy ordered the Interstate Commerce Commission to end segregation on buses and all facilities involved in interstate travel. As a result, about 120 bus terminals were immediately desegregated.

**fundamentalists** People who are associated with a belief in the so-called fundamentals of the faith, including the inspiration and inerrancy of the Scriptures, the virgin birth of Christ, the deity of Christ, the atoning work of Christ on the cross, the physical return of Christ and so on. Fundamentalists usually have a narrow view of *culture** and are generally not involved in cultural issues. Fundamentalists tend to emphasize personal salvation to the exclusion of the other aspects of the Great Commission.

**Garvey, Marcus** (1887-1940) Marcus Garvey was born in Jamaica, West Indies, where he attended high school. After leaving school he began to use his speaking and organizational skills to mobilize fellow Black Jamaicans to fight for their political rights. From 1911 to 1914 he attended college in England and traveled throughout Europe and North America. Later in 1914 Garvey founded and became president of the Jamaica Improvement Association. Two years later (1916) he arrived in Harlem, New York City.

In America Garvey's organization became the United Negro Improvement Association (UNIA). Its official colors were the now familiar red, black and green. The Garvey movement advocated Black pride, Black dignity and Black respect. Its slogan was "One Aim! One God! One Destiny!" Garvey believed that Blacks would never find justice in any country dominated by Whites. Reacting to the god of White *Christianity-ism,** he concluded that Black unity could be accomplished only on the basis of a Black God. He contended that Black people of the world needed to unite into a Black nation in Africa. He established the Black Star Shipping Line and several other businesses to help African-Americans emigrate to Africa.

By the early 1920s the Garvey movement had attracted an estimated two million followers, mostly poor Blacks in the urban North. The European colonial powers became alarmed about Garvey's intention to bring Africa under African-American and African control. Many Whites in America dubbed him subversive, while moderate Blacks (especially those who practiced the "Negro strategy") considered him a threat to their progress.

The Black Star Line fell victim to sabotage. Garvey himself was convicted of mail fraud in 1923, was sent to the federal penitentiary in Atlanta, Georgia, in 1926, was pardoned in 1927 and promptly returned to Jamaica. Without its flamboyant leader, the UNIA declined and disintegrated.

**generic** The basic essence of an idea; that is, the basic underlying pattern of, for example, religion.

**Giovanni, Nikki** Nikki Giovanni was born Yolande Cornelia Giovanni in Knoxville, Tennessee, on June 7, 1943. Her parents, Gus and Yolande, had met as students at Knoxville College. Nikki, the younger of two daughters, spent most of her childhood in Wyoming, Ohio, a suburb of Cincinnati.

In September 1960 Giovanni enrolled at Fisk University (Nashville), a predominantly African-American university. Her independent-mindedness and assertive manner did not win her many friends among authority figures at Fisk. She was placed on probation and eventually suspended. Ironically, at that time Giovanni's political and social philosophy could be described as "right-wing" and conservative. For example, in the 1964 presidential election she supported the candidacy of Barry Goldwater, a conservative Republican.

In 1964 Giovanni reentered Fisk University. She received her B.A. in history, graduating magna cum laude with honors, in February 1967.

Her change in political and social philosophy came while she was involved in the Fisk Writers' Workshop under the direction of John O. Killens, an outstanding author who had a major influence on her. Giovanni became a strong advocate for the Fisk chapter of the *Student Non-violent Coordinating Committee (SNCC).*\* She also organized the Cincinnati Black Arts Festival.

In the years that followed, Giovanni did graduate study at the University of Pennsylvania School of Social Work in Philadelphia and Columbia University School of Fine Arts in New York City. Later, she became assistant professor of English at Queens College of the City University of New York, teaching in the SEEK program. Since 1987 Giovanni has been a professor at Virginia Polytechnic Institute in Blacksburg.

Through her prose and poetry, Giovanni became a major player in the Black Consciousness Movement. Her philosophical journey continued from Black militancy to a more introspective and personal phase, a journey that is reflected in her succession of poetic volumes. Her militant phase was expressed in *Black Feeling, Black Talk* (1967) and *Black Judgement* (1968); her well-known poem *"The Great Pax Whitie"*\* appeared in the latter (the two books were republished in 1970 in one volume, *Black Feeling, Black Talk, Black Judgement*). Giovanni's introspective and personal phase is reflected in her books *Re-creation* (1970), *The Women and the Men* (1972), *My House* (1972), *Cotton Candy on a Rainy Day* (1978) and *Those Who Ride the Night Winds* (1983). Giovanni published three volumes of cleverly written children's poetry as well: *Spin a Soft Black Song: Poems for Children* (1971), *Ego-Tripping and Other Poems for Young People* (1973) and *Vacation Time: Poems for Children* (1980).

Giovanni also published several essays, including *Gemini: An Extended Autobiographical Statement on My First Twenty-five Years at Being a Black Poet* (1971), *A Dialogue: James Baldwin and Nikki Giovanni* (1973), *A Poetic Equation: Conversations Between Nikki Giovanni and Margaret Walker* (1974) and *Sacred Cows and Other Edibles* (1988). More recent works include *Appalachian Elders: A Warm Heart Sampler* (with Cathee Dennison, 1991), *Grandmothers: Poems, Reminiscents and Short Stories About the Keepers of Our Traditions* (1994) and *Racism 101* (1995).

**gospel** The good news that God through Christ has accomplished the solution to the human problem of unrighteousness and God's revealed wrath on humankind. The gospel reveals that God, by way of his Spirit, has delivered his people from his wrath and is developing

in them the will and the power to pursue his *righteousness*.* God
applies this salvation by his grace through *faith*—faith that is a gift
of God's *grace*.* In other words, the gospel tells us that God does
transform those who properly respond to him from the practice of
negative *religion*\* to positive religion.

**gospel music** A twentieth-century expression of the Black theological dynamic (*see* soul dynamic). Its roots go back to the *spirituals*\*
and the *blues*.* It often employs simple melodies and harmonies,
driving syncopated rhythms and repetitive pithy phrases, most of
which are imported directly from historic Southern Black theology.

Gospel music is celebrative and moving. By design it sweeps the
listener into a joyful and warm nostalgia regarding God's works of
grace. Today gospel music also incorporates *jazz, rhythm and blues,*\*
and even *rap.*\*

**grace (God's grace)** The unmerited favor of God toward humanity.

**"grace"** (always with quotation marks to distinguish it from God's
grace) The world of God and the angels—that is, the "sacred" world,
which has little to do with the "secular" world.

**Grace, Bishop Charles Emmanuel** *See* **"Daddy" Grace**

**"The Great Pax Whitie"**

In the beginning was the word
And the word was
Death
And the word was nigger
And the word was death to all niggers
And the word was death to all life
And the word was death to all
    peace be still

The genesis was life
The genesis was death
In the genesis of death
Was the genesis of war
    be still peace be still

In the name of peace
They waged the wars
   ain't they got no shame
In the name of peace
Lot's wife is now a product of the Morton company
   nah, they ain't got no shame

Noah packing his wife and kiddies up for a holiday
row row row your boat
But why'd you leave the unicorns, noah
Huh? why'd you leave them
While our Black Madonna stood there
Eighteen feet high holding Him in her arms
Listening to the rumblings of peace
   be still be still

CAN I GET A WITNESS? WITNESS? WITNESS?
He wanted to know
And peter only asked who is that dude?
Who is that Black dude?
Looks like a troublemaker to me
And the foundations of the mighty mighty
Ro Man Cat holic church were laid

   hallelujah jesus
   nah, they ain't got no shame

Cause they killed the Carthaginians
in the great appian way
And they killed the Moors
"to civilize a nation"
And they just killed the earth
And blew out the sun
In the name of a god

Whose genesis was white
And war wooed god
And america was born
Where war became peace
And genocide patriotism
And honor is a happy slave
cause all god's chillun need rhythm
And glory hallelujah why can't peace
    be still

The great emancipator was a bigot
    ain't they got no shame
And making the world safe for democracy
Were twenty million slaves
    nah, they ain't got no shame

And they barbecued six million
To raise the price of beef
And crossed the 16th parallel
To control the price of rice
    ain't we never gonna see the light

And champagne was shipped out of the East
While kosher pork was introduced
To Africa
    Only the torch can show the way

In the beginning was the deed
And the deed was death

And the honkies are getting confused
    peace be still

So the great white prince

Was shot like a nigger in texas
And our Black shining prince was murdered
like that thug in his cathedral
While our nigger in memphis
was shot like their prince in dallas
And my lord
ain't we never gonna see the light
The rumblings of this peace must be stilled
    be stilled be still

aah Black people
ain't we got no pride?

**Hampton, Fred, and Mark Clark** Fred Hampton, age twenty-one, was the chairman of the Illinois chapter of the *Black Panther Party.*\* Mark Clark, age twenty-two, was a key leader of the group. The chapter was located in Chicago's west side. The FBI, under the paranoid leadership of J. Edgar Hoover, infiltrated the group with an informer. The FBI became even more suspicious when the party instituted a breakfast feeding program for African-American school-children in the poor community. The Panthers' willingness to form a coalition with the Blackstone Rangers, a major street gang, served to exacerbate the suspicions of the FBI and the local police.

Eventually Hampton was arrested on dubious charges. While he was incarcerated, the police raided Black Panther headquarters in Chicago. The Panthers' attempt to resist the raid resulted in a hail of gunfire. In the wake of the raid, several party members and police were wounded. The police arrested seven Panthers and torched the headquarters.

In time Hampton was released from prison. However, tensions between the Black Panther Party and the police increased.

On December 4, 1969, at 4:45 a.m., the police raided Hampton's apartment. Hampton and Clark were killed. Seven other Panthers survived, but four of them were wounded. According to state's attorney Edward Hanrahan, the occupants of the apartment had opened fire on the police. However, this allegation was never established. An investigation revealed that all but one of the almost one hundred shots came from the police. According to all the evidence, this appeared to be an illegitimate police execution.

In the end all charges against the Black Panthers were dropped. The families of the apartment occupants sued the government for civil rights violations. After several years the Chicago police department, along with the state and federal governments, paid the plaintiffs an out-of-court settlement of $1.8 million.

**Harlem Renaissance** With the great migration of African-Americans to Northern urban centers came a more militant stance against racism and social injustice. The chosen outlets of expression were the creative arts. Thus the Harlem Renaissance emerged—a great proliferation of African-American prose, poetry and theater. This phenomenon was also called the Negro Renaissance or the New Negro Movement.

The Harlem Renaissance (which was not confined to Harlem) reached its peak in the 1920s. It was aided by the Association for the Study of Negro Life and History (now called the Association for the Study of Afro-American Life and History), founded by Dr. Carter Goodwin Woodson (1875-1950) in 1915. The renaissance was marked by a dramatic change from a creative philosophy of impressionism to one of expressionism.

Many Black writers from the 1870s to the 1920s had committed themselves to giving the general public the impression that Blacks were "respectable" because they shared the values of the White middle class. The arrival of the 1920s saw the emergence of the "Harlem School" of thought, a sense of racial pride and realistic self-expression regarding the raw realities of the Northern urban African-American experience. A major outlet for Black poets and writers during this period was a magazine called *Opportunity: Journal of Negro Life.*

Though the writings of *W. E. B. Du Bois*\* and *Frederick Douglass*\* eloquently articulated African-American issues, the larger White society had ignored them for the most part. This changed after 1912, when James Weldon Johnson (1871-1948) published *The Autobiography of an Ex-*

*Colored Man.* This work sparked national recognition of Black culture and set the precedent for a more honest self-expression. In 1913 Johnson followed up his national notoriety by publishing *Fifty Years,* a poem commemorating the fiftieth anniversary of the Emancipation Proclamation. After World War I he went on to publish *American Negro Poetry* and *God's Trombones,* a volume of folk poems.

Many regard Claude McKay (1889-1948) as the leading and most militant poet of the Harlem Renaissance. He articulated the gut-level realities of ghetto life in his works *Home to Harlem* and *Harlem Shadows.*

Philosopher Alain LeRoy Locke (1886-1954) did much to define this movement. In 1923 he published an anthology of Black writings called *The New Negro.* He described these writers as having a "deep feeling toward race" and a "consciousness of acting as the advanced guard of African peoples in their contact with 20th century civilization." Like Du Bois, Locke had Pan-African leanings.

A similar phenomenon was happening in Black theater. During World War I Black drama had been relegated to obscure theater houses. However, in the early 1920s hundreds of theaters and tent shows became showcases for live Black entertainment. Eventually these theaters were organized into the Theater Owners Booking Association (T.O.B.A.). Since it was their only outlet, many Black entertainers nicknamed T.O.B.A. "Tough On Black Asses."

Among the prominent theater companies of this period were the Ethiopian Art Players (Chicago), the Harlem Community Players and the Dunbar Players (both of Harlem), and the Krigwa Players (founded by Du Bois).

Among the outstanding individuals of this period were playwrights such as Garland Anderson, George Douglass Johnson, Willis Richardson and Eulalie Spence; singer/actor Paul Robeson; writers such as Ralph Waldo Ellison (author of *Invisible Man*), Claude McKay (poet), Richard Wright (author of *Native Son*), Langston Hughes (poet) and Jessie Fauset (who articulated the problems of the Black middle class). But in spite of the quality, productivity and popularity of these artists, they were never taken seriously by the American intellectual and artistic establishment.

Finally, the Harlem Renaissance was a major catalyst for a number of economic rights and civil rights organizations in the late 1920s and the 1930s, including the *National Urban League,* * the National Negro Business League and the Citizens' League for Fair Play.

**history**  A record of significant events of the past—events whose significance is determined by *consciousness.* *

**Iranian hostage crisis**  The crisis erupted on November 4, 1978, when a massive wave of angry Iranian protesters stormed the U.S. embassy in Tehran, taking its personnel hostage. Jimmy Carter was president.

The roots of the crisis go back to the early 1950s, when, with the help of the CIA, the Shah of Iran (a secular ruler) came to power. He quickly exiled most opposition leaders. One of these exiles was an aging Shiite Muslim cleric known as the Ayatollah Khomeini. For many years he lived in a villa outside Paris. As Islamic fundamentalism grew in Iran, the Shah's regime became more repressive.

Because the Shah was backed by the United States, as hatred for the Shah grew, so did hatred for America. In the days leading to the hostage crisis, hundreds of thousands of protesters marched on the U.S. embassy threatening violence and yelling, "Death to Carter! Death to America!"

The Ayatollah Khomeini became the living symbol of this growing movement, while the Shah came to symbolize anti-Islamic secularism and the "imperialistic influence of America, 'The Great Satan.' "

Eventually the fundamentalist movement overwhelmed the repressive power of the Shah. He fled the country days before the triumphal return of the Ayatollah. Out of concern for the embassy personnel, America refused to grant the Shah asylum. He ended up in Panama, where he discovered he was dying of cancer. For humanitarian reasons, the former Shah was then flown to a New York hospital to undergo surgery. It was his admission into the United States that provoked the protesters to storm the embassy.

Just days after the hostages were taken, the Ayatollah ordered the release of almost all of the African-Americans among them. The Iranian hostage crisis had a major effect on the 1980 presidential election, helping to facilitate the landslide victory of Ronald Regan. The remaining fifty-one hostages were finally released on the day of President Reagan's inauguration (January 20, 1981) after 444 days of captivity.

**Islam-ism** Non-Islamic religious practices expressed in the language of Islam—for example, those of the Nation of Islam.

**Jackson, Jesse Louis** On October 8, 1941, in Greenville, South Carolina, a child was born to a seventeen-year-old high-school student named Hellen Burns. She named him Jesse Louis Burns. His father was Noah Robinson, a middle-class neighbor with a family of his own. Hellen Burns eventually married Charles Henry Jackson, and in 1957 he adopted Jesse.

In 1959 Jesse Jackson entered the University of Illinois on a football scholarship. The following year he transferred to North Carolina Agricultural and Technical College, a predominantly African-American institution in Greensboro. There he excelled as an honor student, quarterback for the football team, president of the student body and officer in his fraternity.

While a student at North Carolina A & T, Jackson joined the Greensboro chapter of the *Congress of Racial Equality (CORE)\** and organized several civil rights demonstrations, including marches and sit-ins. His bold leadership won him the respect of many who were involved in the Civil Rights Movement. He was named field director of southern operations for CORE and elected president of the North Carolina Intercollegiate Council on Human Rights.

Jackson received his B.A. in 1964 and entered Chicago Theological Seminary on a Rockefeller grant. While in Chicago, he worked with the Coordinating Committee of Community Organizations.

In 1965, during the *Battle of Selma,\** Jackson joined the *Southern Christian Leadership Conference (SCLC).\** The following year he left seminary to work full time with SCLC. Jackson was instrumental in Dr. Martin Luther King Jr.'s Chicago campaign for open housing in

1966. That same year Jackson launched Operation Breadbasket, an SCLC organization designed to pressure White-owned businesses to hire African-Americans and to stock African-American-made products.

In 1969-1970 Jackson led a campaign at the Illinois capitol in Springfield to call attention to the problem of hunger. He also unsuccessfully ran for mayor of Chicago in 1971. That same year Jackson resigned from SCLC over a dispute with Ralph David Abernathy, then president of SCLC. Jackson then organized *People United to Save Humanity (PUSH).* * The objectives of PUSH were similar to those of Operation Breadbasket. One of the outstanding aspects of Jackson's new programs was PUSH-Excel, encouraging academic excellence and providing job-placement assistance for urban youth.

Between 1979 and 1984 Jackson emerged as a skilled negotiator on the international scene. For example, in 1984 he secured the release of Lieutenant Robert Goodman (Goodman, an African-American navy pilot, had been shot down and taken hostage by Syria). That year he also arranged the release of several political prisoners from Cuba.

In 1984 Jackson also ran for the Democratic presidential nomination. Though he did not win, he had a strong showing, capturing 3.5 million votes. In the 1988 presidential campaign Jackson proved to be a serious candidate in the New Hampshire primary election. On March 8, 1988, he won the "Super Tuesday" primaries with victories in five Southern states as well as the South Carolina caucuses. On March 15 he came in second in the Illinois caucuses, and on March 25 he won the Michigan primary. Though Michael Dukakis eventually prevailed and captured the nomination, Jackson's victories almost derailed Dukakis's campaign.

Later Jackson moved to Washington, D.C. There he was elected the "statehood senator," a largely ceremonial position created by the District of Columbia government to pressure Congress to grant statehood to the city.

**Jim Crow backlash** After President Rutherford B. Hayes ended the post-Civil War Reconstruction in 1877, the old Southern White elite reestablished White supremacy by various means, including terrorism. Many Whites believed that Blacks were inherently inferior and that the former slaves had made too much progress too fast. Thus by the late nineteenth century Southern state legislatures had passed "black codes," laws that created a racial caste system through segregation and political disenfranchisement. Soon every realm of Southern life was segregated, including public transportation, restaurants, schools, health-care institutions and even cemeteries. Having recently gained the right to vote, the former slaves were stripped of their voting rights through devices such as literacy tests, the poll tax and the grandfather clause.

All this became known as the "Jim Crow backlash." Jim Crow himself was a stereotyped Black character from an antebellum minstrel show. He had been popularized by a hit song written by Thomas R. Rice called "Jump Jim Crow." The first verse went as follows:

Come, listen, all you gals and boys,
I'm just from Tucky-hoe,
I'm goin' to sing a little song,
My name's Jim Crow.

The refrain continued:

Wheel about, an' turn about,
And do jis so;
Eb'ry time I wheel about,
I jump Jim Crow.

Even the federal government participated in the Jim Crow backlash. The U.S. Supreme Court declared the Civil Rights Act of 1875 unconstitutional. In 1896 the high court ruling in the *Plessy* v. *Ferguson* case affirmed the principle of "separate but equal."

**Jonestown tragedy** Jonestown was the name of a defunct settlement near Georgetown in Guyana. It was named after Jim Jones, a religious leader. Jones, a White man, started as a *fundamentalist\** preacher in Indiana and eventually became active in the cause of racial integration. Later he established the People's Temple in San Francisco. His constituents were poor and mostly African-American.

As time passed, Jones began to turn against God and the Bible and proclaim himself to be God. He became a tyrant, demanding unconditional loyalty as he fell into drug abuse and sexual perversions. Out of fear of nuclear war, Jones moved his congregation to rural California and finally to what became Jonestown, Guyana. It was in Guyana that Jones's philosophy became a strange mixture of fundamentalist rhetoric, Soviet-style communism and paranoid demagoguery.

When complaints began to filter out, an investigation was launched by U.S. Congressman Leo J. Ryan. On November 17, 1978, Ryan arrived in Jonestown with an investigative delegation of staffers, relatives of Jonestown residents and journalists. The next day, as Ryan, his delegation and some dissatisfied members of the congregation were departing Jonestown, they were ambushed and gunned down just as they were about to board their planes at the Port Kaituma airstrip. Several were wounded, and Congressman Ryan, NBC reporter Don Harris, NBC cameraman Robert Brown and *San Francisco Examiner* photographer Gregory Robinson were killed. Jones had ordered the murders.

In his paranoid irrationality, Jones then corraled the remaining members of Jonestown and mandated that they commit suicide by drinking Kool-Aid laced with cyanide. Some devoted followers went to their deaths willingly. Others were coerced at gunpoint. Minutes after this mass suicide, the eerie silence of Jonestown was shattered by a shot from an unknown assailant killing Jim Jones himself.

In the wake of Jonestown's demise, almost eight hundred corpses lay bloated and decomposing in the steaming Guyanese jungle. A handful of Jones's followers survived to tell the story.

**Ku Klux Klan (KKK)** The Klan is a terrorist secret society committed to intimidating and blocking the advance of Black people, Jews, Roman Catholics and other minority groups. They believe the White race is superior and intend to maintain its "purity." Because it erroneously claims to be Christian, the KKK represents White *Christianity-ism\** at its worst. Members wear robes and pointed hoods. Their symbol is the burning cross, and with it they try to intimidate their victims.

The Klan was started in 1865 in Pulaski, Tennessee, by several Confederate army veterans who wanted to keep African-Americans from exercising their voting and civil rights. They wanted to drive Blacks out of the political life of the South. When President Ulysses S. Grant sent federal troops to the South, the Klan disappeared. After these troops were withdrawn by President Rutherford B. Hayes, however, the Klan reemerged with a vengeance and became the spearhead of the *Jim Crow backlash.**The Klan and its sympathizers were key catalysts for the numerous lynchings of Blacks in the South.

Today the Klan is trying to project a respectable image, but its goals and methods have not changed.

**Lewis, John R.** John Robert Lewis is one of the unsung heros of the early days of the Civil Rights Movement. He was born in Troy, Alabama, on February 21, 1940. In his youth Lewis showed intense interest in serving God as a pastor. In his teens, having overcome a problem with stuttering, he preached regularly in pulpits throughout the Troy area. Lewis was most inspired by the weekly radio sermons of Martin Luther King Jr.

In 1957 Lewis moved to Nashville, where he attended the American Baptist Seminary. Later he transferred to Fisk University, a predominantly African-American institution in Nashville, where he received his B.A. in philosophy in 1967. In 1960, under the tutelage of James Lawson, Lewis and several other African-Americans had begun to conduct sit-in demonstrations at various "White only" lunch counters in Nashville. In spite of constant harassment and brutality from angry White citizens, Lewis and his companions continued to stage their protests. Soon other student protesters throughout the South joined forces and formed the *Student Non-violent Coordinating Committee (SNCC).**

Because of Lewis's unswerving dedication to nonviolence and the cause of civil rights, he emerged as a prominent leader of the movement. In 1965 he was elected chairman of SNCC. That same year Lewis played a key role in other historic protests, including the *Freedom Rides** and the *March on Washington.** Lewis also provided

courageous leadership in the early days of the *Battle of Selma**
(1964-1965).

In 1966 a more militant group within SNCC gained prominence
and elected *Stokely Carmichael** as the new chairman. Lewis soon
resigned from SNCC and returned to Nashville, where he became
director of community organization projects for the Field Foundation.
In 1970 Lewis moved to Atlanta and became director of the Field
Foundation's Voter Education Project (VEP). President Jimmy Carter
appointed Lewis as the director of U.S. operations for ACTION, a
federal agency coordinating community-based economic development programs.

Eventually, because Lewis wanted to be serving the poor more
directly, he became involved in politics. In 1982 he was elected to the
Atlanta City Council. As a city councilman, Lewis gained a reputation
for being sensitive to the needs of the poor and elderly. His compassion
won him the strong support of those he represented.

In 1986 Lewis won a special run-off election for the Democratic
nomination for the U.S. Congress, defeating his articulate and longtime SNCC ally Julian Bond. Lewis decisively won the general
election to represent the fifth congressional district.

**liberalism (theological)** A nineteenth-century movement that attempted to do *theology** without Scripture as a base. Liberalism was
not bound by the teachings of orthodox theology such as the infallibility of the Scriptures, the deity of Christ and the sovereignty of God.
According to liberalism, human social progress will result in an ideal
society. "Man come of age" became the rally phrase of liberalism early
in the twentieth century. But the horrors of World War I shattered its
optimistic assumptions. Today conservative Christians use this term
to refer to those whose view of the authority of Scripture, the deity of
Christ and the sovereignty of God is less strict than their own.

**March on Washington** The March on Washington (August 28,
1963) is generally considered the high point of the Civil Rights
Movement. Over 200,000 people from across America (including
Blacks and Whites) converged on the Lincoln Memorial in Washing-

ton, D.C. They came to spur Congress to pass the Civil Rights Bill, submitted by President John F. Kennedy. The march also dramatized the problem of Black unemployment. It was organized by the major civil rights organizations.

At the height of the gathering, Dr. Martin Luther King Jr. delivered his eloquent "I Have a Dream" speech. This speech electrified those at the Lincoln Memorial as well as many who viewed it on TV.

In 1964 the Civil Rights Bill was passed by Congress and was signed into law by President Lyndon B. Johnson. The phrase "I have a dream" became a major civil rights theme and legacy of Dr. King.

**Marshall, Thurgood** Thurgood Marshall is best known for his successful argument before the United States Supreme Court in the 1954 *Brown* v. *Board of Education of Topeka* case (see *segregation, unconstitutional\**), which banned racial segregation in the public schools. He is also known for his distinguished career as a Supreme Court justice. Marshall was born on July 2, 1908, in Baltimore, Maryland. In 1925 he enrolled at Lincoln University, a predominantly African-American institution near Philadelphia. There Marshall earned a reputation for being mischievous and was expelled twice for his fraternity pranks. In spite of this he graduated cum laude, receiving his B.A. in humanities in 1930. That year he entered Howard University's Law School, a predominantly African-American institution in Washington, D.C. At Howard, Marshall was inspired by Professor Charles H. Houston to commit himself to ending racial segregation in America.

In 1933 Marshall earned his LL.B., graduating first in his class. That year he was admitted to the Maryland Bar Association. He practiced law in Baltimore and became active with the *National Association for the Advancement of Colored People (NAACP)\** as a negotiator. After winning a case to desegregate the University of Maryland Law School, Marshall became the assistant special counsel for the NAACP's national office in New York City. In 1938 he was promoted to the position of head counsel. In this post Marshall championed the cause of desegregation across the country. He passionately opposed the detention of Japanese-Americans as potential enemies during World War II. In 1954 he led the NAACP's legal team in the case of *Brown* v. *Board of Education of Topeka.*

In 1961 President John F. Kennedy appointed Marshall as a judge in the Second U.S. Circuit of Appeals. In 1965 President Lyndon B. Johnson named him U.S. solicitor general. It was under Marshall that the Miranda rule was enacted (the requirement that police advise criminal suspects of their rights). In 1967 President Johnson nominated Marshall to the U.S. Supreme Court. In spite of bitter opposition from Southern Democratic senators, Marshall was confirmed on October 2, 1967.

After an outstanding and outspoken career on the Supreme Court and a succession of health problems, Marshall retired from the court on June 27, 1991. When asked by a reporter why he was retiring, he tersely retorted, "I'm old!" On January 24, 1993, Marshall died of a heart attack.

**McKissick, Floyd**  When the African-American struggle for freedom and dignity was beginning to take a more militant track, Floyd McKissick was a major force in the new movement. Often overshadowed by *Stokely Carmichael,** McKissick nevertheless played a major role in shaping the concept of Black Power. He was born Floyd Bixler McKissick in Asheville, North Carolina, on March 9, 1922. As he grew up in Asheville, he was greatly influenced by his father, who taught him the value of a good education. Both of his grandfathers were ministers who inspired him to develop his speaking ability.

Just after graduating from high school, McKissick was drafted into the army, and eventually he fought in World War II. After the war he studied at Morehouse College, a predominantly African-American institution in Atlanta, and then at North Carolina College, a predominantly African-American institution in Durham, where he received his B.A. During his time at North Carolina College he became youth chairman of the state chapter of the *National Organization for the Advancement of Colored People (NAACP).** McKissick was also involved in a new civil rights organization called the

*Congress of Racial Equality (CORE).**

When he applied to the University of North Carolina at Chapel Hill Law School, he was denied admission on racial grounds. McKissick sued for admission and won. He was represented by *Thurgood Marshall,** an NAACP lawyer. McKissick received his LL.B. in 1951. As an attorney, he defended numerous CORE sit-in demonstrators. As time passed, McKissick became increasingly concerned for those who were trapped and damaged by institutional racism. It bothered him that social change was slow in coming. Thus he began to espouse a power approach in combating racism.

In 1963 McKissick became national chairman for CORE, and in 1966 he succeeded *James Farmer** as national director. Under McKissick, CORE moved decisively toward Black Power. After two years as the head of CORE, however, he resigned and began planning to realize his dream for developing a planned Black community in North Carolina called Soul City. McKissick supported the 1968 presidential candidacy of Richard M. Nixon, and after Nixon won the election, Soul City was federally funded. However, the promised additional federal grants for Soul City never came. McKissick had envisioned Soul City growing to more than forty thousand residents, but its actual population came to only two hundred.

In the fall of 1990 he was named judge in the North Carolina Ninth District Court. In the spring of 1991 McKissick died of lung cancer and was buried in his beloved Soul City.

**melting pot** By the mid-1880s, the Industrial Revolution in the Northern United States was well under way. Because of trade skills acquired during slavery, recently emancipated African-Americans were ideally suited for the skilled jobs demanded by industrialization.

However, Northern racism led to the rise of White-only trade unions. Thus African-Americans were systematically eliminated from the skilled labor force. To make up the labor shortage, Europeans seeking jobs and a better way of life were encouraged to immigrate to the United States. Massive immigration resulted.

Whites sought a way to "Americanize" these immigrants and

preserve White American culture. Hence the melting-pot concept was developed, and all immigrants were pressured to forsake their cultural roots and assimilate into the American way of life. Of course, this "way of life" was largely defined by British and northern European (Protestant) cultural values. The more one's indigenous culture contained these values, the greater one's ability to "melt." Those from other parts of the world who tried to "melt" found it difficult or impossible.

**Memphis Speech** This last speech by Dr. Martin Luther King Jr. was made on April 3, 1968, at a rally in support of a sanitation workers' strike in Memphis, Tennessee. The main issue was the poverty-level wages the workers were being paid. The strike began after two workers were killed on the job and their families were denied compensation.

Because these workers were African-Americans, this labor struggle became a struggle against the White power structure. At the time of Dr. King's speech, the strike had lasted for about three months.

The day after the speech (April 4) a sniper shot and killed King as he stood on the balcony of the Lorraine Motel in Memphis. The assailant was later identified as James Earl Rey, a White man. Rey fled the country. Eventually he was arrested overseas, returned to the United States, tried, convicted and sentenced to ninety-nine years in the Tennessee State Prison.

In 1978 a special committee of the U.S. House of Representatives concluded that it was likely that Rey had had substantial help from others. To date no one has offered a plausible alternative explanation for how he obtained the resources needed to remain at large as long as he did.

**Memphis to Jackson March** In the spring of 1966, in spite of the Voting Rights Act of 1965, African-American voter registration in the Mississippi Delta (the northwest corner of the state) was minimal at best. Black Mississippians were still in a state of forced economic dependence on the White power structure. Thus they were intimidated out of registering to vote for fear of economic reprisals.

To encourage these African-American citizens to register, James

Meredith (the first African-American to be admitted to the University of Mississippi) staged a "march against fear." Meredith began his march on June 5 in Memphis, Tennessee, and planned to finish in Jackson, the capital of Mississippi—a distance of 208 miles (333 kilometers). Two days into the march, however, Meredith was gunned down by a White bigot.

The *Southern Christian Leadership Conference (SCLC),* \* the *Student Non-violent Coordinating Committee (SNCC)*\* and other civil rights groups quickly convened and decided to continue the walk to Jackson in Meredith's honor. They started at the spot where the shooting took place. It was at a rally in Greenwood, the halfway point in the march, that *Stokely Carmichael*\* introduced the slogan "Black Power."

In spite of significant and violent opposition from many White Mississippians, the march gathered momentum and successfully concluded in Jackson on June 16, nineteen days after the shooting.

Meredith survived the attack, was hospitalized and eventually fully recovered, though early news reports stated that he had been killed.

As a result of the march, thousands of African-American Mississippians registered to vote.

**Million Man March** As the 1990s dawned, it became apparent that the quest for freedom and dignity was heating up again. The surviving civil rights leaders from the 1960s had taken the quest as far as they could go. There had been several reenactments of significant events in the Civil Rights Movement, including a commemorative march on Washington in August 1983 (the twentieth anniversary of the original *March on Washington*\*). But the spiritual dimension had not been recaptured.

It was obvious that the next phase in our quest had to be spiritual in nature. But the church continued to stay within the bounds of its traditional concerns—missing a golden opportunity to shape the next phase. A theological and leadership vacuum developed.

*Louis Farrakhan,*\* leader of the *Nation of Islam,*\* sensed this vacuum and sought to fill it. Sometime in late 1994 or early 1995 he began to call for a million African-American men to march on Washington, D.C., on October 16, 1995. The march was billed as "a day of atonement and reconciliation." It was to be a day when African-American men were to "atone for their sins," such as absentee fatherhood and disrespect of women. It was also a day for African-American men to "reconcile themselves to God." Women were encouraged to support the men by staying home. Though the terms *atonement* and *reconciliation* are biblical and appealing to Christians, Farrakhan's meaning was not Christian. According to Scripture, for humans to "atone for their sins" would require a perfect sacrifice. This is impossible for fallen humanity. The only perfect sacrifice in history was made by Jesus Christ (who lived a perfect life) as he died on the cross, atoning for the sins of the world. Furthermore, human beings are unable to "reconcile themselves to God." It is only God who can reconcile us to himself in the perfect righteousness of Jesus Christ.

The march itself was a great success. The National Park Service estimated the attendance at 400,000, but researchers from Boston University, using digital technology, estimated the crowd at 870,000. As an eyewitness, I would agree with the latter estimate as a minimum. The atmosphere at the orderly march was very positive, profoundly affecting all who attended.

At the height of the march, Louis Farrakhan addressed the crowd with a rambling speech that lasted two hours and twenty minutes. (By comparison, Martin Luther King Jr.'s "I Have a Dream" speech lasted only nineteen minutes.) As Farrakhan addressed the participants, he likened himself to a prophet through whom God had called them together.

Those who did not participate in the march had good reason—their concern being Louis Farrakhan and his controversial message. Those who chose to participate also had good reason—to stand with a million men determined to be more righteous. "This isn't a *Farrakhan* thing, it's a *Black* thing!" was a statement frequently heard among the participants. After the march hundreds of thousands of African-American men made moral resolutions to improve their lives.

It is apparent that God's Spirit has moved on men of all races across the United States to "hunger and thirst for righteousness." The awesome turnout for the Million Man March and the tremendous growth of the Promise Keepers movement reveal this phenomenon.

The leaders of Promise Keepers have made a sincere and strong commitment to racial reconciliation. For this we can be truly thankful. It is unfortunate that Promise Keepers, being an evangelical movement, has inherited a legacy it does not want and did not create—evangelicalism's perceived cavalier attitude toward racism. Thus when Promise Keepers made its genuine call to men to stand for righteousness, as far as many African-American men were concerned the negative reputation of evangelicalism overpowered the message. Though Farrakhan's message was fraught with racist overtones and innuendoes, for many African-Americans his voice was not nearly as obstructed as the evangelical voice. Hence when Farrakhan's call went out for a "day of atonement and reconciliation," it resonated with African-American men's desire for righteousness.

**Muhammad, Elijah** (1897-1975) Robert Poole was born in Sandersville, Georgia, the son of an itinerant Baptist minister. In the rural Georgian educational system he managed to get as far as the fourth grade—a significant accomplishment in those days. In 1923, in pursuit of a better way of life, he and his family moved to Detroit, Michigan. In 1931 Poole met W. D. Fard, a mysterious White man of Turkish origins, founder of the Temple of Islam. Poole soon became First Minister of Islam and changed his name to Elijah Muhammad. After Fard's disappearance in 1934, Elijah Muhammad became leader of the sect and assumed the title "Messenger of Allah" until his death. He also changed the name of the organization to the *Nation of Islam.*\* During World War II he served a four-year prison term (1942-1946) for refusing to register for the draft. He was succeeded by his son, Warith Deen Muhammad.

**Muhammad, Warith Deen** Warith Deen Muhammad is best known as the titular head of American Sunni Muslims. He was born Wallace D. Muhammad, son of Elijah Muhammad, on October 30, 1933. Not much is known about his early life. He was trained as a welder at the University of Islam, a small elementary and high school run by the *Nation of Islam*\* in Chicago. Before he was born, W. D. Fard, founder of the Temple of Islam, the forerunner of the Nation of Islam, had predicted that Elijah Muhammad's next child would be a boy and would succeed his father. This turned out to be Warith.

Warith Muhammad became close friends with Malcolm X, and together they discovered that the teachings of Elijah Muhammad were non-Qur'anic. Warith left the Nation with Malcolm. After Malcolm's assassination, Warith drifted in and out of the Nation for several years. In 1969 his father restored him to the Nation of Islam and in 1974 to the ministry, giving him freedom to preach what he pleased. Elijah Muhammad died February 25, 1975, and the following day the Nation pronounced Warith D. Muhammad its new leader.

Under Warith Muhammad's leadership, Nation of Islam went through several name changes and was transformed into an orthodox community of Sunni Muslims. During this transition several factions broke with Warith Muhammad and started their own sects, reestablishing the old teachings of Elijah Muhammad. Among these defectors was *Louis Abdul Farrakhan*.\* Warith Muhammad's organization, now known as the American Muslim Mission, was decentralized in 1985.

**Nation of Islam** It is easy to identify the Nation of Islam only with *Louis Farrakhan*.\* However, since 1978 at least five distinct Muslim groups have sprung up in the African-American community, each calling itself "Nation of Islam." Following is a brief history of how they came about.

Clarence 13X was a member of the Nation of Islam's Temple No. 7. He began to teach that the Black man was the God of the universe and had his origins in Mecca. His iconoclastic teachings resulted in his suspension from the Nation of Islam. In 1964 he founded the Five Percent Nation of Islam (also known as the "Five Percent Nation" or the "*Five Percenters*\*"). In 1969 Clarence 13X died of suspicious causes at the age of forty. Those who followed him referred to him as "Father Allah."

On February 25, 1975, *Elijah Muhammad\** died of congestive heart failure. The following day the Nation held its annual Savior's Day Rally in his honor. There *Warith D. Muhammad\** (son of the late Elijah Muhammad) was named the new leader. Under his leadership, the former Nation of Islam became an orthodox community of Sunni Muslims.

In spite of the reforms of Warith Muhammad, there remained four reactionary factions within this Muslim community. They resisted the changes and held to the doctrine of Elijah Muhammad.

The leader of the first splinter group was Silas Muhammad. In 1976 he broke with Warith Muhammad and founded the "Lost, Found Nation of Islam," restoring all of Elijah Muhammad's myths and teachings.

Louis Farrakhan broke with Warith Muhammad in December 1977 and founded the Nation of Islam. Farrakhan now refers to himself as the "National Spokesman for the Honorable Elijah Muhammad."

Another leader of a splinter group was John Muhammad. In 1978 he broke with Warith Muhammad and founded a new "Nation of Islam." Finally, in 1978 Caliph Emanuel broke with Warith Muhammad and founded yet another "Nation of Islam."

**National Association for the Advancement of Colored People (NAACP)** The NAACP is the oldest existing civil rights organization in the United States. It was founded in 1909. In 1910 it began publishing *The Crisis* magazine. From its founding until World War II the NAACP was primarily concerned with halting lynchings and other acts of violence against African-Americans. It also fought job discrimination and other legal barriers to racial equality. The organization sought to do all this through litigation and legislation.

After the war Thurgood Marshall, an NAACP lawyer who would later be the first Black Supreme Court justice, successfully argued against segregation before the Supreme Court. The decision was *Brown* v. *Board of Education of Topeka* (Kansas).

During the height of the Civil Rights Movement, the NAACP added direct action to its repertoire of strategies. The organization was instrumental in the passage of several key civil rights bills in Congress, among them

☐ the Civil Rights Act of 1957, which established the Civil Rights Division of the Justice Department and the Commission on Civil Rights

☐ the Civil Rights Act of 1964, which forbade racial discrimination in public places and established the Equal Employment Opportunity Commission (EEOC)

☐ the Voting Rights Act of 1965, which eliminated the barriers against Black voter registration in the South

**National Urban League** This organization, founded in 1910, is mainly focused on fighting racial discrimination and enhancing the economic and political power of African-Americans and other minorities. It seeks to influence national policy regarding equal employment and welfare reform. The Urban League is also active in community programs including job training, job placement, health care, housing and voter education. Its research on the challenges facing the African-American community has been a valuable contribution to our struggle for freedom and dignity.

**"nature"** (always with quotation marks) The world of people and their environment—that is, the "secular" world, which is independent from the "sacred" world.

**neo-orthodoxy** This early-twentieth-century response to liberalism affirmed many theological formulations that sounded more traditional and orthodox. In many cases it reaffirmed the centrality of the Bible for theological reflection. More conservative theologians dubbed the movement "neo-orthodoxy," however, because they believed that adherents held an inadequate doctrine of revelation and yielded too much ground to modern critical theories of the Bible.

**Neo-Pan-Africanism** Pan-Africanism was a movement that emerged in the antebellum North. From the founding of the Free African Society in 1787, Christian thinkers began to affirm a strong kinship with all people of African descent. Concurrent with this was a great deal of interest in African-American nationalism and African identity. This movement became a major force in the 1840s and 1850s and shaped both the *theology\** and the early concept of missions in the Northern indigenous African-American church. It also influenced the ministry of the African-American church during Reconstruction.

Among the leaders of the movement were the Reverend James Theodore Holly, the Reverend Martin Robinson Delany and the Reverend Alexander Crummell. (Crummell was a major influence on *W. E. B. Du Bois.\**) They advocated the formation of a strong Black nation and the spiritual and economic "uplift" of Africa. For them biblical truth was the key to accomplishing these goals.

The foundations of the movement were laid in the mid-1820s by leaders such as the Reverend Nathaniel Paul, who advocated the return of African-Americans to participate in Africa's "regeneration." He believed that the descendants of Africa would return to their motherland and spread the gospel of Christ.

Thus, contrary to popular thought, Pan-Africanism originally emerged from the African-American church. The Pan-Africanism that emerged in the Black movement, however, had a radically different foundation and philosophy, namely secular humanism and Marxism. Hence I refer to this later movement as Neo-Pan-Africanism.

**New York 13** On April 2, 1969, several members of the New York chapter of the *Black Panther Party\** were rounded up in a series of predawn police raids. Twenty-one in all were arrested in the sweep. They were charged with plotting to bomb commuter train facilities, five department stores and the New York Botanical Gardens. They were indicted on thirty counts of arson, conspiracy, possession of dangerous weapons, attempted murder and several other charges. Most people came to call them the "Panther 21."

Thirteen of these defendants (eleven men and two women) were tried together and became known as the "New York 13." If they had been convicted on all the charges, each of them would have faced 309 years in prison.

The trial became a spectacle peppered with diatribes hurled back and forth. Presiding Judge John M. Murtagh seemed bent on preserving the status quo, while the defendants were determined to dramatize the "corruptness" of the legal system by making a mockery of it.

The trial lasted for eight months and cost $2 million—the longest and most expensive trial in New York history. Yet when the case went to the jury in May 1971, they took only ninety minutes to return a not guilty verdict on all charges.

Because of the prohibitively high bail set by the court, many of the "New York 13" had been incarcerated for well over a year in the dreaded Manhattan Men's House of Detention, also known as "The Tombs."

**Newton, Huey P.** Huey Percy Newton (1942-1989) was a charismatic leader who came to symbolize the ideals of the Black revolution. Born in Monroe, Louisiana, on February 17, 1942, Newton grew up surrounded by poverty in Oakland, California. At an early age he began to display antisocial behavior. Suspended from school dozens of times, at the age of fourteen he was arrested for gun possession. He managed to finish high school but was left functionally illiterate. Inspired by his older brother, who had earned a masters degree, Newton overcame his academic handicap and earned an associate degree at Merritt College in Oakland. At Merritt he met *Bobby Seale,** with whom he cofounded the *Black Panther Party** in October 1966. Seale became chairman of the party, and Newton was appointed minister of defense.

Newton and other leaders of the Black Panthers increasingly came under police surveillance and harassment. In the fall of 1968 he was convicted of voluntary manslaughter in a shootout that resulted in the death of an Oakland police officer. During his incarceration, "Free Huey" was a rallying cry for many radical groups. In 1970 Newton's conviction was overturned. Upon his release he resumed his leadership role in the party. After two subsequent trials failed to bring a conviction, the charges against him were dropped.

In 1980 he earned a Ph.D. in social philosophy from the University of California at Santa Cruz. By then, however, his life had begun to deteriorate. The Black Panther Party had disintegrated. In 1974 Newton himself had fled to Cuba for three years because he was implicated in the murder of a seventeen-year-old prostitute. Upon his return to the United States in 1977, Newton was tried twice for murder, but the charges against him were dropped because of deadlocked juries. Eventually Newton was convicted of weapons violations and pleaded no contest to the charge of misappropriation of Black Panther funds. He was later charged with parole violation for possession of narcotics paraphernalia. Huey Newton's life came to a violent and tragic end on August 22, 1989. He was shot dead by a twenty-five-year-old drug dealer outside an Oakland "crack house" in a drug deal gone bad.

**Niagara Movement** The forerunner of the *National Association for the Advancement of Colored People (NAACP),** the Niagara Movement was established to fight racism in the United States. It clearly identified the White community as the cause of America's racial problems, demanded Black voting rights, fought school segregation and worked for the election of candidates who were committed to ending racial discrimination. At one time it had thirty chapters in several U.S. cities.

At the time  many African-Americans considered the Niagara Movement too m itant. Thus the organization never attracted a broad base of support, and it lasted only six years (from 1905 to 1910). However, many ideas of the Niagara Movement were incorporated into the strategy of the more moderate NAACP.

**non-Whiteness** The absence of European characteristics and perspectives (*see* Whiteness).

**Pan-Africanism** *See* Neo-Pan-Africanism

**Parks, Rosa** Rosa Louise McCauley Parks is widely regarded as the "mother of the Civil Rights Movement." She was born on February 4, 1913, in Tuskegee, Alabama, where she grew up. She attended Alabama State College, a predominantly Black college in Montgomery. She married Raymond Parks in 1932, and together they became active in the *National Association for the Advancement of Colored People (NAACP).** In 1955 Rosa Parks found employment as a tailor's assistant at Fair Department Store in Montgomery. She also became a part-time seamstress for Virginia Durr, a White political activist who was sympathetic to the civil rights cause.

Montgomery's segregated bus system was particularly demeaning to African-Americans. The "colored section" was in the back of each bus. Blacks had to enter through the front door, pay their fare, exit the front door, then reenter through the rear door. After they paid their fare, it was common for White bus drivers to drive away before they could reenter the bus. When the "White" seats were full, the bus driver would enlarge the "White section," displacing those seated in the "colored section."

To challenge these humiliating policies, a test case was needed. That opportunity came in March 1955, when a fifteen-year-old high-school student named Claudette Colvin was arrested for refusing to give up her seat to a White passenger. The NAACP met and prepared to organize a bus boycott. But when Colvin discovered she was pregnant, the proposed bus boycott was called off. Just five minutes of intercourse thus kept buildings, streets and institutions from being named after Colvin as the "mother of the Civil Rights Movement." Those five minutes changed the course of history.[2]

On December 1, 1955, the second opportunity to challenge Montgomery's segregated bus system came. Too tired to move, Parks refused to give up her seat to a White man when the "White section" was enlarged to include her seat. Mrs. Parks was arrested and fined fourteen dollars. Because of this incident she lost her job at Fair Department Store, but it was the spark that ignited the 381-day Montgomery Bus Boycott—a boycott that launched the Civil Rights Movement.

In 1957 Raymond and Rosa Parks moved to Detroit, Michigan. There Mrs. Parks continued her career as a seamstress. Eventually Congressman John Conyers hired her as a staff assistant.

In 1969 Detroit's 12th Street was renamed in Rosa Parks's honor. In 1980 the Martin Luther King Jr. Center for Non-violent Social Change awarded her the Martin Luther King Jr. Non-violent Peace Prize. That same year the readers of *Ebony* magazine chose her as the living Black woman who had contributed most to the advancement of African-Americans. Over the years since the Montgomery Bus Boycott, Mrs. Parks has received scores of other awards and honorary degrees. In 1987 she founded the Rosa and Raymond Parks Institute of Self Development, a career training institution for African-American youth.

**People United to Save Humanity (PUSH)** From 1966 to 1971 the Reverend Jesse Louis Jackson was the director of the *Southern Christian Leadership Conference's** Operation Breadbasket. Under his leadership the organization successfully persuaded several White-owned companies to hire African-Americans and to sell African-American-made products. In 1971, however, the Reverend Jackson resigned from Operation Breadbasket and founded PUSH, an organization with similar goals and objectives. In 1976 PUSH launched the PUSH Excel program. Its aim was to inspire and empower African-Americans toward excellence in education.

In 1984 Jackson resigned from PUSH to run for the Democratic Party's presidential nomination.

**post-Martin riots** The hardest-hit cities in the 1968 riots were Baltimore; Chicago; Kansas City, Missouri; and Washington, D.C. In all, these riots (along with riots in 121 other cities) resulted in forty-six deaths, more than twenty-six hundred injuries and $45 million in property damage.

**Prohibition** The idea of Prohibition, a ban on alcoholic beverages in America, can be traced back to the colonial years. However, it was encapsulated in the charter of the Prohibition Party, organized in 1869 in Chicago. The party was never politically successful, but its philosophy influenced other social institutions. The ascendancy of Prohibition was largely due to the influence of *fundamentalism.** It generally increased in popularity through World War I and culminated in the passage of the Eighteenth Amendment, which banned the manufacture, importation, exportation, transportation and sale of alcoholic beverages. Among the fundamentalist groups that became identified with Prohibition was the Women's Christian Temperance Union.

As it turned out, national Prohibition was unenforceable. It never succeeded in eliminating the alcoholic beverage industry. It only drove the industry underground, facilitating the proliferation of organized crime. Prohibition was repealed in 1933 by the Twenty-first Amendment. This represented a major repudiation of the cultural influence of fundamentalism.

**racism in the Muslim world** There are numerous examples of negative stereotypes about Black people in the Muslim world. "The most frequent are that the black is stupid, that he is vicious, unfaithful and dishonest, that he is dirty in his personal habits and emits an evil smell. The black's physical appearance is described as ugly, distorted, or monstrous."[3]

A tenth-century Muslim "man of discernment" described Black Africans as "overdone in the womb until they are burned, so that the child comes out something between black, murky, malodorous, stinking, and crinkly-haired, with uneven limbs, deficient minds, and depraved passions."[4]

**rap** Rap employs a heavy rhythm line with intense, rapid-fire lyrics that are recited, not sung. The content of the recitation tends to be protest, a sharp commentary about some social ill or doctrinaire message. The tone of rap is most often angry.

There is considerable disagreement about whether rap can be classified as music.

**Reformed** A position associated with the classic creeds and confessions of the Reformation. While Reformed Christians essentially agree with *fundamentalists** and *evangelicals** in regard to the so-called fundamentals of the faith, they distinguish themselves from these other groups by their highly rational theological systems which deal with many aspects of life and *culture.* * Reformed Christians are usually quick to point out that their *theology** gives greater weight to the sovereignty of God than does the stance of their evangelical and fundamentalist counterparts. However, by and large this well-worked-out view of the Great Commission remains theoretical for them; it has yet to be fully worked out in real life.

**religion** The human response to the revelation of God's wrath or its effects. Religion can be positive or negative. Positive religion seeks God and his solution. Negative religion tries to avoid God and seeks its own solution. Positive religion is accomplished by God's *grace,* * and negative religion is carried out by human effort.

**rhythm and blues (R & B)** Another name for R & B is "soul music." Its roots are in the big band swing music of the 1940s and the *blues.* * Rock 'n' roll emerged from it. When White rock 'n' roll (often called "rockabilly") split off into its own musical genre, the Black branch became known as R & B.

In its heyday (the late 1950s through the mid-1960s) R & B was most influenced by the "Motown sound," characteristic of artists such as The Temptations, Diana Ross and The Supremes, The Impressions, and Smokey Robinson and The Miracles.

**righteousness** The perpetual pursuit of God and his revelation in every area of life, both individually and corporately. It consists of seeking to live by the principles of the kingdom of God—principles that manifest themselves in qualities such as justice, equality, integrity, compassion, grace and love. Righteousness is the fulfillment of god-liness and liberation. Without the pursuit of righteousness, neither godliness nor liberation is possible. Righteousness is also the fruit of *faith.* *

**Rodney King incident** In Los Angeles, late on the evening of March 2, 1991, policemen ordered a Black motorist named Rodney King to pull over. King attempted to flee the scene in his car. A high-speed chase ensued. Just after midnight on March 3, King was overtaken by several White police officers and stopped. He was ordered out of his car, but as he emerged the policemen felt it necessary to subdue him by force. King was dealt fifty-six blows with police batons and was kicked and stomped on. He sustained life-threatening injuries and subsequently required extensive hospitalization.

The beating was secretly captured on videotape and later broadcast The world was stunned by this display of brutality.

The police officers were tried for the use of excessive force.

However, at the request of the defense, the venue for the trial was changed from Los Angeles to Simi Valley (a middle-class and upper-middle-class, predominantly White suburb). On April 29, 1992, the mostly White jury acquitted the four officers of all but one charge, and there was a hung jury on that one.

The world was outraged by the verdict. To residents of South Central Los Angeles this case demonstrated that "the system" was still racist and unjust. The Rodney King incident ignited smoldering frustrations. As a result, riots erupted in Los Angeles—the worst in American history thus far—and lasted from the day of the verdict until May 3. Unlike the rioters of the sixties, these rioters and looters were racially and ethnically integrated. Over sixty people were killed, and over $700 million worth of property was destroyed. Violent incidents also broke out in Atlanta, San Francisco, Seattle, Pittsburgh and other cities. Many warned that this was the beginning of a new wave of urban riots.

**Scopes trial** In 1925 John T. Scopes, a high-school biology teacher in Dayton, Tennessee, was accused of teaching Charles Darwin's theory of evolution in violation of a newly passed state law prohibiting "high school and college teachers from teaching any theory which denies . . . creation." The prosecution team featured such notables as William Jennings Bryan, a leading *fundamentalist** lawyer and political leader. The defense included Clarence Darrow The trial attracted worldwide attention.

The trial came to a climax when Bryan allowed Darrow to interrogate him as a hostile witness for the defense. This proved to be a fiasco for Bryan. Through intense and clever questioning about the Bible, Darrow revealed Bryan's inadequate intellectual savvy. The larger fundamentalist movement was disgraced.

In the end, Scopes was found guilty and fined one hundred dollars. But the trial was a blow from which fundamentalism never recovered. The fundamentalists won the battle but lost the war, as their cultural and intellectual respectability plunged in the years following.

**Seale, Bobby** On October 22, 1936, Robert George Seale was born to poverty-stricken parents in Dallas, Texas. Eventually the Seale family settled in Oakland, California. Bobby Seale dropped out of high school and joined the U.S. Air Force; however, after a three-year stint he was discharged for bad conduct. Upon his return to Oakland, he finished high school and found employment in several aircraft plants.

In 1959 Seale enroled at Merritt College (in Oakland), where he joined the Afro-American Association (AAA). This Black nationalist campus group advocated self-reliance and separation from White society. Seale met *Huey Newton** through the AAA in September 1962. His close friendship with Newton shaped and sharpened his philosophy of Black revolutionism.

Eventually Seale saw AAA's program as ineffective, particularly for those trapped in the ghetto. He was attracted to Malcolm X's call to armed resistance as the vehicle for freedom from White racism. For Seale, the force of arms was the great equalizer for the ghetto masses as they faced the realities of White power. The assassination of Malcolm X in 1965 exacerbated Seale's rage at the White power structure. As a result, in 1966 he and Huey Newton founded the *Black Panther Party.**

As chairman of the Black Panthers, Seale saw solidarity among radical groups as the key to fighting racism. Thus in 1968 he founded the Peace and Freedom Party, a coalition with several White radical groups.

Seale was a participant in the notorious anti-Vietnam War demonstration at the 1968 Democratic National Convention (Chicago). At this protest the actions of the police quickly degenerated into brutality, and that triggered rioting among the demonstrators. Seale along with seven others was indicted for inciting to riot. Among his fellow defendants were Jerry Rubin and Abby Hoffman (founders of the Youth International Movement, better known as the Yippies) and Tom Hayden and Bennie Davis (founders of Students for a Democratic Society, the SDS). On September 24, 1969, these radical leaders, known as the "Chicago Eight," went on trial before U.S. district judge Julius Hoffman.

Shortly before the trial, Seale asked for a postponement to give his attorney, Charles Garry, a chance to recover from surgery. Judge Hoffman denied Seale's request. Eventually, on the advice of his attorney, Seale requested permission to be his own legal counsel. Hoffman denied this request also.

Because Seale believed the judge's actions violated his constitutional rights, he disrupted the courtroom proceedings by repeated diatribes against Hoffman. Finally the judge had Seale bound to his chair with handcuffs and leg irons and gagged with cloth and tape. In spite of this, Seale continued to disrupt the proceedings. Eventually Hoffman separated Seale's case by declaring a mistrial for him. As a separate defendant, Seale was found guilty of sixteen counts of contempt of court; Hoffman sentenced him to four years in prison. After he had served two years, however, the federal government dropped all charges against him.

In March of 1971, while he was still in prison, Seale was tried in New Haven, Connecticut, for conspiracy to kidnap and murder in the death of Alex Rackley, a suspected police informant. On May 2, 1971, a mistrial was declared because of a deadlocked jury. Subsequently all charges against Seale were dropped.

After Seale's release, he began to purge the Black Panther Party of criminal elements and move it in the direction of practical community services, such as breakfast programs for urban children and free health clinics. During this time Seale published his book *Seize the Time,* for which he won the 1971 Martin Luther King Memorial Prize.

In 1973 Seale ran for mayor of Oakland and finished second in a field of nine candidates. Having become frustrated with the limited focus of the Black Panther Party, in 1974 he resigned from the party and organized Advocates Scene, an organization designed to empower people to form grassroots political coalitions.

*A Lonely Rage: The Autobiography of Bobby Seale* was published in 1978. By the early 1980s Seale had become a strong and outspoken advocate for handgun control. For the rest of the decade Seale served as a community liaison for the African-American Studies Department of

Temple University (Philadelphia). He also became a barbecue gourmet; *Barbeque'n with Bobby* was published in 1987. The proceeds from this book funded nonprofit, community-based social organizations.

**second exodus** The notion that African-American history and Hebrew history have parallels. This is one of the basic motifs of historic Black *theology.\** American slavery was seen in terms of Hebrew slavery in Egypt, and the White slavemasters were seen as Pharaoh. During slavery the North was seen as the temporal promised land and heaven as the eternal promised land. After Emancipation the eternal promised land remained the same, but the temporal promised land came to stand for true freedom and human dignity. Our post-Reconstruction period has been seen as the wilderness wandering.

**segregation, unconstitutional** Until 1954 America's racial policy was governed by *Plessy* v. *Ferguson* (1896), in which the Supreme Court ruled that "separate but equal," the basis of racial segregation, was constitutional. This ruling was overturned with the famous *Brown* v. *Board of Education of Topeka,* in which the court ruled that segregation is indeed unconstitutional.

**slavery in the Muslim world** The enslavement of Black Africans in the Muslim countries of the Middle East is well documented. The people most victimized were the Zonj of East Africa, who were enslaved for civilian and military use.

Slavery in the Muslim world was quite brutal. A typical attitude toward these slaves was expressed by Egyptian writer al-Abshihi (1388-1446): "Is there anything more vile than black slaves, of less good and more evil than they? . . . The better you treat him [a Black or Mulatto slave], the more insolent he will be, the worse you treat him, the more humble and submissive."[5] Massive numbers of Blacks were pressed into involuntary slavery—so many that the Arabic word for slave *(ab'd)* became a synonym for "Black African."

Even today, attitudes toward Blacks in the Islamic world are not much different. A popular and often quoted poem by al-Mutanabbi, a well-known Arab poet, says in part, "Do not buy a slave [African] without buying a stick with him, / for slaves [Africans] are filthy and of scant good."[6]

The push for the abolition of slavery in the Muslim world came in the nineteenth century. Ironically, this came as a result of the imposition of imperial military power by Britain and later France, Holland and Russia. Yet slavery was only suppressed, not abolished. Because "the institution of slavery" was so "strongly defended by conservative religious opinion," abolition never really succeeded in the Islamic countries of the Middle East.

In the United States the legacy of slavery is a large population of African-Americans. In the Middle East and North Africa, by contrast, the Black population today is minimal. There are two reasons for this. First, Black male slaves were routinely castrated. Second, Black slaves had a high death rate and a low birth rate.[7]

**soul dynamic** The core of the African-American culture that developed in the context of White oppression and Black resistance to oppression. This dynamic is a combination of two main components:

□ A theological dynamic—an oral tradition that emerged from the historic African-American church experience. It captures nuggets of biblical truth in forceful, effective phrases and mental images out of life experience.

□ A cultural dynamic—deeply moving expressions of African-American consciousness that emerge from the very roots of their humanity and experience, from levels where the image of God cannot be suppressed.

Because these expressions are aligned with the power of God's Word, they have the power to deeply affect others who encounter them.

**Southern Christian Leadership Conference (SCLC)** The SCLC was founded by Dr. Martin Luther King Jr. in 1957. It was established to assist, coordinate and advise those involved in direct action for civil rights in the South. Other functions included leadership training and voter registration drives. During the height of the Civil

Rights Movement, the SCLC was the major catalyst.

After King's assassination, the Reverend Ralph David Abernathy assumed the leadership of the organization. He continued the basic philosophy of nonviolence. Since Abernathy's death (April 1990) the organization has continued its historic strategy under the leadership of the Reverend Joseph Lowery.

In 1971 the Reverend Jesse Jackson, a key leader, left the organization and founded *People United to Save Humanity (PUSH).** Since then the SCLC has lost much of its momentum.

**Student Non-violent Coordinating Committee (SNCC)** The SNCC, often called "Snick," was founded by Black and White college students in 1960. SNCC was instrumental in desegregating lunch counters in Nashville, Tennessee; Greensboro, North Carolina; and other cities in the South. It was heavily involved in Black voter registration in the South. For example, in 1964 thousands of Mississippi Blacks registered to vote as a result of the Mississippi Project.

In 1966 *Stokely Carmichael** took over SNCC's leadership from John Lewis. Under Carmichael SNCC became less involved with civil rights and more concerned with Black power.

In 1967 *H. Rap Brown** succeeded Carmichael. The organization came to advocate Black nationalism and, in February 1968, joined with the *Black Panther Party** in calling for a Black revolution. To reflect this change in philosophy, SNCC changed its name to the Student National Coordinating Committee in 1969.

When SNCC changed its focus from Southern civil rights concerns to Northern Black power issues, the organization lost most of its constituency. It never recovered its momentum.

**spirituals** The first indigenous expressions of historic Black *theology.** These songs were sung by slaves in the South. Some of the melodies originated in Africa. The tunes were very simple, using the pentatonic scale. They were usually sung a cappella.

Most of the spirituals were based on biblical characters and stories that resonated with the slaves' experience. It was in the spirituals that the slaves began to use double-meaning language.

**theological dynamic** *See* soul dynamic

**theology** The application of God's Word by persons in every area of life.

**Thirteenth, Fourteenth and Fifteenth Amendments** These amendments to the U.S. Constitution were largely concerned with the constitutional status of the newly freed slaves.

The Thirteenth Amendment (ratified on December 18, 1865) buttressed the Emancipation Proclamation. It extended the abolition of slavery to the North and West as well as the South.

The Fourteenth Amendment (ratified on July 28, 1868) proclaimed that the former slaves were full citizens of the United States, entitled to civil rights and due process of law.

The Fifteenth Amendment (ratified on March 30, 1870) forbade any state from depriving its Black citizens of the right to vote because of their race or their former status as slaves.

**toning** Preaching in a musical tone. Toning is often accompanied by *whooping**\* in traditional Black preaching.

**trial of O. J. Simpson** Orenthal James Simpson is one of the best-known African-American sports icons. He gained considerable renown as an outstanding college and professional football player and increased his popularity as a film actor and sports commentator.

Simpson was born on July 9, 1947, in San Francisco. He studied at the University of Southern California in Los Angeles and later graduated from City College of San Francisco. In 1968, during his years as a college player, he was awarded the coveted Heisman Trophy by the New York Downtown Athletic Club. He was also voted College Football Player of the Decade by ABC Sports.

From 1969 to 1978 O. J. Simpson played halfback for the Buffalo Bills, and during the 1978-1979 season he played for the San Francisco Forty-niners. His teammates affectionately called him "Juice" because the initials O.J. are often used to refer to orange juice. As a professional athlete Simpson received further honors; for example, he was named to the American Football League All-Star Team (1970) and inducted into the Football Hall of Fame (1985).

The life of O. J. Simpson took a dramatic turn in the summer of 1994. On the night of Sunday, June 12, his former wife, Nicole Brown Simpson, and her friend Ronald Goldman (both White) were brutally stabbed to death just outside Nicole's condominium in the pricy Brentwood area of Los Angeles, California. Within an hour of the murders, Simpson was boarding a flight to Chicago for a scheduled business trip. When Simpson was informed of the murders, he immediately returned to Los Angeles and gave a statement to the police without his lawyer present. A murder weapon was never found, nor were there any known witnesses to the crime.

Within days, based on circumstantial evidence, O. J. Simpson was considered the only suspect. On the morning of June 17 Simpson's lawyer informed him he was about to be arrested and charged with the double murder. Simpson dropped out of sight with his longtime friend A. C. Cowlings. At 6:45 p.m. they were spotted by two motorists on the San Diego Freeway, headed in the direction of Simpson's estate (also located in Brentwood). Cowlings was driving a white Ford Bronco, and Simpson was lying on the back seat distraught, with a gun to his head. Within minutes a number of Los Angeles police cars were in a close low-speed pursuit of the Bronco. It was a bizarre scene as they passed thousands of people standing on the side of the freeway yelling, "Go Juice!" When the Bronco arrived at Simpson's estate, Simpson turned himself over to police custody. At his arraignment on June 20 he pleaded "absolutely, 100 percent not guilty!"

Jury selection began on September 26, 1994, the jury was sworn in on December 8, and opening arguments began on January 24, 1995. By the end of the trial (October 3, 1995) the jury consisted of nine African-Americans, two Whites and one Hispanic. There were ten women and two men.

The prosecution lawyers were Marcia Clark (lead counsel), Christopher Darden (the only African-American on the team), William Hodgman, Cheri Lewis and Lisa Khan. Their strategy was to present circumstantial evidence to the jury to prove Simpson's guilt—evidence that included the latest in DNA technology as well as evidence of past spousal abuse on Simpson's part. The defense lawyers were Johnnie Cochran (lead counsel, African-American), Robert Shapiro, F. Lee Bailey, Carl Douglass (also African-American), Gerald Uelman, Barry Scheck and Alan Dershowitz, all famous and outstanding lawyers; the press often referred to them as the "dream team." Their strategy was to discredit the evidence by showing that it was tainted by sloppy police work. They also intended to show that some officers who discovered and collected the evidence were racists and therefore had reason to plant evidence to frame Simpson.

Mark Fuhrman, lead police detective in the case, testified that he found incriminating evidence on Simpson's property, including a bloody glove whose mate was at the murder scene. Under cross-examination Fuhrman emphatically denied that he was a racist and said that over the previous ten years he had never referred to African-Americans as "niggers."

At the insistence of the prosecution, the court ordered Simpson to try on the bloody gloves linked to the crime, but the gloves were too small.

In September the jury heard taped excerpts from a 1988 interview in which Fuhrman was clearly heard referring to African-Americans as "niggers." The transcripts that accompanied the tapes revealed Fuhrman's profound racism. In the end, Fuhrman and the gloves destroyed the prosecution's case, and on October 3 the jury found Simpson not guilty.

The sheer scale of this trial was gargantuan:

☐ Simpson spent 474 days in jail.

☐ The jurors were sequestered for 266 days.

☐ More than fifty thousand pages of court transcripts were produced.

☐ Coverage of the trial dominated the electronic media. Cable News Network (CNN) alone devoted nine hundred hours to the case.

☐ The verdict was watched by about 150 million Americans as well as tens of millions more around the world.

☐ The cost to Los Angeles County was a record $9.1 million.

But the real significance of this trial is in what it revealed—deep divisions between African-Americans and Whites. For example, after the verdict, 74 percent of Whites thought Simpson probably committed the murders while 66 percent of African-Americans thought he probably did not.[8] According to a Celinda Lake/Ed Goeas poll (October 3-5, 1995), 70 percent of African-Americans believed that the jury acquitted Simpson based on the facts of the case and 53 percent of Whites believed the acquittal was based on other factors.[9] Sixty-six percent of African-Americans believed the trial revealed that police often frame innocent people, as compared to only 28 percent of Whites.[10] More than 60 percent of African-Americans said that the trial showed there is a different justice for African-Americans and Whites, while 70 percent of Whites said there is no difference.[11]

According to Brent Staples, an editorialist for *The New York Times,* "Blacks in a White context are suspected" of not sharing their values. The trial uncovered a "social cold war" that had been smoldering for many years. Many in America were shocked at this revelation.

All the men I interviewed at the *Million Man March*\* cited the O. J. Simpson trial and the issues surrounding it as major factors that motivated them to participate.

**Trotter, W. Monroe** (1872-1934) A militant Northern adversary of White racism in the late nineteenth and early twentieth centuries. This brilliant man graduated with honors (Phi Beta Kappa) from Harvard University. In 1901 he founded *The Guardian,* a newspaper that spoke forcefully against racial discrimination. In 1905 Trotter cofounded the *Niagara Movement*\* with *W. E. B. Du Bois.*\* He did not join Du Bois in the formation of the *National Association for the Advancement of Colored People*\* because to him it was too moderate. Instead he founded the National Equal Rights League.

His efforts against racism were not confined to the United States. He attempted to persuade the Paris Peace Conference (following World War I) to outlaw racial discrimination. However, partly because the U.S. State Department denied him a passport and in other ways opposed his intentions, his efforts in Paris were unsuccessful.

From the perspective of the 1960s, Trotter's methods did not appear to be overly militant. For example, his strategy of direct-action demonstrations was adopted by the Civil Rights Movement.

**Truth, Sojourner** (1797-1883) Sojourner Truth was born Isabella Baumfree in Ulster County, New York. She was freed from slavery at the age of thirty with the New York State Emancipation Act of 1827. She sensed a call to the ministry and eventually adopted the name Sojourner Truth, believing this was the name God had given her for the mission he had called her to. This mission involved traveling (sojourning) across the United States, spreading the truth. This gifted woman became a dynamic, quick-witted orator who attracted huge crowds.

An active participant in the abolition movement, Sojourner Truth prophetically spoke out against the evils of slavery. When the U.S. Civil War erupted, she was active on the side of the Union. She was also instrumental in helping escaped slaves obtain employment and housing. Once the war was over, Sojourner Truth became an important spokesperson for African-American concerns.

**Tubman, Harriet** (1820-1913) Harriet Ross Tubman is best known as the "conductor" on the Underground Railroad, a network of people and safe houses through which slaves escaped to Northern "free" states and Canada. Tubman was born in Dorchester County, Maryland (about 1820). In 1848 she managed to escape from slavery, leaving her husband, John Tubman, behind. After she gained her freedom, she began to develop strategies to help other slaves to freedom. During the next ten years she made some twenty trips to the South to rescue other slaves. She prayerfully looked to God for guidance as she passed through the dangerous phases of each trip. She ended up safely delivering over three hundred slaves to freedom. She was considered so dangerous that a reward of forty thousand dollars was offered for her capture.

In 1860 Harriet Tubman became a noted spokesperson for women's rights and the antislavery movement. Just months before the outbreak of the U.S. Civil War, she was forced to flee to Canada. Once the war had begun, she played a key role in the Union army as a spy, a nurse, a scout and even a soldier. She was awarded many honors, but she lived her last years in poverty. To make matters worse, the U.S. government was thirty years late in giving her the pension she earned during the Civil War.

**Turner, Nat** (1800-1831) Nat Turner was born in Southampton County, Virginia, on a plantation. His parents and grandparents instilled in him a love for education and freedom. The son of one of his owners taught him to read and write, and he became a voracious reader of the Bible. He sensed a call to the ministry and became a powerful preacher. Turner soon came to the conviction that his mission was to free the slaves. This conviction led him to plan a rebellion.

In 1831 the Reverend Turner and about sixty-five other slaves took up arms and struck out against those who held them in bondage. This was the most famous slave revolt in American history.

In the wake of Nat Turner's revolt, sixty Whites were dead, including his owners (the Joseph Travis family). A Southampton County vigilante group eventually captured Turner and sixteen of his cohorts, who were tried and hanged. In a fit of vengefulness, angry Whites killed about one hundred more slaves who had nothing to do with the revolt. This incident also provoked the Southern states to pass restrictive laws governing the movement of slaves, especially those who were ministers.

**Two-Thirds World** The peoples outside the developed, industrialized nations (the United States, Western Europe and Japan). The Two-Thirds World comprises the developing and underdeveloped nations, which make up approximately two-thirds of the global population.

**Underground Railroad** *See* Tubman, Harriet

**urban riots in 1965** The *Watts riot\** prompted urban riots in several other cities in 1965. The major ones occurred in Chicago (August 12-14), Springfield, Massachusetts (August 13), and Philadelphia (August 16).

**Vesey, Denmark** (1767-1822) Denmark Vesey was born a slave in Charleston, South Carolina. His master was a seaman named Captain Vesey. Denmark sailed with his master throughout the Caribbean for about twenty-six years until he bought his freedom for six hundred dollars.

Vesey was a very bright young man who learned to read and write. He also possessed exceptional leadership skills. As a free man, he settled in Charleston and later sensed a call to the ministry in the Methodist Church. Eventually his biblical studies convinced him to lay his own freedom on the line in an attempt to free his slave brothers and sisters. The Reverend Vesey planned to accomplish this by overthrowing the government of Charleston. Hundreds of slaves supported this plan, which was to be executed in July 1822.

However, Vesey was betrayed by a fellow slave. As a result, many of those involved were arrested. Vesey himself was tried, sentenced to death and hanged with several of his collaborators on July 2, 1822.

**Washington, Booker T.** (1856-1915) Booker Taliaferro Washington was born a slave in Hales Ford, Virginia. After the end of slavery in 1865, his family moved to Malden, West Virginia. He attended Hampton Institute (Hampton, Virginia) from 1872 to 1875, and in 1879 he became a teacher there.

In 1881 he founded Tuskegee Institute and became its principal. The school taught trades and trained teachers. Washington felt that Blacks would be best served by vocational education rather than a college education.

When the *Jim Crow* * lynchings of Blacks dramatically increased in the 1880s, Washington advised African-Americans to stop demanding their rights and to try harder to get along with Whites. He also advised Whites to hire Blacks in better jobs. In his speeches he never publicly supported causes that were displeasing to Southern Whites. Because of this, his speeches provoked great controversy and criticism from more militant Black thinkers like *W. E. B. Du Bois.* *

Although Washington appeared to acquiesce in the face of the Jim Crow backlash, his true sympathies revealed him to be far more militant. He supported several Black newspapers. He also secretly financed many lawsuits opposing segregation and affirming voting rights for Blacks.

**Watts riot** On August 11, 1965, at 7:45 p.m., a White California highway patrolman stopped Black motorist Marquette Frye (age twenty-one) on suspicion of drunk driving. This happened in the Watts section of Los Angeles, a 95 percent Black community. In the time it took the patrolman to give Frye a sobriety test, about twenty-five people gathered around them. Among them was Frye's mother.

When Frye failed the test, his mother began to berate him. Agitated by this scolding, Frye struck out at the policeman. A scuffle broke out as the officer tried to force Frye into his patrol car. The bystanders became restless. Tensions escalated as more police arrived on the scene and the crowd grew. Officers with riot guns tried to force the crowd to move back. By that time the crowd had swelled to about six hundred. Finally tempers overflowed and the crowd went on a rampage, smashing windows, stoning vehicles and looting stores. By 1:30 a.m. on August 12, Watts was in the grips of a full-fledged riot. More than one thousand people were in the streets, looting and burning. The crowd of rioters eventually numbered over ten thousand.

In addition to the police, it took over twelve thousand National Guardsmen to quell the riot. Thirty-four people (twenty-eight Blacks and six Whites) lost their lives, more than one thousand were injured, and over $200 million worth of property was destroyed.

**White humanism** A belief that White people and White cultural standards are the final reference point for all truth, or that Whites are not really affected by unrighteousness.

**Whiteness** A perspective on reality based on the cultural *consciousness** (including sense of *history** and *destiny**) of Euro-American people.

**whooping** An abrupt guttural sound that punctuates phrases in some traditional Black preaching. The whoop is a kind of oral exclamation point and is usually used in conjunction with *toning.**

**Zoroaster** Zoroaster, also known as Zarathustra, was a great Median religious reformer who lived during the seventh and sixth centuries B.C. There is some uncertainty about the exact dates of his life. Some scholars say he lived from 630 to 553 B.C.; others say 628-551, while others say 618-541. In any case, he lived during the time of the prophet Daniel.

By the dawn of the seventh century B.C., Media and Persia were decadent societies, under the influence of polytheism and in the iron grip of a group of corrupt magi (priests). The political and military leaders, along with the general population, were fed up. But there was no ideological consensus around which to mobilize the population to overthrow the power of the priests. Zoroaster, however, was able to inspire a new consensus with a revolutionary theology based on an old idea, worship of the one true God.

A case can be made that Zoroaster was influenced by the prophecies of Isaiah, who lived a century earlier. By the seventh century the truths Isaiah spoke had spread throughout the known world over well-traveled trade routes. Moreover, according to 2 Kings 17:6 some from the defunct northern kingdom of Israel had settled "in the towns of the Medes." Maybe they were acquainted with Zoroaster. Zoroaster himself was probably familiar with Daniel's powerful ministry in Babylon.

Zoroaster's theological system dispensed with most of the corrupted sacrificial system of the magi, thus rendering the priestly function superfluous. Originally Zoroastrianism was a unitarian system, similar to modern Judaism and Islam.

Zoroaster had a profound effect on both Media and Persia. His clear and simple ethical teaching electrified the Medes and the Persians, helping to galvanize them into a unified kingdom. The power of the corrupt magi was swept away in the resulting cultural revolution. In 539 B.C., within twenty years of Zoroaster's death, King Cyrus led the Medio-Persian army in the conquest of Babylon, and Media-Persia became an undisputed world power.

Eventually the magi recovered their strength and once again gained dominance in Persian religion. Polytheism was reestablished, and the Persian empire went into decline. In the third century A.D., however,

Christianity began to sweep across Persia. To blunt the advance of the gospel, the Sassanian dynasty sponsored the development of Neo-Zoroastrianism, a dualistic monotheism. Neo-Zoroastrianism saw Ahura Mazda, the divine source of good, locked in a battle with Ahriman, the principle of evil. Neo-Zoroastrianism became the official religion of Persia.

In the seventh century the region was conquered by Islam, and Neo-Zoroastrians came under persecution. They fled to India, and today their religion is known as Parseeism.

## Notes
### Chapter 1: Toward a Promised Land
[1]Martin Luther King Jr., *Why We Can't Wait* (New York: Mentor, 1963), from the back cover (his emphasis).

### Chapter 2: Picking Up the Pieces
[1]Frederick Douglass, *Narrative of the Life of Frederick Douglass: An American Slave* (New York: New American Library, 1968), p. 120. Emphasis mine.

[2]By *humanism* I do not mean humanitarianism, which is the affirmation of the dignity of human beings. We should all be humanitarian. But humanism, as we shall see, leads to the erosion of the very possibility of humanitarianism.

[3]Denis Osborne, *The Andromedans and Other Parables of Science and Faith* (Downers Grove, Ill.: InterVarsity Press, 1977), pp. 29-31. Used by permission.

[4]I recognize that this is a redundant phrase. However, I use it deliberately because it matches the vernacular of many African-Americans.

[5]*The Willowbank Report: Gospel and Culture,* Lausanne Occasional Papers 2 (Wheaton, Ill.: Lausanne Committee for World Evangelization, 1978), p. 6.

### Chapter 3: "Oh, Freedom!"
[1]James Cone, *Black Theology and Black Power* (New York: Seabury Press, 1969).

[2]Because of gravity, the air around us weighs about fifteen pounds per square inch. This is called air pressure, and it pushes on everything equally on all sides. When a wing passes through the air, the air flowing over the top travels faster than the air flowing under it. This causes the pressure on top to be less than the pressure on the bottom. The wing is pushed up as a result, causing lift.

When the upward pressure is greater than the downward pressure and the weight of the plane, the plane flies. This upward pressure is due to gravity, and so the lift of the wing is an expression of the law of gravity.

## Chapter 4: Soul Dynamic

[1]Ray Dillard, professor of Old Testament, Westminster Theological Seminary, Philadelphia.

[2]Edward W. Blyden, *Christianity, Islam and the Negro Race* (Edinburgh: Edinburgh University Press, 1967), pp. 114-15.

[3]Scholars B. F. Wright and M. A. Smith have confirmed that Augustine was born of African parents. Actually, Augustine, Tertullian and Origen were brown North Africans and not Black sub-Saharan Africans. They have been classified as Caucasian by some. However, if these men had been Americans they would have been classified as Black, and it is the American classification that I use here.

[4]Blyden, *Christianity, Islam and the Negro Race,* p. 114.

[5]Charles H. Wesley, *In Freedom's Footsteps,* International Library of Negro Life and History (New York: Publishers, 1966), p. 7.

[6]Chancellor Williams, *The Destruction of Black Civilization* (Chicago: Third World Press, 1976), pp. 101-2, 156-58, 164-65, 208-18.

[7]Columbus Salley and Ronald Behm, *What Color Is Your God?* (Downers Grove, Ill.: InterVarsity Press, 1981), pp. 18-19.

[8]LeRoi Jones, *Blues People* (New York: William Morrow, 1963).

[9]Salley and Behm, *What Color Is Your God?* p. 20 (their emphasis).

[10]Ibid., pp. 20-21.

[11]An illustration often used by Dr. Henry Mitchell, author of *Black Preaching* (New York: Harper & Row, 1970) and *Black Belief* (New York: Harper & Row, 1975).

[12]Charles Tabor, "Is There More Than One Way of Doing Theology?" *Gospel in Context* 1 (January 1978): 6.

[13]James Cone, *God of the Oppressed* (New York: Seabury Press, 1975), pp. 54-55, my emphasis.

## Chapter 5: A Formative Phase

[1]In the antebellum North many Christian leaders developed a strong interest in African identity and African-American dignity. This movement emerged in the 1820s and became a major force in the 1840s and 1850s. It shaped the theology of the indigenous African-American church. A major spokes-

man for this movement was W. C. Pennington. Pennington was fiercely anticolonialistic. He was also instrumental in coordinating African-American missions on a national scale, both in the United States and in Africa.

[2]Lerone Bennett Jr., *Before the Mayflower* (New York: Penguin Books, 1962) pp. 183-84.

[3]A fuller discussion of Jim Crowism is found in ibid., pp. 220-41.

[4]Thom Hopler, *A World of Difference* (Downers Grove, Ill.: InterVarsity Press, 1981), pp. 157-74.

[5]Walter Rauschenbusch, *Christianity and the Social Crisis* (New York: Macmillan, 1907).

[6]Andrew E. Murray, *Presbyterians and the Negro: A History* (Philadelphia: Presbyterian and Reformed, 1966), p. 3.

[7]Lenard Broom and Norral Glenn, *Transformation of the Negro American* (New York: Harper & Row, 1965), pp. 9-15.

[8]Columbus Salley and Ronald Behm, *What Color Is Your God?* (Downers Grove, Ill.: InterVarsity Press, 1981), p. 32.

**Chapter 6: Two Streams**

[1]"The Atlanta Exposition Address, 1895," in *Black Protest Thought in the Twentieth Century,* ed. Francis L. Broderick and August Meier, American Heritage Series (Indianapolis: Bobbs-Merrill, 1971), pp. 4-6.

[2]Malcolm X with Alex Haley, *The Autobiography of Malcolm X* (New York: Grove, 1964), pp. 40-41.

[3]Ibid., pp. 54-55 (his emphasis).

[4]Columbus Salley and Ronald Behm, *What Color Is Your God?* (Downers Grove, Ill.: InterVarsity Press, 1981), pp. 46-47.

[5]Ibid., p. 47.

**Chapter 7: "De Lawd"**

[1]Martin Luther King Jr., *Stride Toward Freedom* (New York: Harper & Row, 1958), p. 33.

[2]Ibid., pp. 43-44.

[3]Ibid., p. 46.

[4]Ibid., p. 54.

[5]Ibid., p. 56.

[6]Ibid., p. 59.

[7]Ibid., pp. 59-60.

[8]Martin Luther King Jr., *Strength to Love* (Cleveland: Collins World, 1963), p. 151.

[9]King, *Stride Toward Freedom,* pp. 61-63.

[10]Ibid., p. 63.

[11]Ibid., pp. 69-70, 84.

[12]Martin Luther King Jr., *Why We Can't Wait* (New York: Mentor, 1963), p. 25.

[13]Ibid., p. 50.

[14]Ibid., pp. 76-95.

[15]Ibid., p. 61.

[16]Material in italics from King, *Why We Can't Wait,* p. 101; other material is from an interview with Andrew Young, *Bill Moyers' Journal,* PBS, aired on WHYY Philadelphia, April 2, 1979.

[17]King, *Why We Can't Wait,* p. 101.

[18]Ibid., p. 30.

[19]Ibid., p.39.

[20]John Frame, lecture outline for "Doctrine of the Christian Life" course (Philadelphia: Westminster Theological Seminary, 1979), p. 112 (his emphasis).

[21]Ibid., pp. 112-13.

[22]King, *Why We Can't Wait,* p. 112.

[23]*Bill Moyers' Journal,* April 2, 1979.

[24]King, *Strength to Love,* pp. 147-51.

[25]Ibid., p. 151.

[26]Columbus Salley, address to the National Black Evangelical Association (NBEA) Convention, New York, 1970.

[27]King, *Strength to Love,* p. 27.

[28]King, *Why We Can't Wait,* pp. 123-24.

[29]J. M. Kik, *Church and State in the New Testament* (Philadelphia: Presbyterian and Reformed, 1962), p. 46.

[30]King, *Why We Can't Wait,* p. 34.

[31]John Frame, lecture outline for "Doctrine of the Knowledge of God" course, part 2 (Philadelphia: Westminster Theological Seminary, 1976), p. 3.

[32]Ibid., p. 4.

[33]Frame, "Doctrine of the Christian Life," p. 1 (my emphasis).

[34]Cornelius Van Til, *Christian Theistic Ethics,* vol. 3 of *In Defense of the Faith* (Nutley, N.J.: Presbyterian and Reformed, 1977), p. 87.

[35]Stokely Carmichael and Charles V. Hamilton, *Black Power: The Politics of Liberation in America* (New York: Vantage Books, 1967), p. 55.

[36]Louis E. Lomax, *To Kill a Black Man* (Los Angeles: Holloway House, 1968), p. 190.

[37]Malcolm X, *Malcolm X Speaks,* ed. George Breitman (New York: Ballantine Books, 1965), p. 74.

[38]Quoted from *Bill Moyers' Journal,* April 2, 1979.

**Chapter 8: "A Shining Prince"**
[1]Eldridge Cleaver, *Soul on Ice* (New York: Delta, 1968), p. 74.

[2]Louis E. Lomax, *To Kill a Black Man* (Los Angeles: Holloway House, 1968), p. 121.

[3]Columbus Salley and Ronald Behm, *What Color Is Your God?* (Downers Grove, Ill.: InterVarsity Press, 1981), p. 65.

[4]In the mid-1820s the Reverend Nathaniel Paul, pastor of the African Baptist Society in Albany, New York, began to express his view that the "regeneration" of Africa was the special duty of African-American Christians. To that end he advocated the emigration of African-Americans to Africa. (See *Neo-Pan-Africanism.**)

[5]Malcolm X with Alex Haley, *The Autobiography of Malcolm X* (New York: Grove, 1964), pp. 4, 2.

[6]Ibid., p. 37 (his emphasis).

[7]Ibid.

[8]Ibid., p. 154.

[9]Ibid., p. 155.

[10]Ibid., p. 156.

[11]Ibid.

[12]Ibid., pp. 158-59 (his emphasis).

[13]Ibid., pp. 163-65.

[14]Ibid., pp. 165-68.

[15]Ibid., p. 299.

[16]Ibid., p. 307.

[17]Ibid., p. 387.

[18]Ibid., pp. 344-46 (his emphasis).

[19]Ibid., pp. 324-40, 348.

[20]Ibid., p. 349.

[21]Bernard Lewis, *Race and Color in Islam* (New York: Octagon Books, 1979), pp. 3-4.

[22]"Slavery," *Newsweek*, May 4, 1992, pp. 30-38.

[23]Malcolm X, *Autobiography*, p. 371.

[24]Malcolm X, *Malcolm X Speaks*, ed. George Breitman (New York: Ballantine Books, 1965), pp. 63-64; emphasis added.

[25]Malcolm X, *Autobiography*, p. 375 (his emphasis).

[26]Cornelius Van Til, *Christian Theistic Ethics*, vol. 3 of *In Defense of the Faith* (Nutley, N.J.: Presbyterian and Reformed, 1977).

[27]Quoted in Malcolm X, *Autobiography*, p. 451.

[28]Cleaver, *Soul on Ice*, p. 59.

[29]Malcolm X, *Malcolm X on Afro-American History*, ed. Betty Shabazz (New York: Pathfinder, 1970), p. 2.

[30]Malcolm X, *Autobiography*, p. 432.

[31]Ibid., pp. 432-33.

[32]Ibid., p. 434.

[33]Ibid.

[34]Ibid.

[35]Malcolm X, *Malcolm X Speaks*, pp. 76, 24.

[36]Lomax, *To Kill a Black Man*, p. 172.

[37]Malcolm X, *Malcolm X Speaks*, pp. 43-44.

[38]Marshall Frady, "The Children of Malcolm," *The New Yorker*, October 12,

1992, p. 77.

[39]Stokely Carmichael and Charles V. Hamilton, *Black Power: The Politics of Liberation in America* (New York: Vantage Books, 1967), pp. 37-38, 44.

[40]"Niggers Are Scared of Revolution," The Last Poets—Douglas3, East Wind Associates.

[41]"STOP" (a song), lyrics and music by Henry Greenidge, 1970, sung by Soul Liberation.

[42]Malcolm X, *Malcolm X Speaks,* pp. 76-77.

[43]Thom Hopler, "The Dynamics in the Black Church: The Interaction of Pan-Africanism, Church Growth and Foreign Missions in the American Black Church from 1790-1975," "The First 25 Unbelievable Years, 1875-1900," and "Review of the Black Missionary Effort," typescripts, Fuller Theological Seminary, Pasadena, California, 1974-1975.

[44]As early as 1787, Northern antebellum Black Christian thinkers began to affirm a strong kinship with all people of African descent. This was often referred to as Pan-Africanism. (See *Neo-Pan-Africanism.* *)

[45]*Truth Is on Its Way,* Nikki Giovanni and the New York Community Choir, Right On Records, RR95001.

[46]Malcolm X, *Malcolm X Speaks,* pp. 19-20.

[47]Translated by Abdullah Yusuf Ali, revised and edited by The Presidency of Islamic Researches, IFTA, Call and Guidance, King Fahd Holy Qor'an Printing Complex.

Footnote 432 in this passage says the following: "The 'face' *(wajh)* expresses our Personality, our inmost being. White is the colour of Light; to become white is to be illuminated with Light, which stands for felicity, the rays of the glorious light of Allah. Black is the colour of darkness, sin, rebellion, misery; removal from the grace and light of Allah. These are the Signs of heaven and hell. The standard of decision in all questions is the justice of Allah."

[48]The Nation of Islam became the Billilian Community, which in turn became the World Community of Al-Islam in the West, which in turn became the American Muslim Mission.

[49]Lomax, *To Kill a Black Man,* p. 170.

[50]Malcolm X, *Autobiography,* p. 428.

[51]Ibid., p. 421.

### Chapter 10: A Little "White" Lie in the Name of Black Truth

[1]Augustine, *The City of God,* trans. Marcus Dods (New York: Random House, 1950), pp. 345-668.

[2]Robert Knudsen, *History* (Cherry Hill, N.J.: Mack, 1976), p. 15.

[3]Robert Knudsen, *The Secularization of Science* (Memphis, Tenn.: Christian Studies Center, 1954), pp. 8-9.

[4]Knudsen, *History,* p. 15.

[5]Knudsen, *Secularization of Science,* p. 9.

[6]Louis L. Knowles and Kenneth Prewill, eds., *Institutional Racism in America* (Englewood Cliffs, N.J.: Prentice-Hall, 1969), pp. 142-43.

[7]Malcolm X with Alex Haley, *The Autobiography of Malcolm X* (New York: Grove, 1964), p. 369 (his emphasis).

**Chapter 11: "Busting Out"**
[1]Duke Ellington, "Something About Believing," *Second Sacred Concert,* Prestige, 1974, P-24045.

[2]Hermann Hanse, "κατέχω," in *Theological Dictionary of the New Testament,* ed. Gerhard Kittel and Gerhard Friedrich, 10 vols. (Grand Rapids, Mich.: Eerdmans, 1964), 2:829.

[3]Osadolor Imasogie, "African Traditional Religion and Christian Faith," *Baptist Theological Journal* 70 (Summer 1973): 289-90.

**Chapter 12: "That Boy Sho' Can Preach!"**
[1]Dizzy Gillespie.

[2]Charlie Parker.

[3]Billie Holliday.

[4]Miles Davis, "On Green Dolphin Street," *'58 Sessions,* Columbia/Legacy (CD) CK47835.

**Chapter 13: Cultural Seeding**
[1]Marvin Gaye, *What's Going On?* Motown (CD) 09036MD (original 1971).

[2]Stevie Wonder, *Music of My Mind,* Motown (CD) MOTD-314 (original 1972); *Talking Book,* Motown (CD) MOTD-318 (original 1972); *Inner Visions,* Motown (CD) MOTD-326 (original 1973); *Fulfillingness First Finale,* Motown (CD) MOTD-332 (original 1974); *Songs in the Key of Life,* Motown (CD) MOTD2-340 (original 1976).

[3]Marvin Gaye, "Let's Get It On," *Let's Get It On,* Motown (CD) MOTD-5192 (original 1973).

[4]Joshua is the Hebrew form of the Greek 'Ιησοῦς (Jesus). *X* is the first letter in the Greek title Χριστός (Christ). Davidson is another way of saying "Son of David" (Matthew 1:1).

**Chapter 14: New Vistas**
[1]W. A. Pratney, *Leadership Training Manual* (Los Angeles: Black Ministries Unlimited, 1975), p. 45 (emphasis mine).

**Chapter 15: The Fields Are *Black* unto Harvest**
[1]Carl F. Ellis Jr., *Beyond Liberation: The Gospel in the Black American Experience* (Downers Grove, Ill.: InterVarsity Press, 1983), p. 181.

[2]Ibid., pp. 183-84.

[3]Ibid., p. 188.

[4]Ibid.

[5]James Weldon Johnson, "Lift Every Voice and Sing," Edward B. Marks Music Corporation. Used by permission.

## Glossary of People, Events and Terms

[1]Bernard Lewis, ed. and trans., *Religion and Society,* vol. 2 of *Islam: From the Prophet Muhammad to the Capture of Constantinople* (Oxford: Oxford University Press, 1974), p. 210.

[2]Bernard Lewis, *Race and Color in Islam* (New York: Octagon Books, 1979), p. 96.

[3]David J. Garrow, *Bearing the Cross: Martin Luther King Jr. and the Southern Christian Leadership Conference* (New York: William Morrow, 1986), pp. 15-16.

[4]Quoted in Lewis, *Religion and Society,* p. 162.

[5]Quoted in Lewis, *Race and Color in Islam,* p. 97.

[6]Quoted in ibid., p. 79.

[7]Ibid., p. 88.

[8]*Newsweek,* October 16, 1995, p. 39.

[9]*U.S. News & World Report,* October 16, 1995, p. 34.

[10]Ibid., p. 50.

[11]Ibid.